ANDREW CRAWFURD'S COLLECTION OF BALLADS AND SONGS

Lithograph of Andrew Crawfurd

ANDREW CRAWFURD'S COLLECTION OF BALLADS AND SONGS

Volume I

EDITED BY

E. B. LYLE

The Scottish Text Society
Edinburgh
1975

Reprinted 1997

Printed by
William Blackwood & Sons Ltd., Edinburgh

Reprinted by
BPC - AUP Aberdeen Ltd.

TO MY MOTHER
AND THE MEMORY OF
MY FATHER

CONTENTS OF VOLUME I

PREFACE

THIS VOLUME marks a new departure in the policy of the Scottish Text Society, and I should like to express my pleasure that the Society is prepared to help in the task of making available the manuscript song-collections which represent one facet of our heritage. It should be said that the new format in which this volume appears has taken shape under the eye of Professor William Beattie.

The Crawfurd collection became known to me some years ago through the pioneering bibliographical work done by Dr William Montgomerie, and I began to prepare this edition in the summer of 1969. Through Professor John MacQueen's acceptance of the value of what I was attempting, I was granted a Senior Scholarship (1970–72) by the Carnegie Trust for the Universities of Scotland and have been able to work in the School of Scottish Studies at Edinburgh University. To my colleagues here I am deeply indebted for stimulus and advice, and my debts extend widely also to a number of knowledgeable people who, in conversation and by letter, have offered information or suggestions on individual points concerning songs or historical source material or, in the case of Mr David Murison, the meanings of words. I am grateful, too, to the librarians in many libraries where manuscript, broadside and chapbook collections have been made available to me, and am particularly indebted to Mrs A. Mackenzie and the staff of Paisley Central Library where the Crawfurd manuscripts lie, and to the Trustees there for giving me permission to publish this edition. The lithograph that is reproduced as the frontispiece to this volume is in Paisley Central Library and was photographed by the Frank Hardy Studios, Paisley. The songs in the appendix appear by courtesy of the Trustees of the British Museum and the Librarians of the University Libraries of Cambridge, Glasgow and Harvard.

E. B. L.

EDINBURGH
1 October 1974

ABBREVIATIONS

GENERAL

BM	British Museum
Bronson	Bertrand H. Bronson *The Traditional Tunes of the Child Ballads* 4 vols. Princeton 1959-72
Child	Francis J. Child *The English and Scottish Popular Ballads* 5 vols. Boston 1882-98, reproduced New York 1965
Greig *NE*	Gavin Greig *Folk-Song of the North-East* Peterhead 1909, 2nd series 1914, reproduced in one volume with *Folk-Song in Buchan* Hatboro, Pa. 1963
GUL	Glasgow University Library
Laws	G. Malcolm Laws *American Balladry From British Broadsides* Pennsylvania 1957
LC	The Lauriston Castle collection of chapbooks in the National Library of Scotland
Madden	The Madden collection of broadsides in Cambridge University Library
Opie	Iona and Peter Opie *The Oxford Dictionary of Nursery Rhymes* Oxford 1951, reproduced Oxford 1962
RB	*The Roxburghe Ballads* ed. William Chappell and J. W. Ebsworth 8 vols. Ballad Society, Hertford 1871-99
Simpson	Claude M. Simpson *The British Broadside Ballad and its music* New Brunswick and New Jersey 1966
SMM	*The Scots Musical Museum* ed. James Johnson 6 vols. Edinburgh 1787-1803; 1853 edition reproduced in two volumes Hatboro, Pa. 1962

MANUSCRIPTS

Buchan *Ancient Ballads*	Peter Buchan *Manuscript Collection of Ancient Ballads of Scotland* 2 vols.; BM Additional MSS 29,408-9
Buchan *Secret Songs*	Peter Buchan *Secret Songs of Silence*; Harvard College Library MS 25241.9
Creighton MS	Collection of Elizabeth Creighton's songs; Ewart Library, Dumfries, Db 151
Duncan *Tunes*	James B. Duncan *Folk-Song Airs of the North-East;* Aberdeen University Library MS 786
Greig *Tunes*	Gavin Greig *Folk-Music* 4 vols.; Aberdeen University Library MSS 705-8
Greig *Words*	Gavin Greig *Folk-Songs. (Words.)* 64 vols.; Aberdeen University Library MSS 711-74
Kinloch MSS	William Macmath's copy of George Ritchie Kinloch's song-collection now in Harvard College Library, MS 25242.12; Hornel Library, Broughton House, Kirkcudbright
Macmath MSS	Collection of material relating to ballads and songs made by William Macmath; Hornel Library, Broughton House, Kirkcudbright
Motherwell *Ballad Book*	Volume of ballads and songs compiled by William Motherwell; Glasgow University Library MS Murray 501
Motherwell *Notebook*	Collection of songs and related notes made by William Motherwell; Pollok House, Glasgow
St Clair MS	Song-collection made by Elizabeth St Clair (the Mansfield MS); Hornel Library, Broughton House, Kirkcudbright
White MS	Collection of songs and poems owned by Robert White; Newcastle University Library MS B/W 3

GENERAL INTRODUCTION

ANDREW CRAWFURD's parents were Andrew Crawford, partner in William Caldwell & Co., a firm of cotton-spinners in the village of Lochwinnoch near the Ayrshire border of Renfrewshire, and Jean Adam, daughter of William Adam, portioner of Johnshill in the same village.[1] There were four children of the marriage: William (who became a surgeon in practice in Port Glasgow), Andrew, Barbara and Mary. Andrew was born on 5 November 1786,[2] and received his schooling in Lochwinnoch. Then 'in compliance with his father's inclination to make him a manufacturer' he worked as a clerk for some years, first to Mr Abercrombie, bleacher, Calderhaugh Field, Lochwinnoch, and then to MacCauley & Hart, manufacturers in Causeyside, Paisley. In the meantime, however, he took lessons in Latin and eventually entered Glasgow College in November 1810. He proved an able student who was awarded prizes in the Greek, Logic and Ethic classes,[3] and in 1818 he was granted a diploma by the Faculty of Physicians and Surgeons of Glasgow. Early in that year, at the age of thirty-one, Crawfurd began practice at Rothesay, but apparently he did not intend to continue in the profession of surgeon for he applied for a post in the teaching of Natural Philosophy at the newly established Dollar Institution (now Academy).[4] His application was successful, but in December 1819, before he could take up his appointment, he caught typhus fever from his patients. This was nearly fatal and, although Crawfurd did make a recovery, it was 'with the loss of speech, the amputation of one leg above the knee, and palsy on the

[1] Crawfurd wrote a brief third-person autobiography in his manuscript *Cairn of Lochunyoch Matters* 46 vols. (Paisley Central Library PC 1407-52) 1.21b, and this supplies the information given here that is not referred to other sources.

[2] Scottish Record Office CH3/456/1 *Burntshields Associate Congregation.*

[3] W. Innes Addison *The Matriculation Albums of the University of Glasgow From 1728 to 1858* (Glasgow 1913) No 8259; and W. Innes Addison *Prize lists of the University of Glasgow from Session 1777-78 to Session 1832-33* (Glasgow 1902) pp. 146, 158-9, 164-5 and 170.

[4] Obituary notice in *The Paisley Journal and Renfrewshire Gazette* 20 January 1855 p. 5 col. 1.

right side of the body'.[5] Thereafter, he was confined for the most part to his home in Johnshill but his disabilities did not isolate him from the community. 'He encouraged his friends to visit and talk to him, and it was wonderful how easily and gracefully he managed to keep them going with an occasional laugh, shake of the head, "aye, no, ou-aye, etc." His part of the conversation was supplied by writing, when needful.'

Before his illness, Crawfurd was active in the literary world and contributed to three periodicals: *The Scotchman* (Paisley 1813), *Attic Stories* (Glasgow 1817) and *The Visitor* (Greenock 1818). After his illness there is a silence until William Motherwell in his *Minstrelsy: Ancient and Modern* (Glasgow 1827) acknowledged receiving help from his friend 'Dr Andrew Crawford of Lochwinnoch' (introduction p. civ). Crawfurd's song-collecting was limited almost entirely to the years 1826-28 and was at its peak in the early part of 1827 when he was forty years old. He lived on till the age of sixty-eight, dying on 27 December 1854,[6] and gave his mind energetically to antiquarian matters during his later years. He left a large manuscript compilation of miscellaneous material, particularly strong in local family history, which he called his *Cairn of Lochunyoch Matters* (see note 1), and it is quite often possible to glean from it some information on the singers who contributed to his song-collection. He also put together a five-volume *Eik to Jamieson's Dictionary*[7] and this reflects the fact that, while he cared deeply for everything old and Scottish, he had a particular enthusiasm for the Scots language. He regretted the change to an Anglified spelling and felt quite free to approximate older Scottish forms, in accordance with the views expressed in a pronouncement attached to a rendering of a poem by Alexander Wilson into thicker Scots than that originally used: 'The Scots o Wilson, as weil as the Scots o the lave of our poets, for a quhyle bygane, has been sair shachlit, with a missettand gate o spellin, barrowit frae our Southland neibours. Sae the publishar thinks he dis a leil turn, baith to the poet an the Scots leid, quhan he ettles to restore the

[5] This and the following quotation are from an account by Crawfurd's nephew, Andrew Crawford Young, drawn upon by George Williamson in *Old Greenock* Second Series (Paisley and London 1888) p. 273.

[6] *The Paisley Journal and Renfrewshire Gazette* 30 December 1854 p. 4 col. 5.

[7] National Library of Scotland MSS 6512-16.

trew spellin.'[8] It was his preference for Scots that led to his choice of the spelling 'Crawfurd' for his own name, instead of the 'Crawford' used by other members of his family.

The songs Crawfurd collected are principally contained in three volumes which were presented to Paisley Central Library by Crawfurd's niece, Miss Mary Young, probably between 1903 and 1910,[9] and have the press-marks PC 1453-5. The first two volumes are devoted in the main, though not exclusively, to ballads and songs, and Crawfurd appears to be referring to these volumes alone when he includes in a list of his activities the statement, 'I collected 2 volumes of manuscript of Auld Ballads in aiding my friend Mr Motherwell for his Minstrelsy, 1827' (*Cairn* 1.21d). The third volume is a more miscellaneous collection which includes a certain number of songs, but Crawfurd treats all three volumes as a unit to which he provides a general index. The volumes are in their original binding done by Crawfurd himself[10] of marbled boards with calf spine. Pasted on the outside of the front cover of each is a slip with the title and appropriate volume number made out in ink: *Auld Ballats, With Lochwinioch Matters. In 3 Quairs. I. / II. / III.* Pasted above this slip in each case is a printed slip with numerals in ink which runs: *Auld Ballats, with Lochunyoch Matters. Quair I. / II. / III.* and there are signs that this slip was also pasted on the spine of each volume, although very little of the paper remains. Inside the front cover of each volume is a printed slip serving as a book-plate with the wording: *And. Crawfurd, Umquhyle Surgeon, St. Johnshill. No.*

Volume 1 measures 7·4″×6·2″ and has 364 pages. The book formerly began with page 7 where the original pencilled title, although faint, can be made out to be: *Old Ballads and Scots Songs copied after the[ir] recitation at Johnshill volume I.* Although there are a number of insertions, the basic paper in the portion of the book at

[8] Note to 'The Laurel Dispuitit' in a contribution by Crawfurd to *The Visitor* (Greenock 1818) 2.170; 'missettand gate' = displeasing way, 'leid' = tongue and 'ettles' = attempts).

[9] Mary Young, whose name appears on library book plates inside the front covers of the three volumes as 'Miss Young, 7 Foremount Terrace, Dowanhill, Glasgow', inherited the whole estate of her brother Andrew Crawford Young on his death on 8 April 1903 and herself died on 26 June 1910.

[10] Williamson, p. 273, speaks of manuscript volumes of Crawfurd's 'mainly or altogether stitched and bound with his left hand, aided by the very slight help which his right arm and hand were latterly trained to afford'.

pages 7-198 is striated and has a watermark which includes the date 1821, while pages 1-6 and 199-364 are of an inferior paper without watermark. The fresh title written in ink on page 1 runs: *Old Ballads; &c. taken down from the Recitation of various Persons, who got them by Oral or Traditional Communication. In three volumes Vol. I 1827, &c. By A. Crawfurd, Johnshill, for William Motherwell, Paisley, aiding him with his Minstrelsy.* The contents of the volume are listed at pages 3-7. Volume 2 measures 7·8″×6·4″ and has 382 pages. There is a title written in ink on page 3 which runs: *Old Ballats; &c. taken from the Recitation of various Persons, who got them by Oral or Traditional Communication. Collectit be And. Crawfurd, Johnshill; For Wm Motherwell, Paisley, for assisting him with his Minstrelsy. In three volumes. Vol. II. 1827, &c.* and the contents are listed at pages 5-8. The third volume measures 7·7″×6·3″ and has 460 pages. There is no list of contents at the beginning but at pages 435-56 there is a general index headed 'Contents of the three volumes of Auld Ballats, with Notices of Lochwinioch Matters'. The main title is written in ink on page 1: *Old Ballats; taken from the Recitation of Sundry Persons, who got them by Oral or Traditional Communication; – Together with Notices of Lochwinioch Matters. Colleckit be And. Crawfurd, Johnshill. In three volumes. Vol. III. 1827, &c.* and there is another one on page 5, also in ink but not so formally set out: *Ballads, Sang*[*s*], *and Local Rhymes, collected by Andrew Crawfurd, at Johnshill, Lochwinioch, chiefly for Motherwell for his Ministrelsy printed in 1827.* There are a number of different types of paper at various points in volumes 2 and 3 but the basic paper is plain and without watermark.

Crawfurd was inclined to reorganise materials in his manuscript collection after they had been listed according to his original arrangement, and there are clear signs that he removed a number of items from these three volumes. However, most of the traditional songs he removed are to be found in a volume of 360 pages, measuring 13·1″×8·2″ which is also available in Paisley Central Library (PC 2846, volume 8) having been presented by Miss Mary Love of the Knowes, Lochwinnoch, in 1964. This volume, which has been rebound in brown boards by the library with the title *Lochwinyoch Matters* on the spine, bears on page 1 the title *Lochwinioch Matters. VIII* written in ink at the top, a printed slip reading [*L*]*ochunyoch Matters. Folio. Quair VIII* in the centre and Crawfurd's printed book-plate at the foot. Crawfurd employed the term

'Folio' to refer to the set of manuscript books of which this volume is the eighth, and I accordingly use the abbreviation 'F' for this volume while referring to the three volumes of *Auld Ballats* by the numbers 1-3 simply. The transfer of material to F was evidently made for ease of reading since the songs concerned were written from top to bottom of sheets that are slightly over 12″ long which could be easily bound as they were written in this volume but in the small volumes had had to be folded in two in such a way that the writing appeared sideways. The transfer seems to have been made between 1839 and 1844.[11]

Since Crawfurd's pagination is erratic with omissions and duplications of numbers, I have renumbered all four of the volumes containing songs, and references are normally to this new numbering. When there is occasion to refer to Crawfurd's page numbers, which I have lightly deleted, I state this fact. Crawfurd in many cases puts Roman figures before the songs and other items in his collection but, as they are not consecutive and as there are many gaps in the sequence of numbers, I have not found them very helpful although it is possible that they may sometimes indicate order of recording.

Crawfurd's repeated statements in his titles and elsewhere make it abundantly clear that his song-collecting was connected with the publication of William Motherwell's *Minstrelsy: Ancient and Modern* but, although this work did not appear as a bound volume until December 1827, the first of the parts in which it was published had come out in 1824 and the bulk of the book had been completed by November 1826 when the Crawfurd collection was begun. Indeed, Motherwell evidently felt in that month that his work was nearly over for he mentioned in a letter to Robert A. Smith written on 24 November 1826 that he hoped 'to have the *Minstrelsy* lumbering about in the Book market' in January.[12] An undated letter from Motherwell to Crawfurd, from which the following extract was made by Philip A. Ramsay,[13] may have been

[11] The latest dated item in F is a letter of 3 September 1839 (p. 189) and the date 1844 is included in material Crawfurd wrote on pages of the *Auld Ballats* that replace the removed sheets (1.140). The printed title and book-plate slips may have been added about this time for dated items of the same kind printed by Crawfurd are mainly of the years 1838-9 with one item of 1842.

[12] GUL MS Robertson 3 *Letters R. A. Smith & Motherwell* f. 90v.

[13] Ramsay wrote this on a page immediately before the introduction in Motherwell's interleaved copy of the *Minstrelsy*, GUL Bh19 - e.4.

written shortly afterwards:

> I am nearly finished with my volume. I may mention that it was not projected by me, but the editorship I was obliged to take upon myself after 3 or 4 parts had been published. When finished it will look pretty well, notwithstanding many defects which partially disfigure it. Other two parts, or thereabouts, have been printed, but these are kept up till we can bring out the whole, which will be, I expect, in something less than a month. Indeed the great delay is attributable to my own indolence in deferring from day to day to write out an Introduction to the vol.; and the difficulty of doing so is pretty apparent, for there is much to say on the subject, and little space.

It was accordingly only in the last parts of the *Minstrelsy* to be completed, the introduction and the appendix, that Motherwell could make use of the Crawfurd material. The Paisley collection (2.199-201 No 182) includes a draft or copy of Crawfurd's reply to a query of Motherwell's relating to his appendix:

> Friday morning, Sept. 1827.
>
> Dear Motherwell
>
> I received (your munificent present to the Loch[winnoc]h Library) and the Opera Divi Joannis Gersonis. This same John Gerson[14] seems to shew his vast labour, (but) not (to) the edification of his readers.
>
> And also I got your last letter written on Sunday - but [received?] onWednesday - about John Tamsoun's man.
>
> I looked over since that time Ramsay'[s] Evergreen, Sir David (Linds) Lindsay's Works by Chalmers, and Kelly's Proverbs.[15] I find no (any) allusion to John Tamson except (in Kelly) that in Kelly under B, proverb No 122. as follows
>
> Better be John Tamson's man, than Ring and Dinn's, or John Knox's.
>
> Kelly's own Gloss on it is,

[14] The French theologian Jean Charlier de Gerson (1363-1429).

[15] Allan Ramsay *The ever green* (1st edn. Edinburgh 1724), *The Poetical Works of Sir David Lyndsay of the Mount* ed. George Chalmers (London 1806), see 1.257, and James Kelly *A Complete Collection of Scotish Proverbs* (London 1721), see p. 72.

"John Thomson's man is he that is complaisant to his wife's humours, Ring and Dinn's is he whom his wife scolds, John Knox's is he whom his wife beats."

I used to hear about him, at Loch[winnoc]h and perhaps in some other places, as if any company were sitting together socially and one neighbour coming (into) in, it is customary to welcome him thus, Cum awa, we're aw John Tamson's bairns.

I will cast my eye to this eccentric (John Tamsoun) and *hamard*[16] John (Th) Tamsoun. I will send you any facts if I can find them.

Gynkertoun

Fra play, thow leit me never rest,
Bot gynkertoun* thow luffit ay best;
And ay, quhen thow come fra the scule,
Than I behuffit to play the fule."

Chalmers has a note about Gynkertoun,

Gynkertoun; the name of a Scottish tune, which tradition has not preserved.

May this allusion suit to your Minstrelsy.[17]

Crawfurd kept his promise to look out for further material and managed to collect two verses on John Tamson's wallet and a rhyme beginning 'Jon Tamson an his man' (2.202-4) which Motherwell printed along with the other John Tamson information Crawfurd sent him in his introductory remarks to *John Thomson and the Turk* in his appendix, p. x.

One of the two verses on John Tamson's wallet was from Meg Walker, Mrs Caldwell, whose songs are included in this volume. As it appears in Crawfurd's collection it runs (2.202):

About his wallet there was a dispute
Sum said it was made of the skin of a brute
But I do believe it was made of the best of ben
John Thamson's wallet frae end to end

[16] *I.e.* homely.

[17] In prose quotations manuscript deletions are enclosed in round brackets, and editorial additions are enclosed in square brackets.

The *Minstrelsy* appendix is indebted to Meg Walker at another point also. Her variant of *Jamie Douglas* which is No 50 in the present volume was one of the sources of Motherwell's composite text *Lord Jamie Douglas* (appendix pp. v–ix). Child recognised that Motherwell's final three stanzas, which are close to Meg Walker's, were from a source unknown to him and distinguished them as a separate variant (Child 204 *Jamie Douglas* N).

The introduction of the *Minstrelsy* quotes four Crawfurd texts in notes at pages lxxi, lxxiv–v, xci and xcix: a verse of *The Battle of Otterburn* (Child 161 E), the whole of *The Fause Knight upon the Road* (Child 3 A), two verses of *The Wylie Wife of the Hie Town Hie* (Child 290, note to B) and two verses of *Bonnie Annie* (Child 24 B, vs. 15–16 and note). The appendix also includes among the detached verses given with the music, ten which are equivalent to opening verses of ballads in the Crawfurd collection. These are: 5 *Lord Bengwill* (Child 5 *Gil Brenton*), 6 *Babe Norice* (Child 83 *Child Maurice*), 7 *Sir Hew or The Jews Daughter* (Child 155), 8 *Earl Richard* (Child 68 *Young Hunting*), 10 *Ochiltree Walls* (Child 217 *The Broom of Cowdenknows*), 12 *The Three Ravens* (Child 26), 17 *Amang the Blue Flowers and Yellow* (Child 25 *Willie's Lyke-Wake*), 18 *Young Johnston* (Child 88), 23 *Lady Jean* (Child 52 *The King's Dochter Lady Jean*) and 29 *Ricadoo* (Child 281 *The Keach i the Creel*).[18] Motherwell also wrote into his interleaved copy of the *Minstrelsy*[19] variations from his printed text of *Willie and May Margaret* (pp. 155–8) which are taken from a Crawfurd variant of *The Mother's Malison, or, Clyde's Water* (Child 216, note to B).

The overlap with the Crawfurd collection is not limited to the *Minstrelsy*, however, for Motherwell's manuscript *Ballad Book* contains eighteen Crawfurd items. The titles of the first five of these appear in the list of contents in darker ink than the surrounding titles and three of them are squeezed between the lines as normally

[18] The titles listed are those at the head of the verses; three of the titles above the music are the shorter forms 7 *Sir Hew*, 12 *Three Ravens* and 17 *Blue Flowers and Yellow*, and two differ from the verse headings, 5 *Lord Bingwell* and 18 *Willie and the Young Cornel*. Motherwell may have sent a full text of 29 *Ricadoo* to Peter Buchan for an abstract of a letter of his to Buchan dated 8 March 1827 (GUL MS Robertson 9 f. 12r) states, 'Sends him a version of the Auld Wife and the Peet Creil', and this is the Crawfurd title of the ballad (No 25 in the present volume); *cf.* Buchan's reference to a text received from Motherwell in a note to *The Cunning Clerk* in *Ancient Ballads and Songs of the North of Scotland* (Edinburgh 1828) 1.319, and Child 5.121.

[19] Glasgow University Library Bh19 - e.4.

spaced.[20] It can be inferred that these items are later additions, and this inference is confirmed by the appearance of the texts which, as with the titles, are in darker ink than the surrounding texts. Each takes up only a single page, and it seems that they have been inserted to fill up pages previously left blank.[21] These five items are: *The Queen's Mary* (Child 173 K) at page 96, *The Deil's Courting* (Child 2 I) at page 103, *Mild Mary* (Child 91 E) at page 123, *The Deil's Wowing*, which is not a Child ballad, at page 309, and *Rosie Ann* (Child 51 B) at page 398. Probably the first Crawfurd ballad written into his book by Motherwell was *Bob Norice* (Child 83 C) at pages 510-13, which is followed almost immediately by *The Laird o' Ochiltree Wa*'s (Child 217 D) at pages 517-21, and after a wider gap by *The Burning o' Loudon Castle* (Child 178 G) at pages 543-8. Finally, at pages 635-61, there is a block of ten Crawfurd ballads: *The Earl of Aboyne* (Child 235 F), *The Water o' Ganrie* (Child 215 G), *Johnston Hey and Young Caldwell* (Child 88 D), *Wee Messgrove* (Child 81 G), *The Unco Knicht's Wowing* (Child 1 C), *The Twa Brithers* (Child 49 C), *The High Banks o Yarrow* (Child 24 B), *Jamie o' Lee* (Child 244 C), *The King's dochter Lady Jean* (Child 52 A) and *Robin Hood* (Child 250 C). Comparison with the material in the *Minstrelsy* shows that the two verses of *Bonnie Annie* in the introduction belong to *The High Banks o Yarrow* and that the single verses of *Babe Norice*, *Ochiltree Walls* and *Lady Jean* in the appendix belong to *Bob Norice*, *The Laird o' Ochiltree Wa's* and *The King's dochter Lady Jean*.

Seven of the full texts mentioned above were derived from Mary Macqueen, the wife of William Storie. Motherwell's most detailed heading concerning her is attached to *Bob Norice* which, as already noted, was probably the first of the ballads he copied. He says, 'This ballad was forwarded to me by my good friend Andrew Crawfurd of John's hill Lochwinnoch. He wrote it from the recitation of Mrs. Storie wife of William Storie labourer in Lochwinnoch. It was a song of Mrs. Storie's Grandmother.' He also notes that *The Deil's Wowing*, *Rosie Ann*, *The Laird o' Ochiltree*

[20] These three titles in the list of contents are *The Queens Mary*, *The Deils courting* and *The Deils Wowing*. The titles mentioned in the text are spelt as in the headings.

[21] Four of the pages had not been written on, but *Mild Mary* at p. 123 is written over three verses of a text in pencil. These verses come at the close of *Little Musgrave* which was written out in pencil on pages 120-3 and then written over more tightly in ink, so that the ballad was completed on page 122 and the first copy of the verses on page 123 made redundant.

Wa's, *The Unco Knicht's Wowing* and *The King's dochter Lady Jean* are from the 'singing' (pp. 309, 517) or 'recitation' (pp. 398, 647, 657) of Mrs Storie. As William Montgomerie has observed,[22] 'recitation' as used by the nineteenth-century ballad collectors may refer to singing and no distinction is being drawn. Motherwell does not credit Mrs Storie with the text of *The Fause Knight upon the Road* that he printed in his introduction but the Crawfurd MSS indicate that it was derived from her.

The ten detached verses linked with the music were also, it seems, from Mrs Storie. As three of these are the same as full texts, this gives seven additional items from this singer. The fourteen items from Mrs Storie which were included by Motherwell in his *Minstrelsy* and *Ballad Book* were available to Child, who printed all of them apart from *The Deil's Wowing* (41 *The Deil's Courtship* in the present collection) which fell outside his compass.[23] The following table shows the occurrence of full texts and first verses derived from Mrs Storie in Francis J. Child's *English and Scottish Popular Ballads* and Bertrand H. Bronson's *Traditional Tunes of the Child Ballads*. The Child numbers and titles are followed in brackets by the numbers of the ballads in the present collection.

		Child		*Bronson*	
1	Riddles Wisely Expounded (45)	C	full		
3	The Fause Knight upon the Road (31)	A	full		
5	Gil Brenton (1)	[F]	v. 1	2	v. 1
25	Willie's Lyke-Wake (16)	D	v. 1	3	v. 1
26	The Three Ravens (40)	b	v. 1	2	v. 1
51	Lizie Wan (46)	B	full		
52	The King's Dochter Lady Jean (36)	A	full	1	v. 1
68	Young Hunting (37)	[F]	v. 1	6	v. 1
83	Child Maurice (2)	C	full	4	v. 1
88	Young Johnstone (5)	F	v. 1	2	v. 1
155	Sir Hugh, or, The Jew's Daughter (10)	R	v. 1	56	v. 1
217	The Broom of Cowdenknows (32)	D	full	9	v. 1
281	The Keach i the Creel (25)	note	v. 1	1	full

Where Child had a single verse to consider, he generally treated it as an independent fragment (as in his Nos 25, 26, 88, 155 and 281)

[22] 'Sir Walter Scott as Ballad Editor' *Review of English Studies* NS 7 (1956) pp. 160–2.

[23] Child's only reference to Crawfurd is at 2.274 where he quotes Motherwell's note to *Bob Norice* and comments, 'The affected spelling I suppose to be Crawfurd's'.

except where he included it as a part of a full text from Mrs Storie (as in his Nos 52, 83 and 217), but there are two exceptions which are indicated by the use of square brackets in the above table. In these two cases, Nos 5 and 68, he was ready to match the single verses with texts in Motherwell's collection which do not have as strong a claim as the texts of Mrs Storie that are now available. The wording of the narrative lines in 5 *Lord Bengwill* (Child 5 *Gil Brenton*), 'Seven ladies liv'd in a bower, / And aye the youngest was the flower', is exactly the same as that in the Crawfurd MSS text of this ballad, whereas Child's F text, with which he matches this verse, has the rather different, 'There were three sisters in a bouir, / And the youngest was the fairest flour.' There is some room for doubt in the case of 8 *Earl Richard* (Child 68 *Young Hunting*) for the opening verse of this ballad is very similar in form in several texts. In the first line, the F variant which Child points to and the verse in Motherwell's appendix both have 'a hunting' where the Crawfurd text has 'to the hunting', but in lines 2 and 4 the advantage lies on the other side, both the appendix and Crawfurd texts having the wording 'As hard as he could ride' and 'his broad sword' where Child F has 'As fast as he can ride' and 'a small sword'.

Besides the fourteen items from Mary Macqueen and the contribution to a composite text of Motherwell's from Meg Walker which relate to the present volume, there are fifteen Crawfurd texts and fragments in Motherwell's *Minstrelsy* and *Ballad Book* which come under the scope of the second of the Scottish Text Society volumes. These items, all of which are Child ballads,[24] were collected from a number of different singers by Mary Macqueen's brother, Thomas Macqueen, whose handwriting as it appears in the Crawfurd MSS identifies him beyond doubt as the poet (1803-1861) who published several volumes of verse in Scotland and later emigrated to Canada where he became a newspaper editor.[25] An account of the expenses of gathering materials for the

[24] They appear in Child's collection as 2 I, 24 B, 49 C, 81 G, 88 D, 91 E, 161 E, 173 K, 178 G, 215 G, 216 note to B, 235 F, 244 C, 250 C, and 290 note to B.

[25] See Andrew Haydon *Pioneer Sketches in the District of Bathurst* (Toronto 1925) 1.237-85 'Thomas Macqueen - Poet, Journalist, Politician' and W. Stewart Wallace *The Dictionary of Canadian Biography* (2nd edn. Toronto 1945) 2.431. There are examples of his handwriting in the Beith Papers, Glasgow University Archive, Nos 1035-6. I have used Thomas's spelling of the surname for all members of the family.

Minstrelsy contained in Motherwell's *Notebook* (pp. 156-7) has four consecutive items that relate to sister and brother:

	£	s	d
To Mrs. Storie Lochwinnich	1	1	
To James Macqueen to enable him to go to Ayr in quest of Ballads		10	6
To expense of bringing Mrs. Storie to Paisley & getting her airs noted		17	
To filling up Macqueen with a pack and dispatching him thro' Ayr & Galloway on the old quest	2	2	

and later there is the further item:

To paid Macqueen		3	6

The use here of the Christian name 'James' seems to be a slip,[26] for it is quite certain that Thomas Macqueen collected for Motherwell as a letter from him in the Crawfurd MSS bears witness (2.335). His two expeditions took place about January and March-April 1827, and Mrs Storie's visit to Paisley may also have occurred in the early months of 1827. In Paisley, her airs would have been noted by Motherwell's music collaborator, Andrew Blaikie, who was session-clerk and precentor of Paisley Abbey Church and had an engraving business at 7 Abbey Street.[27] It may have been on the occasion of Mrs Storie's visit that Motherwell heard her sing *Bob Norice*. Apparently he had in front of him his copy of Crawfurd's text of the ballad in his *Ballad Book* and made a few alterations to it as she sang. He comments (p. 513), 'The interlineary corrections were made in consequence of Mrs Storie singing the ballad over to myself'. There is no clear evidence that she sang any other ballads for Motherwell, and Motherwell may or may not have been present when Blaikie noted the tunes of the ten opening verses of ballads that have been mentioned above. Blaikie may well have recorded more of Mrs Storie's airs, but the only ones known to be extant are those that he engraved for the *Minstrelsy*.

[26] Perhaps 'James' occurred by association with James Macqueen, editor of the *Glasgow Courier*; he was succeeded in this post by Motherwell in 1830.

[27] For further information on Blaikie, see E. B. Lyle, 'The Matching of Andrew Blaikie's Ballad Tunes with their Texts' *Scottish Studies* 16 (1972) pp. 175-80.

INTRODUCTION TO VOLUME 1

THE FIRST of the two volumes in which Crawfurd's collection is to be published includes the songs from Mary Macqueen (Mrs Storie), the principal singer represented in it, and also those from three other singers who made a sizable contribution, Meg Walker (Mrs Caldwell), William Gemmel and John Smith. Most of the songs printed in this volume were written by Crawfurd himself (those in volume 1 of his collection in pencil and the rest in ink), but there are two other hands besides his. One complete ballad (45) and part of another (46) from Mary Macqueen were written in pencil by her brother, Thomas Macqueen, and ten of the songs from Meg Walker (48-56 and 64), all eight songs from William Gemmel (65-72) and one from John Smith (75) were written in ink by Crawfurd's Lochwinnoch friend and contemporary William Orr, nicknamed 'the merchant' or 'the young merchant'.[28] Crawfurd recorded directly from Mary Macqueen but the songs from Meg Walker and John Smith which appear in his hand may quite likely have been copied from records made by William Orr, and it is also possible that a number of the Mary Macqueen songs were taken down by an intermediary, most probably Thomas Macqueen, and copied by Crawfurd. In the case of 46 *Rosianne*, the main part which is found in Crawfurd's hand was apparently copied from a text written down by Thomas Macqueen, the ending of which has been preserved.

Thomas Macqueen is the only one of the three men who wrote down these songs to record them in the normal Scots spelling generally used by educated ballad-collectors of this period. Crawfurd chose a deliberately antique way of spelling which allows variation in the letters between different occurrences of the same word. Since the ballads and songs were written from oral sources, the principal concern is whether the manner of setting them down accurately reflects the words as sung and, although Crawfurd's

[28] The son of William Orr, merchant in Lochwinnoch, and Margaret Lang, he was born 8 August 1785 and died in 1847 (*Cairn* 18.117). There are signed letters in his hand at *Cairn* 6.20 and 14.92.

method does not achieve any close phonetic exactness, it seems to give as accurate a rendering as the standard method. At one point, indeed, in its use of the 'and' ending for the present participle, it can be claimed to be more precise for it retains the distinction between the participle and the gerund which was still operative in Lochwinnoch at this time, as Crawfurd tells us.[29] Crawfurd's preference for older Scottish forms led him to substitute a number of words of his own choosing for those used by the singers, but these substitutions are generally overt and the singers' words deleted by Crawfurd are given in the present texts. There are occasions, however, when Crawfurd appears to have made silent alterations of this type, and although I have retained 'the strein' and 'bespak' in the texts there is good cause for thinking that the words sung may have been 'yestreen' and either 'and spak' or 'then spak'. Orr's spelling is not standard and may present some difficulties to the reader. The spelling 'the' usually denotes 'the' or 'they' but stands for 'thee' at 48 13.3; the spelling 'they' usually denotes 'they' or 'thy' but stands for 'the' at 64 7.7 and 71 8.2, and for 'there' at 53 19.3. The spelling 'thy' denotes 'thy' or 'they', and 'there' denotes 'their' as well as 'there'. The single letter 'e' may be used in the creation of a syllable where 'ie' is generally used, as in 'lasse' and 'weared'. The spelling 'kind' is written for the sense 'kine' in 53, and 'kine' for 'kind' at 71 5.6; similarly 'mine' is written for the sense 'mind' at 71 5.8. The letter 'a' is employed where it would be usual to find 'aw', 'ay' or 'ae' in the following words:

bra	=	braw	fra	=	frae
sa	=	saw	ga	=	gae
sha	=	shaw	ha	=	hae
a	=	ay	na	=	nae
ga	=	gay	sa	=	sae
sa	=	say	ya	=	yae

The word 'yae' (single) is also denoted by 'ye' at 66 7.3, and the word 'sae' (so) by 'say' at 53 21.2. Orr's use of apostrophes is very

[29] In his *Eik to Jamieson's Dictionary* (1.47, 51) Crawfurd says with reference to the older Scottish practice, '*and* or *an* is always the sign of the participle, and with regard to *in* or *ing*, it is the constant sign of the gerund' and goes on to state that 'the country people of Scotland' say, 'He is *improvan* (participle) his land, and he is become ritch by *improving* (gerund) his farm.' *Cf. Cairn* 11.338-48 where Crawfurd refers specifically to Lochwinnoch.

uncertain. He sometimes correctly indicates omission as in 'dash'd' 64 4.6, but he also uses the sign where there is no omission as in 'lou'd' and 'looke'd' 53 5.2, 19.2, or indicates the omission in the wrong place as in 'c'a' for 'ca'' (call) 53 17.1. He also inserts the apostrophe in some plurals, as in 'A my pretty palace's for to vew' 50 3.2, perhaps through confusion with the possessive use which he occasionally indicates correctly, as in 'another man's bride' 66 4.7. However, Orr's irregular use of apostrophes does not make for such difficult reading as his frequent omission of the apostrophe 's' both in the possessive, as in 'Lord Bangwell gate' at 75 8.1, and as the abbreviation of 'is' or 'has', as in 'Ga mak for my Lady that comming' at 53 18.1 and 'he tean her up' at 65 4.3. Orr's prose is without sentence division and in the quotations below all full stops and the capitals following them are editorial.

The songs from the four singers have been extracted from various points in Crawfurd's volumes and I list below the items as they occur there under the name of each singer and also add information about the singers and relate the variants sung by them, wherever possible, to the songs as they are known to occur elsewhere. In the lists the Crawfurd number is shown at the left and the number of the song in this edition follows the title in brackets. The date of recording is included wherever Crawfurd made a note of it.

Mary Macqueen (Mrs Storie)

All the songs known to be from Mary Macqueen are in the first volume of Crawfurd's collection, and take up nearly two-thirds of the book. They form two main blocks at pages 8-122 and 169-218, and the only items not apparently from her within these blocks are two songs at pages 96-101 and 201-3. The blocks are separated by an inserted gathering (pp. 123-68) which consists basically of material collected by Thomas Macqueen, and which includes four of the songs given here. Crawfurd's numbering appears to indicate that the songs in the inserted gathering belong at a later point in the collection that the present page order would suggest and so I have placed these four between a first section where the Crawfurd numbers run up to 21 and a later section where the numbers run from 54. In addition two separate ballads from Mary Macqueen occur later in the volume at pages 275-80 and 316-21.

The fourteen items marked ★ are not specifically ascribed to Mrs Storie, but in the sequences of songs taken down from her Crawfurd gives her source at the head (see notes to individual songs), and this practice links with her all these items except 47 *The Prince of Orange* where no source is given but which has been included here on the rather slight ground that it comes in Crawfurd's numbering between two songs that are known to have been derived from Mary Macqueen. In the case of 45 *The Unco Knicht's Wooing* and 46 *Rosianne*, which were written by Thomas Macqueen, there is no note about source in the Crawfurd MSS and the ascription to Mrs Storie rests entirely on Motherwell's *Ballad Book*.

		1826	
1	Bob Norrice (2)	20 Nov	1.8–12
2	The Laird of Ochiltree Walls (32)	12 Nov	1.13–19
3	Lord Bangwell's Adventure (1)		1.21–6
	★The Hawthorn Green (4)	Dec	1.27–8
4	William and the Young Colonel (5)		1.29–34
5	The Bush of Broom (27)		1.35–7
	★Fair Rosalind (6)	Dec	1.38
6	The Cruel Stepmother (7)		1.39–42
	★The Reeking House (24)		1.43–5
	★The Grazier's Dochter (8)		1.46–53
7	Lady Jean (36)	30 Nov	1.54–8
8	Lord Meanwell (9)	30 Nov	1.59–65
9	Earl Richard (37)	1/2 Dec	1.66–70
10	Sir Hugh (10)	Dec	1.71–5
11	The King's Dochter Jean (11)		1.76, 78–9
	The Laird o' Kelty (38)	Dec	1.80, 85–6
	The Mason's Dochter (39)	Nov	1.81–4, 87–8
	list of song titles		1.89
12	The Cruel Mother (12)	2 Dec	1.91–5
13	Lord Gregory (13)	Dec	1.102–7
14	My Lord Derwater (3)	12 Dec	1.108–11
19	The Deil's Courtship (41)	Dec	1.113–16
	★The Wandering Lover (14)	31 Dec	1.117–18
21	The Squire's Son of Aizling Town (15)	31 Dec	1.119–22

		1827	
20[30]	The Merry Lykewake (16)	4 Jan	1.169-70
	*Young Betsy (17)	8 Jan	1.171-3
		1826	
18	Fair Rosanne (18)	12 Dec	1.175-9
	*The Bonnie Blue-Eyed Lassie (33)		1.180-1
15	The Auld Wife and the Peat Creel (25)	12 Dec	1.182-5
	Mother Bunch (28)	12 Dec	1.186-90
	*The Hills o' Gowrie (29)		1.191
	*Willie Taylor (19)		
	*The Yorkshire Rambler (26)		
16	The Three Ravens (40)		1.192-5
17	Lord Level (20)	12 Dec	1.196-8
27	The Unco Knicht's Wooing (45)		1.127-30
		1827	
49	The Shepherd's Son (30)	18 Jan	1.147-50, 155
	*Slighted Love (43)	Jan	1.156-7
24	Rosianne (46)		1.159-63
58	*The Penitent Bride (21)		1.199-200
59	*The Prince of Orange (47)		1.204-5
	Mall Bowie (35)		1.206-8
55	The Fause Knicht (31)		1.209-10
60	*The Three Jolly Butchers (22)		1.211-13
54	Poor Greeting Wilsie (42)		1.214-16
	Wise Willie (23)		1.217-18
67	The Ensign and the Lady Gay (44)		1.275-80
68	May Colyean (34)		1.316-21

Crawfurd identifies this singer in an incidental comment relating to a William Sempill, portioner of Little Cloak or Boghead in

[30] The XX appears to have been altered from XXII, and the number XX seems formerly to have been given to *The Wandering Lover* (1.117-18) but has been deleted there.

Lochwinnoch parish (*Cairn* 1.238-40). He remarks that Sempill, after the death of his wife, Mary Boyd, 'cast a love eye to his servant Mary Macqueen of a travelling or some such a tinklar family who (were) had taken their quarters in the houses of the Boghead, after the Boghead mill was burnt.[31] Mary McQueen had some beauty but she refused his addresses and married Willie Story son of old Will Storie, in the old town all weavers, and went to america - in this year 1828. Old Will and his wife, viz. Elizabeth Stewart, Young Willie with his wife, viz Mary Macqueen and 4 children, and Rab Storie another son of old Will Storie - a youth very fond of whisky. The same Mary Macqueen has a great number of auld ballads which I had fished out of her for Mr William Motherwell.' The family party described by Crawfurd landed in Canada on 2 May 1828, and went to stay temporarily with young William Storie's brother James in the township of Macnab by Hull in Upper Canada[32] before setting up on their own about ten miles away. Crawfurd's *Cairn* contains copies of three letters from the emigrants (13.57-65) and the one from Mary Storie is addressed to her father Osburn McQueen, Kilbirnie. Possibly her mother, from whom she learnt many of her songs, was 'Elizabeth Copland Spouse to Osbourn McQeen' who died in Kilbirnie parish in 1831.[33] Mary also learnt songs from her brothers 'Tam' (Thomas, the poet) and Hamilton, both of whom worked as masons.[34] Thomas, who was born on 9 October 1803, was aged twenty-three in the early part of 1827 when he went on his collecting expeditions. I have not discovered the date of Mary's birth, but her marriage to William Storie was proclaimed on 25 August 1821,[35] and, if she is assumed to have married at twenty, she would have been twenty-five or twenty-six at this time.

[31] The mill was burnt about 1813 (*Cairn* 11.33).

[32] James Storie had written from Canada encouraging his father to emigrate in a letter of 3 September 1826, an extract from which was published anonymously in *The Paisley Advertiser*, 13 January 1827, p. 1 cols. 4-5; Crawfurd identifies the author in his *Newspaper Cuttings* Vol. 1 (Paisley Central Library PC 1456) pp. 72-3.

[33] Kilbirnie Parish Register, 596/2, 29 January 1831. The Lochwinnoch Parish Register, 570/3, records the birth of a daughter, Marjory Young McQueen, on 18 November 1819 to 'Ozborn McQueen and Elizabeth Copland in Boghead'.

[34] Crawfurd links the two brothers when he mentions the marriage to Agnes Mackie of 'Hamilton McQueen mason Kilbirnie the brother of the poet' (*Cairn* 12.277).

[35] Lochwinnoch Parish Register, 570/3; this volume of the register also records the birth of twin sons, William and John, 'to William Storie and Mary McQueen in Lochwinnoch' on 12 December 1822.

Mary Macqueen's songs in this edition have been grouped according to source. The first twenty-seven were family songs, No 1 deriving from her great-grandmother, Nos 2-3 from her grandmother, Nos 4-23 from her mother and Nos 24-7 from her brothers. Nos 28-31 were learnt in Galloway, 32-5 in Ayr and 36-42 in Lochwinnoch. Nos 43-4 were learnt from named people who are not located, and no information on source is available for Nos 45-7. Within each of the above groups, songs are given in the order in which they have been listed here, except that all songs from the same person are brought together at the point where the first item occurs.

Twenty-two of the songs recorded from Mary Macqueen are Child ballads: 1-3, 5, 9-13, 15-16, 20, 25, 30-32, 34, 37, 40 and 44-46. All are separate variants except 34 *May Colyean* which is similar to the D text of Child 4 *Lady Isabel and the Elf-Knight*, a chapbook form of the ballad. *May Colyean* is closest to D.d *The historical ballad of May Culzean* (Child 1.485, 488-9) which occurs in a collection of chapbooks printed in Ayr in the National Library of Scotland (LC 2790:3 Ayr n.d. pp. 2-6; 4 n.p. n.d. pp. 2-8) and so, as Mary Macqueen learnt this song from a Mrs Smith in Ayr, there is some likelihood that it stemmed from a chapbook printed in that town. 30 *The Shepherd's Son* comes rather closer at some points to a chapbook form with the same title (LC 2842:3 Glasgow 1816 pp. 6-[8]) than to any of the variants of Child 112 *The Baffled Knight* printed by Child or Bronson. The relevant verses (2, 3 and 11) are quoted here:

He looked east, he looked west, he's ta'en another look,
And there he spied a fair maid a-swimming in a brook.

O do not touch my mantle, but let my cloaths alone,
And you shall have a good reward if you conduct me home.

* * *

There is a flower in our garden, they call it marigold,
And he that would not when he could, he should not when he
would.

Seven of Mary Macqueen's songs are listed by G. Malcolm Laws in his *American Balladry From British Broadsides:* 17 *Young Betsy* (M 20 *Betsy is a Beauty Fair*), 19 *Willie Taylor* (N 11 *William Taylor*), 21 *The Penitent Bride* (P 31 *The Nobleman's Wedding*), 22 *The Three*

Jolly Butchers (L 4 *The Three Butchers*), 35 *Mall Bowie* (O 14 *Pretty Polly*), 43 *Slighted Love* (P 25 *Love Has Brought Me to Despair*) and 47 *The Prince of Orange* (P 12 *Nancy II*). *Young Betsy* has a general resemblance to two chapbook and broadside forms, *Pretty Betty* (*e.g.* chapbook GUL BD20 - i.10:20 n.p. n.d. pp. 2-5) and the more widespread one often called *The Betrayed Maiden* (*e.g.* broadside BM 1875.d.16 f. 3, chapbook GUL Bh13 - d.2:4 Glasgow 1800 pp. 3-5; C. H. Firth *An American Garland* Oxford 1915 pp. 69-70), but it is not very close to either. William Taylor occurs in a number of different versions, but the verse quoted by Crawfurd is particularly close to the opening of *Revengeful Lover* (*e.g.* chapbook LC 2856:2 Kilmarnock n.d. pp. 6-8):

William was a youthful lover,
  Full of pride and lovely air,
And he did his mind discover
  To a charming lady fair.

The song called by Laws *The Nobleman's Wedding* was adapted by William Allingham and his version of it was current in broadsides (*e.g.* Madden 25:179), but of the older form represented by *The Penitent Bride* I have seen only a single broadside copy which is reprinted in the appendix (No 3 *The Wedding*). Although *The Three Butchers* was widely current in several different broadside versions, I have not observed one that comes very close to the present variant, which is like that printed by Greig (Greig *NE* 36). *Mall Bowie* is similar to *Honest Mall Boye* (*e.g.* chapbook LC 2899:6 n.p. 1794 pp. 5-7). The song *The Prince of Orange* or *Nancy II*, which is best known in Scotland as *The Rambling Beauty* (Greig *NE* 142), occurs in a number of different forms on broadsides and in chapbooks (*e.g.* Madden 4:362, 5:1274, 16:15, 17:135; Newcastle University Library, Robert White collection of chapbooks 12:31 Glasgow 1805 pp. 5-6). 43 *Slighted Love* may have lost from its opening some narrative material which is found in other variants of *Love Has Brought Mε to Despair*. All the verses except the last have equivalents in the broadside song beginning 'Near Woodstock town in Oxfordshire' which was current in the seventeenth and eighteenth centuries with the titles *The Constant Lady and False-hearted Squire* and *The Oxfordshire Tragedy* (*RB* 8.635), but the presence of the last verse indicates that it is more likely to relate directly to forms of which I have not noticed any broadside or chapbook texts.

There are also among Mary Macqueen's songs several lengthy broadside pieces not mentioned by Laws. 7 *The Cruel Stepmother* is widely found and appears in print as *The Lady Isabella's Tragedy; Or, The Step-Mother's Cruelty* (*RB* 6.651-2; chapbook GUL Mu52 - e.17:25 Edinburgh n.d. pp. 2-5). It is clear from the printed copies that the stepmother's message to the cook originally referred to a 'doe' and not a 'dove' as in Mary Macqueen's variant. The change has evidently come about through the intermediary Scots word 'doo' (dove), which occurs together with 'dove' in this song as recorded from Elizabeth Creighton (Creighton MS p. 76). 8 *The Grazier's Dochter* appears to be an adaptation of *The Kentish Garland* (Julia H. L. De Vaynes *The Kentish Garland* Hertford 1881-2, 1.227-33). The only other instance of the adapted form I know of is *The Unfortunate Grazier's Daughter* printed at Belfast in 1767 which is given at the end of this volume (Appendix No 1). 18 *Fair Rosanne* tells the story of Rosamund de Clifford, mistress of Henry II, and is the treatment of the story which is entitled *The Unfortunate Concubine; Or, Rosamond's Overthrow* (*RB* 6.676-8). It is interesting to compare Mary Macqueen's variant not only with this widely found form but also with the Irish broadside text called *Fair Rosamund* (Appendix No 2) which begins at the same point as *Fair Rosanne* and, like it, omits the second part of the narrative found in *The Unfortunate Concubine.* At the end of this song, Crawfurd has the note: 'She heard there are 4 songs on this subject - and [did] not recollect [whether] her mother had them all - and (h) she is certain that her mother had another one'. One of the additional three songs may have been *The Life and Death of Fair Rosamond, King Henry the Second's Concubine* by Thomas Deloney (*RB* 6.673-5) and another the anonymous ballad beginning 'In Woodstock Bower, once grew a Flower' (BM 12330.a.24 *The Unfortunate Concubines* London 1717 pp. 79-82 *A Song on the Death of Fair Rosamond*). Other possibilities are *Queen Eleanor's Confession* (Child 156; *RB* 6.680-1) where Queen Eleanor confesses that she 'poisoned Fair *Rosamond*, all in fair *Woodstock* bower' and the song concerning Edward IV's mistress, *The Woful Lamentation of Mrs. Jane Shore* (*RB* 1.483-92), which begins with a reference to 'Rosamond that was so fair'. It seems almost certain that the lurid murder narrative 39 *The Mason's Dochter* circulated on broadsides but I have not located it in print. I have seen it elsewhere only in the Greig collection where it is called *Fair Isabel* (Greig *Words*

10.82–5, 55.111–15). This text, from Alexander Robb, is shorter than Mary Macqueen's (fifty-six lines as against eighty) but it does include an additional verse which comes in after verse 12 of her variant:

> Oh little did fair Isabel's mistress know
> The pain & the anguish she did undergo,
> But in two or three weeks she grew healthy & well
> But still he bore kindness to his bonnie Isabel.

Further broadside and chapbook songs with a slighter narrative content than those just discussed are 24 *The Reeking House*, 26 *The Yorkshire Rambler*, 27 *The Bush of Broom*, 28 *Mother Bunch*, 29 *The Hills o' Gowrie* and 38 *The Laird o' Kelty*. In the case of *The Yorkshire Rambler* and *The Hills o' Gowrie* Crawfurd gives only the first four lines, probably feeling that the songs were modern and generally available. The first, which is most often called *The Yorkshireman in London* or *Quite Politely* (*e.g.* chapbook GUL Mu52 - e.17:11 Edinburgh n.d. pp. 6–8, broadside BM 1875.d.5 No 144; Frank Purslow *The Wanton Seed* London 1969 pp. 55–6), tells how a Yorkshireman who is being duped by a London girl has had the forethought to sew fish-hooks in his pockets and succeeds in going off with her diamond ring. The four lines headed *The Hills o' Gowrie* are the opening of the song called *The Lass o' Gowrie* which is found in chapbooks in two forms, one with three eight-line verses and the other with two additional ones (*e.g.* LC 2856:52 Kilmarnock n.d. pp. 6–7, 3 verses, LC 2853:15 Greenock n.d. pp. 2–3, 5 verses; Robert Ford, *The Harp of Perthshire* Paisley and London 1893 pp. 116–17). A song with this title by Carolina Oliphant, Lady Nairne, (Ford, pp. 118–19) has the same opening lines, but it seems more likely to have been the anonymous chapbook song that was known to Mary Macqueen. *Mother Bunch* occurs in the chapbook and broadside press with the title *Andrew Carr* (*e.g.* chapbook LC 2826:20 Falkirk 1816 pp. 2–4, broadside BM 1870. c.2 No 316). *The Reeking House*, *The Bush of Broom* and *The Laird o' Kelty* appear in a number of collections derived from Scottish oral tradition but I have seen only one instance of each in broadside or chapbook and I include these items in the appendix (No 4 *Neighbour Hark*, No 5 *Bonny Bush of Broom* and No 6 *The Pretty Parks of Cailty O*).

41 *The Deil's Courtship* is a variant of a song often called *A*

Pennyworth of Pins or *The Keys of Canterbury*. The form with the devil in place of a human wooer seems to have found favour in Scotland and may be a distinctively Scottish development (see Robert Chambers, *Popular Rhymes of Scotland* Edinburgh and London 1870 pp. 61–2 *The Tempted Lady*, and Kinloch MSS 6.57–9 *The Devil's courtship*). 42 *Poor Greeting Wilsie* is the song called *Kind-Hearted Nansy* in Herd's collection (*Songs from David Herd's Manuscripts* ed. Hans Hecht, Edinburgh 1904 p. 155 No 46) which is treated as a cognate form of Opie 317, although it might possibly be regarded as falling within the group of songs listed under this number. 4 *The Hawthorn Green* is of considerable interest since it is a variant of the song called *A mery Ballet of the Hathorne tre* in the fifteenth-century manuscript BM Cotton Vespasian A.25 (*Jahrbuch für romanische und englische Sprache und Literatur* NS 2, 1875, pp. 360–2). This early text was printed by Joseph Ritson in his *Ancient Songs* (London 1790 pp. 146–8), but it does not seem likely that the variant recorded from Mary Macqueen was derived in any way from Ritson's volume. The only other trace I have found of the song is a verse which is equivalent to the fourth printed here that was recovered from tradition in the present century (Fred Hamer *Garners Gay* London 1967 p. 15). 6 *Fair Rosalind* is part of a song of seven eight-line stanzas beginning 'On the bank of a river so deep' which appears in the second volume of a song-book called *The Charmer* (Edinburgh 1782 pp. 73–4). 14 *The Wandering Lover* belongs to the class of night-visiting songs (*cf.* Peggy Seeger and Ewan MacColl *The Singing Island* London 1960 No 19 *Here's a Health to All True Lovers*[36]), and 23 *Wise Willie* is the wren-hunt song (Opie 447) found widely distributed throughout the British Isles. I have not succeeded in tracing 33 *The Bonnie Blue-Eyed Lassie*. Its opening lines are like those in the fourth verse of a quite different piece called *The Queen of Hearts* (BM 11602.gg.30 p. 34; *cf. The Constant Maiden's Resolution RB* 7.539–40):

> I wish I was on yonder high mountain,
> Where gold & silver I could have for counting, . . .

Twenty titles at 1.89, the last two of which are written sideways next the spine, seem likely to be those of songs known to Mary

[36] Bronson (4.20) gives this as variant 10 of Child 248 *The Grey Cock, or, Saw You My Father?* but the connection with this ballad seems tenuous.

Macqueen. In the case of songs found in the Crawfurd MSS and included in this volume I have noted the song number at the side. The letter 'd' following a name indicates that it was deleted by Crawfurd.

28	Mother Bunch d	
25	The auld wife and the Peet Creel d	
20	Lord Level d	
	Donald Macdonald d	
	The faithless Lover	modern
30	The Shepherd's Son d	- baudie
	The unfaithful Lady	modern - baudie
41	The Deil - or Clutie's Courtship d	
	The faithless lover about the Galloway lass	for Motherwell
14	The wandering Lover d	
15	The Squire's Son of Aizling town d	good for Motherw[ell]
	Barbara Allan d	
35	Mall Bowie	modern
	New Barbary d	
	Bess and Jean d	
	The Prentice Boy	
	The nut Bush	
	Jean Lockie	
	A Song about Castlesemple	
	The Other Song about Haizling town or Haizling-green	

Eight of the items listed are clearly the same as songs in this volume recorded from Mary Macqueen, and 'The faithless Lover' may possibly be the same as 43 *Slighted Love*. By 'The Other Song about Haizling town or Haizling-green' Crawfurd apparently means Child 293 *John of Hazelgreen* for he has a side-note to 15 *The Squire's Son of Aizling Town* at 1.119 saying 'Motherwell in his Minstrelsy quotes *Jock o' Hazlegreen*. in the Introduction, p. c.' A variant of it headed 'Johnie of Hazelgrein' was recorded by Thomas Macqueen from his mother (1.268-70). 'A Song about Castlesemple' is probably the song beginning 'Castle-Semple stands so sweet' which is printed among the *Poems and Songs* of Alexander Tait (1790) pp. 183-4. Variants of it were collected by Crawfurd from Peggy Reid and W. Wingate (3.67-8, 291-2).

A number of items not included in the Crawfurd MSS are common in chapbooks, and in these cases I give a reference to a representative example. 'Donald Macdonald' is a song of James Hogg's (*James Hogg: Selected Poems* ed. Douglas S. Mack, Oxford 1970 pp. 111-13; LC 2874:9 Stirling 1824 pp. 2-5) and 'Bess and Jean' seems likely to be *Bess the Gawkie* by James Muirhead (*SMM* 1.4 No 4; LC 2838:6 Glasgow 1802 pp. 2-4). 'Barbara Allan' is Child No 84 *Bonny Barbara Allan* (LC 2892:52 Edinburgh 1823 pp. 2-3) and 'New Barbary' is fairly certainly *Captain Glen's Voyage to New Barbary* (LC 2899:14 n.p. n.d. pp. 4-7) which is Laws K 22A *Captain Glen* and is given by Bronson as an appendix to Child No 57 *Brown Robyn's Confession*.[37] 'The faithless lover about the Galloway lass' is very probably *Fair Margaret of Craignargat* (James Maidment *Scotish Ballads and Songs* Edinburgh 1859 pp. 172-8; LC 2835:33 Glasgow 1802 pp. 2-7).

No certain identification can be made in the case of the song referred to by the title 'The Prentice Boy' but two possibilities are *The Apprentice Boy* or *The Prentice Boy* beginning 'By my indentures I was bound' (LC 2807:6 Edinburgh n.d. pp. 5-7; *cf.* Greig *NE* 64 *The Apprentice Sailor*) and Laws M 12 *The Apprentice Boy* beginning 'As down in Cupid's garden for pleasure I did walk' (Madden 18:609 *The 'Prentice Boy*). I have not found a song called 'The nut Bush' but it may be the same as *The Nut Bushes*, a slip song printed in Glasgow (GUL Mu22 - x. 13 p. 27a), which is a form of Laws P 2 *The Green Bushes*. 'The Unfaithful Lady', which is described as 'baudy', may have been the song sometimes called *The False Bride* which begins (Greig *NE* 24):

I once loved a fair maid both handsome and gay,
I hated all people that against her did say;
But now she's rewarded me ill for my pains,
  For she's going to be wed with another.

and often has a verse or two about the bridegroom wearing the lover's old shoes. I have not been able to trace the song called 'Jean Lockie', and the only suggestion I have to offer is that it might possibly have been a mishearing of the name *Glenlogie* (Child 238).

[37] There is a possibility that the verse and air of this ballad in the appendix of Motherwell's *Minstrelsy* (No 31 *Captain Glen*) were recorded by Blaikie from Mary Macqueen, but in all the known records from her he gives the first verse of the ballad, whereas in this case he gives a later verse.

Meg Walker (Mrs Caldwell)

There are items from Meg Walker in all four of the volumes that contain Crawfurd's song-collection. Those in volume 1 and those transferred to F are in ink in William Orr's hand,[38] and those in volumes 2 and 3 are in ink in Crawfurd's hand. Three items not specifically assigned to Meg Walker (Nos 51, 52 and 56) have been included here since they are grouped with others that are known to be from her. The last two items in the list of contents of the first volume are not in the book and they do not appear in F, although it seems possible that they were removed at the same time as the items at 1.337-44 which do appear there. *The Beltrees Sang* may be the same as *Lady Beltrees* at 2.198, and the title *Lord Bangwell*, which Crawfurd applies in his general index (3.436) to the Mary Macqueen ballad headed *Lord Bangwell's Adventure* at 1.21, may refer to another variant of Child 5 *Gil Brenton*. I have not included here a variant of Child 73 *Lord Thomas and Fair Annet* called *Lord Thomas and Fair Eleanor* (2.295-9) to which Crawfurd attaches Meg Walker's name in the list of contents in volume 2, for the text of this ballad is followed by the ascription 'Mary Wishart a native of Dunse' and I have supposed that Crawfurd marked it as Meg Walker's by a mistake, perhaps arising from the identity of the initials.

[38] Most of the material written by William Orr which has been transferred from volume 1 to F appears on three similar long sheets the last of which is watermarked 1823. On these sheets Orr has written over pencil notes by Crawfurd on the Ewing family. They were numbered by Crawfurd 317-22 (equivalent to pages 337-44 in the fresh numbering used in the list above) and are now F 15-20, with the ending of *Sir Donald and Eliza Lindsay* coming on a smaller piece of paper stuck to F 21. F 22 is blank but F 23-4, which has the watermark M 1824, is another long sheet in Orr's hand which has been transferred from volume 3. This sheet, which contains *Bonnie Belleen*, has on one side (p. 24) the Crawfurd page numbers 180 and 181 and evidently had the position 3.179-82 which is equivalent to 3.199-202 by the fresh numbering. 1.345-56, which contain the final three songs in Orr's hand in the first volume, are of the same paper as this sheet with the watermark M 1824. At 1.322-34 Orr has written on smaller pieces of paper which have been stuck to the pages of Crawfurd's volume. In nine cases he has used the backs of handbills reading, 'Wanted to Borrow Two Thousand pounds, on security over Lands; Interest 4 per Cent, and to be paid yearly. - Apply to John Connell Writer. Lochwinnoch, 15th. April, 1823. Printed by W. Taylor, Lochwinnoch'. These are attached printed side down to pages 322-3 and 329-34. The folio 325-6 was stuck down by Crawfurd to page 324 so that the page I have numbered 325 was obscured, but it has now separated from page 324 except at the spine so that all the writing can be read. Crawfurd copied the contents of page 325 (the last five verses of 48 *The Nut-Brown Bride*) on page 328.

69	The Nut-Brown Bride (48) *March 1827*	1.322-8
70	The Laird o' Ochiltree (49) *March 1827*	1.329-34
	Jamie Douglas (50)	[1.337-8] F 15-16
	The Faughhill Shearing (51)	[1.338] F 16-17
	When My Old Hat Was New (52)	[1.339-40] F 17-18
72	Sir Donald and Eliza Lindsay (53)	[1.340-4] F 18-21
71	The Rose Smells Sae Sweetly (54)	1.345-9
73	The Sun Shines over the Valley (55)	1.350-3
	A Yarmouth Story (56)	1.354-6
	[The Beltrees Sang]	[1.357-?]
	[Lord Bangwell]	[1.359-?]
183	Lady Beltrees (57)	2.198
182	Rhyme on John Tamson's wallet *c. 1 Oct 1827*[39]	2.202
184	Lord Thomas and Lady Margaret (58)	2.273-6
120	Jock t' Leg and the Merry Merchant (59)	3.7-10
208	The Laird of Johnstone and Miss Jean Macdowall (60)	3.71
238	The Braes of Killiecrankie (61)	3.81
	Tradition about the death of Miss Hope	3.84
232	Rhyme on the borrowing days	3.85
	Lord Eglinton's Song (62)	3.86-7
269	Anecdote about the half-wit Will Speir	3.88-9
	Tradition about the death of Mrs Hunter *1828*	3.90

[39] The date is attached to a variant of this rhyme from Mrs Greenfield which comes before Meg Walker's on the same page.

229	The Wee Crap (63) *1828*	3.106-7
250	Legends about Michael Scott	3.169-73
251	Legends about Michael Scott	3.193
	Bonnie Belleen (64)	[3.199-202] F 23-4

Margaret Walker (Mrs Caldwell) is always named Meg or Peggy by Crawfurd, and I call her Meg as he regularly does in the first volume of the *Auld Ballats* where most of her songs appear. At the time the songs were recorded she was a widow, living at Bridgend in Lochwinnoch. Her husband had been John Caldwell, baptised 10 October 1762, the natural son of John Caldwell of Lochside and Margaret Orr who was servant there. The William Orr who took down the songs was the nephew of this Margaret Orr and so was Meg Walker's cousin by marriage. Crawfurd mentions that John Caldwell had the nickname Horn Johnie 'for he was blawing on a horn ilka morning to raise the workers of the cotton mills here' (1.328; *Cairn* 1.296, 304c and 34.119-21). This couple may be the 'John Caldwell and Margaret Walker both of this parish' [of Lochwinnoch] who gave in their names to be proclaimed on 28 November 1795 and who had a daughter Margaret on 12 March 1800.[40] If so, it seems that the daughter did not survive for Crawfurd says they had no children. Crawfurd states that 'Johnie died about 1810 or 1820. Peggie died about 1830 or thereby'. Supposing that the singer was of the same age as her husband, she would have been sixty-four in the early part of 1827, but she may quite likely have been rather younger than this. She evidently had contacts with Ayrshire, for a note at 3.173 on the Michael Scott material states that she 'got the story from Robert Montgomerie of Broadlie' in the parish of Dalry,[41] and there is also a deleted note following the rhyme on John Tamson's wallet saying that Meg Walker 'brought it from Beith'.

[40] Lochwinnoch Parish Registers, 570/2 and 570/1.

[41] This is the Robert Montgomerie (1730-1822) mentioned in James Paterson's *History of the Counties of Ayr and Wigton* (Edinburgh 1863-6) 3.174. Crawfurd published the Michael Scott legends in 'The Deil of Ardrossan' *The Scottish Journal of Topography* 1 (1847) pp. 316-17.

The songs taken down from her include eight Child ballads: 48-50, 53-55 and 58-59, two of which, 49 and 55, are variants of ballads also recorded from Mary Macqueen: Child 217 *The Broom of Cowdenknows* (32) and Child 25 *Willie's Lyke-Wake* (16). 51 *Jamie Douglas* (Child 204) is unusual in two respects. Firstly, it ends with the reinstatement of the lady and the death of the villain. As already noted, the ending of Motherwell's composite version (Child N) is based on the conclusion of this text. Secondly, this variant of *Jamie Douglas* stands alone in having a blackamoor in opposition to the lady, and there is an interesting possibility that this development reflects an incident in the history of the principal family in Lochwinnoch parish in the eighteenth century, the Macdowalls of Castlesemple. Colonel William Macdowall (1677-1748) served in the West Indies, and Crawfurd notes (*Cairn* 29.ix.9-10) that he brought home 'a Negro from St Kitts, as a flunkie, or a body servant, called James Hamiltoun, or commonly called *Col. McDowalls' Black*'[42] and adds a tradition received from William Jack and Robert Hendrie:

> This Blackamore's colour did not suit the refined taste of the Jacobitical Lady McDowall.[43] She waged a constant war with her husband about this Black. She advised the Laird to put the Negro away. One day he ordered his carriage to be prepared for a long journey. She speired at the Laird what was his object. He replied that he cannot live without his favourite Negro, and he was determined to separate from his beloved spouse. She seeing his firmness to his purpose, was obliged to be content with the colour of the Black's skin.

It is by no means certain that this episode affected Meg Walker's *Jamie Douglas*, but there are local references in other songs recorded from her as, for example, in the fragment of *The Collier Laddie* called *The Laird of Johnstone and Miss Jean Macdowall* (60, *cf.* John Ord, *Bothy Songs and Ballads* Paisley 1930, repr. Edinburgh 1973 pp. 40–2). Its situation does not appear to have any close parallel in the Macdowall family history, but there may be a reminiscence of the marriage that took place in 1779 between Miss Mary

[42] He is mentioned in the Lochwinnoch Kirk Session Record as 'Black James (A Heathen)' at Castlesemple, 22 March 1737 (Scottish Record Office CH2/649/1).

[43] The reference is to Colonel Macdowall's second wife, Isabella Wallace, heiress of Woolmet in the parish of Newton near Edinburgh.

Macdowall of Castlesemple and George Houston, Laird of Johnstone in the Parish of Paisley.[44] 57 *Lady Beltrees*, which is a variant of *Mount and Go* (Greig *NE* 158) is related by its title to the family of the Sempills of Beltrees in Lochwinnoch Parish. The song does not commonly include a verse like the one given here, but a Border text of it 'from the Olivers of Chesters' in James Telfer's collection (White MS p. 691) opens:

> The lady looked over her castle wae
> And there she spied her marners all
> And there she spied them one and all
> Saying go and ile go withe you laddie
> Bony laddie munt and go
> Bony laddie munt and go
> Bony laddie munt and go
> Go and ile go with you laddie

62 *Lord Eglinton's Song* is known throughout Britain as *A Sweet Country Life* and was current in chapbooks and broadsides (*e.g.* GUL Bh13 - d.1:32 Glasgow 1802 p. 3, BM 1875.d.16 No 8), but here it is regarded as an Ayrshire song, and is ascribed in a note to the Lord Eglinton who was shot by a poacher on his estates at Ardrossan, *i.e.* Alexander Montgomerie, tenth Earl of Eglinton (1723-1769).

In 51 *The Faughhill Shearing* I have used the spelling 'Faughhill' for Orr's 'fahill' supposing that there is a connection with the place of this name in Roxburghshire, but this may not be so. In the only other text I know of, *The Harvest Song* supplied to Gavin Greig by Bell Robertson (Greig *NE* 98), the place-name is 'Firehall'. The narrative of 56 *A Yarmouth Story* is best known through a song sometimes called *The Box upon her Head* (Laws L 3 *The Undaunted Female*), but Meg Walker's text is close to the older form *The Tinker and Staffordshire Maid* which dates from the eighteenth century (*e.g.* broadside Madden 3:722). A chapbook song of twenty-three eight-line stanzas called *Luckidad's Garland; or, When my Old Hat was New* (*e.g.* LC 2846:16 n.p. n.d. pp. 2-8; James Maidment *Scotish Ballads and Songs* Edinburgh 1859 pp. 134-41) was evidently the source of the fragmentary 52 *When My Old*

[44] The marriage took place on 30 January (Lochwinnoch Parish Register, 570/2). For the family history, see Burke's *Landed Gentry*, *Cairn* 29.ix, and *The Macdowall Family* (MS) in Paisley Central Library, PC 1471.

Hat Was New; Meg Walker knew the full title 'Luckedat Garling or when my old Hat Was New' as in the chapbook. 61 *The Braes of Killiecrankie* was current in Scotland as a fragment (*cf. Songs from David Herd's Manuscripts* ed. Hans Hecht, Edinburgh 1904 p. 153 No 44 *Birks of Abergeldie*). I have not found elsewhere 63 *The Wee Crap*. Crawfurd relates the situation it describes to an account of the dry summer of 1826 which he copied from the *Glasgow Chronicle* of 5 October (2.277 No 230):

> There is an old Scottish saw which runs thus -
>
> A sunnie simmer has ay been
> Auld Scotland's best and chiefest freind, -
> Though aften nipt be cauld and weet,
> Yet ne'er owr brunt wi simmer's heat.
>
> Although this saw may have been verified, yet we have good reason to believe that it is not always the truth, of which I fear this year's crop is a too deep-felt proof. A very large proportion of the best corn lands has produced an uncommonly light crop. The dwarfish stooks were truly pitiful, and the poorly filled stack-yards are no less so.

From its place in the manuscripts, 64 *Bonnie Belleen* was apparently the last of the songs recorded from Meg Walker, and it is conceivable that it was supplied in response to an enquiry about a four-line fragment and summary collected from a Mrs Oliphant (3.330):

> O hae you hard of bonnie Balein
> The flouir of Andalee
> Or hae ye hard of hir brithers twa
> Wha focht be the warlock trie.
>
> Mrs Oliphant forgot all except thir four lines. She minds the story of this ballat. A knight came courting Balein. Her twa brithers were offended. The lovers eloped. The brothers pursued them and slew the knight.

Meg Walker committed this song to memory from a book owned by a Miss Jamieson, but I have not succeeded in finding it in print.

William Gemmel

All but one of the items from William Gemmel are in Orr's hand and occur at four points in the second volume. The material at 2.157-64, 166-70 and 177-9 is in black ink, and the material at 2.207-17 is in brown ink, with some additions in black. The list of contents in volume 2 ascribes 'Black Jock etc.' to William Gemmel and I have taken it that the 'etc.' covers *As I Was A-Walking by yon Green Garden* which comes before *Black Joke* on the same page, and also *There Was an Old Man Was Smoking his Pipe* on the facing page which is in the same ink as the other two and has lines scored through as they do. A further item in the third volume, which is headed 'The last speech of an Old Miser rec[i]ted by old tailor Wm Gemmil', was initially written out in full by Orr but the first six verses now appear in Crawfurd's hand.[45]

	Airlie House (65)	2.157
180	Young Lochinvar's Courtship (66)	2.158-61
179	Traditions about the Earl of Glencairn	2.162-4
	There Was an Old Man Was Smoking his Pipe (67)	2.166
	As I Was A-Walking by yon Green Garden (68)	2.167
	Black Joke (69)	,,
	The Last Speech of Michael Marshall's Tup	2.168-9
	The Tup's Ghost	2.169-70
187	Johnie Miller of Glenlee (70)	2.177-9
139	Linton Race (71)	2.207-12
146	Outline of a song about Johnie o' Moffat	2.213
156	The Wee Wee Man (72)	2.214-15
	The Daft Bargain - by Allan Ramsay	2.216-17
	The Last Speech of a Wretched Miser - by Allan Ramsay	3.207-14

[45] Orr wrote the poem in ink on both sides of two long sheets which are bound in sideways, and are pasted together and to Crawfurd's volume in such a way that the opening six verses are obscured. These verses were written out by Crawfurd right way up on pages that were numbered 189-91 (now 207-9), and the title only in Crawfurd's hand appears on a page numbered 186 which is now the lower half of F 26. This and the other Ramsay poem recorded from William Gemmel are in Volume II of *The Works of Allan Ramsay* ed. Burns Martin and John W. Oliver (Scottish Text Society, Edinburgh 1953) pp. 62-8 and 54-5.

William Gemmel was a tailor who had moved to Lochwinnoch from Cumnock in Ayrshire. He bore the same name as his father, also a tailor, and his mother was called Elizabeth McCleary (*Cairn* 1.74-7, 44.320). Crawfurd states that Gemmel 'died in December 1844 or 1845 aged about 95 years', which would put his date of birth at about 1750/1, but it seems likely that his age had been slightly exaggerated for a record in the New Cumnock Parish Register of the baptism on 29 September 1751 of Janet, daughter of 'William Gemmell and Elizabeth McClearly, in Connelburn'[46] probably refers to his elder sister who is called Jennie in Crawfurd's genealogical notes. If the record in the Old Cumnock Parish Register of the birth on 12 August 1758 of a son Alexander to 'William Gemmil Taylor in Borland and Elizabeth McCorle' refers to the next child after William who is called Sandy, William's birth can be dated between 1752 and 1757, which would mean that in 1827 he would have been somewhere between seventy and seventy-five years of age. In 1776, Gemmel married Jean White, a baker's daughter, in the parish of Old Cumnock, where he was apparently working in the village of Cumnock,[47] and there were eleven children of this marriage. The move to Lochwinnoch does not seem to have taken place before 1789 when the birth of a daughter Anne was recorded in the Old Cumnock Parish Register.[48] In 1813, Gemmel made a second marriage with Janet or Jenny Orr, daughter of James Orr of Strandhead and Isobel Blackburn in Lochwinnoch.[49]

William Gemmel's songs include three Child ballads: 65 *Airlie House*, 66 *Young Lochinvar's Courtship* and 72 *The Wee Wee Man*. Some lines relating to 67 *There Was an Old Man Was Smoking his Pipe* which occur as a scribble in the sole manuscript of William Stewart's *Buik of the Croniclis of Scotland* appear to have been jotted

[46] New Cumnock Parish Register, 608/1.

[47] The Old Cumnock Register of Marriages, 610/3, records that 'William Gemmel & Jane Whyte both in this parish were proclaimed' on 14 and 21 April 1776. In the Register of Births, 610/1, the couple are referred to as 'William Gemmel Taylor in Cumnock and Jean White' (6 January 1785). Jean White's parents may have been 'John White Baxter in Cumnock and Jean Wilson' who had a daughter Elizabeth on 28 October 1758.

[48] 610/3, 18 April 1789.

[49] Lochwinnoch Parish Register, 570/2, records the proclamation of the marriage of 'William Gemmel and Janet Orr both in this Parish' on 4 December 1813. Janet Orr was born in 1771 (*Cairn* 1.390-1).

down in the sixteenth or seventeenth century by a Hew Crawfurd of Cloberhill:

> Ther was ane ould man satt Piping
> He was blind and he could not sie
> Ther was ane ould wyff sat shytting
> Vnder ane greinewod trie
> The ould wyff shott with sick ane Race
> The Sparks off hir ars flew in his face[50]

I do not know of an occurrence elsewhere of 68 *As I Was A-Walking by yon Green Garden.* A variant of 69 *Black Joke* written by Scott Douglas in the margin of a copy of *The Merry Muses of Caledonia* in the late nineteenth century is printed with discussion by Gershon Legman in *The Horn Book: Studies in Erotic Folklore and Bibliography* (New York 1964 pp. 191–3), and a refrain like the one recorded from William Gemmel is quoted in notes on *Black Joke* in *English Dance & Song* 34 (1972) p. 148.

70 *Johnie Miller of Glenlee* is ascribed to Gemmel's father, William Gemmel, and an accompanying note states (2.179):

> This song was made by Wm Gemmel Father by ordors of the E[arl of] D[umfries][51] upon John Miller the justices Clerk brother from his been a notoroes glutton and extrordonry fat. He was so attach to mutton that he in all his tacks with his tenents stipulated that the were to furnish him with a fat weather yearly and he generley came to Glenlee till he (ate) eat them up. At on time dinning with D[umfries] the E[arl] took the liberty of Singing the song to him which much displeasd him.

Gemmel's song evidently had a certain circulation for it occurs in

[50] Cambridge University Library MS Kk. 2. 16 f.171r. The scrap of verse is written two or three words to the line in a space between the two columns of chronicle text. For information on the manuscript, see *The Buik of the Croniclis of Scotland by William Stewart* ed. William B. Turnbull (Rolls Series 6–8, London 1858) 1. vi–vii, and for notes on the Crawfurds of Cloberhill or Cloverhill in the parish of East Kilpatrick, Dunbartonshire, see George Crawfurd's 'Historicall and Genealogicall Deduction of the Several families of the Surname of Crawfurd', National Library of Scotland MS Adv. 34.3.4, ff. 63v–64r.

[51] Orr uses only initials in his note, but some words before the passage quoted run: 'The (original of) song was by the (of E- of Dumf)'. The Earls of Dumfries were the principal land-owners in the Cumnock area and their seat, Dumfries House, was in the parish of Old Cumnock. The reference may be to William, fifth Earl (1742–1768) or Patrick, sixth Earl (1768–1803).

the eighteenth-century collection made by Elizabeth St Clair (St Clair MS p. 300, beginning 'My name is Jock Millar') and was also made available to William Macmath (Macmath MSS S.21 Vol. 1, 16 February 1874, *Turkey Jock Miller* or *The Laird of Glenlee*). Its object was John Miller of Glenlee in the parish of Kells, Stewartry of Kirkcudbright, whose younger brother, Sir Thomas Miller (1717-1789), became Lord Justice-Clerk in 1766.[52] The song must have been composed between that date and John Miller's death on 28 November 1780.[53] The same vigorous vein of satire as in this song is apparent in the following two pieces of verse also ascribed to William Gemmel,[54] the first of which is internally dated in 1765:

The Last Speech of Michael Marshall's Tup

1 In seventeen hundred sixty five
The month of March the time of snow
My errend press'd me very hard
To Galoway I needs must go

2 As Afton watter I went up
I heard a mylancholly bleeting
Between Michal Marshal and his Tup
As the did part at there last meeting

3 Says Michal tell to me Sir Tup
What is the reason ye man die
This year Ill loss my stock of lambs
For my dependence hung on thee

[52] James Paterson, *History of the Counties of Ayr and Wigton* (Edinburgh, 1863-6), 1.723, and George Brunton, *An Historical Account of the Senators of the College of Justice* (Edinburgh and London, 1832), pp. 530-1.

[53] Service of Heirs, 24 April 1781, Scottish Record Office C.22/84.

[54] 2.168-70. I have normalised the titles from 'The last speech of Michal Marshal Tup' and 'The Tup Gost', given capitals to 'March', 'Afton' and 'Mamon', and at II 3.4 emended 'my' to 'thy'. At II 1.2 I have added the 'l' in 'flaicee' = fleecy, but the word is not distinctly written and the reading is doubtful. The words 'mistar of my stones' = function of my testicles (I 5.2), 'Thou' = Though (I 8.1), 'oo' = wool (II 1.2), 'paw' = pawn (II 1.4), 'worset' = worsted (II 2.1), 'spang' = sprang and 'press' = cupboard (II 2.3).

4 While health and strength wi me remaind
I acted like the best of rams
And did exert my natural pours
In ordor to produce you lambs

5 But the vigorous ridding of your ewes
Has dried the mistar of my stones
And this uncommon storm of snow
Has draind the marrow from my bones

6 So waes me ever I was yours
On me has ligtd money a curse
For ye extorcet beith rich and poor
In order to agment your purse

7 My famous wool mor white then snow
Ye'll keep that for yourself to wear
Because ye want to make a show
In sheep's apperal to appear

8 Thou God knows ye ar a greedy whoolf
And every sheep would fain devour
Then Michal stop'd the poor Tup mouth
And wad na let him speak no more

The Tup's Ghost

1 In name of wonder what art thou
So flaicee and cover'd o'er we oo
Thou's like my Tup but can't be him
For shurly I did paw they skin

2 And gart Meg Campble spin the worset
Because my tup said it was curset
And Michal spang behind his press
And to his God made this address

3 Say's Mamon save me from the spirit
Thou knows my worth and knows my merit
That all my life I neir did flinch
From thy commands one single inch

A note after the verses comments: 'The two last was wrot by William Gemmel father upon an old Tylor who was miserably hard and made (up) a large forton on sixpence a day'. This old tailor may quite likely have been the 'Michael Marshall, tailor in Blackwoodhead', protests by whom were recorded on 1 April 1736 and 6 July 1737 in the Register of Deeds for the Regality of Cumnock.[55]

71 *Linton Race* is preceded by an account of the circumstances of the song headed 'The origin of Lintock Race' (2.207-8). This account is in brown ink, but three revisions incorporated in the text below are in black ink like that used for writing out the song. These are the addition of 'at Linton' at the beginning, and the alterations from 'Dumfish' (*i.e.* Dumfries) to 'Loudon' and 'eleven' to 'fifteen' which bring the prose narrative into line with the song.

> A certain Lord Draquar having given a Silfer Cup to be run for at Linton a great number of Gentelmen assembled to wit English and Scoths. Amongst the rest was Lord (Dumfish) Loudon how at that time had a great many exelent Horses. Among the rest was a wall eyd poney. The said horse Vallace the Groom who was (the the the) to be the rider wished to carry with them but this his master would not allow him. An altercation took place and Valance was disbanded his services. He whoever went home and walking about the stables in a dismal manner his mistress surprised at Seeing him demanded his reason for not being with his master. After Stating the cause and likwise that he had got his discharge She desired him to disguise himself and said horse and proceed instantly to run for the Cup and if unsuccessful that neither him nor horse should ever set there face in her prasence again. Valance took the (dis) disguise of a beggar likewise made such alterations on the horse as could be accomplished and outstrip'd the whole that Started (eleven) fifteen in number unhookd the cup that was hung upon the winning pole and went directly home at

[55] SC 6/79/1 ff. 126b and 142, consulted in West Register House, Edinburgh.

> ful speed persued by many a Gentelman all of whom he utstripped and delivered the cup to his mistress. In a short time my Lord arrived and the Lady made enquirey who took the Cup. He said it was won by a beggar how made his elopment and is unknown to ever one but had he not left his wall eyd poney at home he would have sworn it was it. She asked him if he would know the cup if he saw it. He said he would. She presanted it and stated (his) her ordors to Valance. He was restored to his situation and enjoyd a pention till his death.

Written in black ink at the end is the statement, 'I had this traditional storey from a Miss Crawford 50 years ago' and in Crawfurd's hand there follows the note, 'The said Miss Crawfurd was a farmer's daughter about Mauchline - her father was a bankrupt - and he [was] much reduced in his circumstances. Quod William Gemmil'. The song (verse 4) praises the Earl of Wigton, and this implies that it is not later than 1747 when the title became extinct, and suggests that the Linton referred to is West Linton in West Lothian for the Earls of Wigton had possessions near there at Biggar.[56] I can find no record of a race held at West Linton, but advertisements in the *Caledonian Mercury* of the early part of the eighteenth century show that it was customary to hold local race-meetings and that the prize might be a piece of plate given by a nobleman.

William Orr also took down from Gemmel an outline of a song that he could not recall (2.213 No 146 'Tradition'):

> One Johnny the little Scot was a great robber and he [was] call'd o Moffat.[57] Being persued ordred the smith to shoe his horse with his caukers before and (he would be) well payd he should be but as soon as he had done his job he knocked his brains out for fear he tell on him afterwards. There was a song on this subject sung by William Gemmel gran Ant but he remmember it not.

John the Little Scot occurs as a title of *Johnie Scot* (Child 99 T) and Motherwell may be referring to this recollection of Gemmel's in a written comment opposite page c in his interleaved copy of the

[56] William Hunter *Biggar and the House of Fleming* (Edinburgh 1867) p. 563. I have assumed that *Linton Race* is a song, but it should be mentioned that Crawfurd refers to the piece in his general index (3.446) as 'Lintock Race: A Poem'.

[57] The capital 'M' is editorial. Crawfurd apparently read what I take to be 'o' = of as 'a' = the, for he gives this item in the list of contents as 'Johnie the Moffat'.

Minstrelsy: 'Johnnie Scot. I am inclined to think there is yet another ballad of this name not yet printed / Mem. consult A.C's notes)'. The strongest associations of the song summarised here, which may perhaps be called *Johnie o' Moffat*, are with *Archie o Cawfield* (Child 188), several variants of which include a horse-shoeing episode (Child 3.487-90, 4.516-17). Child gives a report of a form of this ballad where the main character belongs to the Johnstone family and the rescuers seek refuge in the mountains of Moffat (Child 3.485), and it seems possible that it was a variant of this kind that was known to William Gemmel's great aunt.

The ballad *The Gypsy Laddie* (Child 200) was not recorded from Gemmel but a tradition he relates about William Cunningham, twelfth Earl of Glencairn (1734-1775), depends on knowledge of the form of it in which the lady who runs off with the gypsies is identified as the Countess of Cassilis (2.162 No 179):

> The last Lord Glencairn and the familey of Cassels in former times used to live at great variance. They whoever met at a large dinner party (at) in the Town of Ayr about the com(men)encement of the Ayr racises where the discourse turned on musick. Lady Glencairn being an old fiddler daughter Casseles gave him the rub by telling him his father in law could play a good bow. He Glencairn retorted by saying he coul'd play the (Giy Gypess) Gyptiess came to Lord Cassils yeat with as bold a bow as ever he heard a man.

Crawfurd printed a flat retelling of Gemmel's story in an article on 'Lady Glencairn and Miller Samson' in *The Scottish Journal of Topography* 1 (1847), p. 19, where the ballad is referred to as *Johnie Faa and the Countess o' Cassillis* and not *The Gypsies Came to Lord Cassilis' Yet* as here. George Ritchie Kinloch heard a similar anecdote when he dined with the Presbytery of Ayr but in his version Glencairn's father-in-law is said to be a piper (Kinloch MSS 5.301-3).

John Smith

All the songs ascribed to John Smith are in the second volume, and occur as a single song and then as two groups separated by only one item. They are written in pencil in Crawfurd's hand with the exception of 75 *Mossgrove* which is written in ink in the hand of William Orr. Orr also made revisions in 76 *The Widow's Dochter.*

152	The Old Bachelor (73)	2.153–5
154	The Blackbird (74)	2.336
131	Mossgrove (75)	2.337–40
133	The Widow's Dochter (76)	2.341–3
153	The Mailin (77)	2.347–8
155	The Weaver's Dochter (78)	2.349
	Jockie and the Fair Maid (79)	2.350–1
173	The Wooer Came to the Widow's Door (80)	2.351–2
	The Maid's Complaint to her Mother (81)	2.353–5

John Smith, like William Gemmel, was a tailor, and he is described by Crawfurd as being 'a very thirsty man'. He came into Lochwinnoch from Stranraer, and was married in Lochwinnoch on 23 February 1783 to Margaret Kirkwood,[58] daughter of John Kirkwood, tailor, and Janet Young, and had several children.[59] In 1830, Crawfurd speaks of him as 'now in Kilbirnie' (*Cairn* 1.91, 4.176–7). All the songs for which he gives a source, and perhaps others also, were learnt in his youth in Stranraer and date from before 1783, by which time he had settled in Lochwinnoch. If he is assumed to have married at twenty, his age in the summer of 1827 would have been sixty-four, and probably we can estimate that he was in his sixties when his songs were recorded.

There is only one Child ballad in this group, 75 *Mossgrove*, which was learnt from an Irish boy. A number of John Smith's other songs relate to chapbook pieces although they are not always close to known texts. 73 *The Old Bachelor* beginning 'I am a man unmarried' occurs in chapbooks as *The Roving Bachelor* beginning 'I am a roving bachelor' (*e.g.* LC 2864:20 Stirling 180[6] pp. 4–6). Smith's variant is of particular interest as it is by his opening line that Burns referred to the song when he noted that his own first song, *O once I lov'd*, was composed to the tune *I am a man unmarried* which was a favourite with the girl he was addressing (*The Poems and Songs of Robert Burns* ed. James Kinsley 3 vols. Oxford 1968, 1.3, 3.1003). Burns did not mention that he had the words of the

[58] Lochwinnoch Parish Register, 570/2.

[59] Crawfurd names three, John, Janet and Agnes, and the Stranraer Parish Register, 899/1, notes the birth on 20 July 1795 of 'Mathew Smith son of John Smith Taylor and Margaret Kirkwood'.

old song in mind, but the line 'Sho is pleasant to the ee' (4.4) seems to be echoed in his third verse:

A bonny lass I will confess,
Is pleasant to the e'e,
But without some better qualities
She's no a lass for me.

The fragmentary 74 *The Blackbird* corresponds to the second half of verse 2 and verses 3 and 5 of *The Hawk* beginning 'Once I had a bird, and a very fine bird' (LC 2844.A:10 Glasgow n.d. pp. 5-6):

But she's ta'en up her flight and has flown away quite,
And there's nobody knows where she's gone,
Brave boys, &c.

Then up the broad meadow and down the broad meadow,
And through the wide forest I ran,
And there I espied my wanton wee hawk
Standing fast by the side of a man, brave boys,
Tied fast to another man's hand.

* * *

He that has got her, oh long may he keep her,
And make the best of her he can;
For I vow and swear, and solemnly declare,
That I'll hawk with her aye when I can,
Brave boys, &c.

It is evident that the 'alake! with her' in the Crawfurd MSS comes from 'I'll hawk with her' as in this chapbook form, and that the song as a whole must once have referred to a hawk. The blackbird of John Smith's variant is a unique feature and may have been introduced through crossing with a song called *The Wandring Black-Bird* (chapbook BM 11621. a. 6:2 n.p. n.d. pp. 6-7) which begins:

I am weary weary wandering,
All day and all night,
Since my Black-bird has left me,
And has taken his flight: . . .

78 *The Weaver's Dochter*, of which Crawfurd gives only the opening verse and a summary, was current in Scottish chapbooks (*e.g.* LC 2807:6 Edinburgh n.d. pp. 2-5 *Dr Stafford, and the Weaver's Daughter*; Greig *NE* 78), and 79 *Jockie and the Fair Maid* (Laws O 9

Branded Lambs) is fairly close to a twenty-eight line chapbook form called *Jockey the Shepherd* (*e.g.* LC 2823:5 Falkirk n.d. pp. 5-6). 81 *The Maid's Complaint to her Mother* is a rather fragmentary recollection of a seventeenth-century broadside song called *The Maulsters* (or *Maltster's*) *Daughter of Malborough*.[60] This song had a broadside reply called *The Young Farmer's Answer To his Sweetheart Nanny* which has been reprinted (*RB* 8.207-8) but the earlier song has not been made available. I include in the appendix (No 7) a chapbook printing of it called *The Longing Maid* which is undated but appears to belong to the eighteenth century. A broken-down form of the song combined with *Whistle, Daughter, Whistle* (Opie 128) occurs in chapbooks and in records from tradition (*e.g.* LC 2838:3 Glasgow 1802 p. 2 *The Whistling Daughter*; Cecil J. Sharp *English Folk Songs* 2 vols. London 1920, reproduced in one volume London 1959, 1.100-1).

I have not found broadside or chapbook equivalents of John Smith's other songs, although one of them, 76 *The Widow's Dochter*, has been recorded fairly frequently from tradition (*e.g.* George Ritchie Kinloch *The Ballad Book* Edinburgh 1827 pp. 1-3 *The Widow o' Westmoreland*). 80 *The Wooer Came to the Widow's Door* appears in Peter Buchan's manuscripts with the title *The Bridegroom Grat When the Sun Gaed Doun* (*Secret Songs* pp. 73-5 and, in modified form, *Ancient Ballads* 1.145v-6v). The line 'Wou'd ye be on, young man, said I' in Buchan's variant provides a link with a maceronic fragment in Manx and English called *Haink Sooreedeyr nish gys Dorrys ven Treoghe* or *A Wooer came to the Widow's Door* (*Journal of the Folk Song Society* 7, 1922-6, pp. 136) which includes the words 'will you be on' in the dialogue. I have not located 77 *The Mailin* elsewhere, but there may just possibly be a link between its refrain and the rather similar one that occurs in a recently recorded variant of *The Waukin' o' the Claes* (*Tocher* 1, 1971-2, pp. 180-1; *cf.* Greig *NE* 98):

> He's providin, he's providin,
> He's providin for me:
> There's a hoose and a bonnie lad:
> He's providin for me.

[60] Pepys Library broadside songs 3.70, Magdalene College, Cambridge; and *Bibliotheca Lindesiana: Catalogue of a Collection of English Ballads of the XVIIth and XVIIIth Centuries* (Aberdeen 1890, reproduced New York 1962) No 823.

TITLES

1 LORD BANGWELL'S ADVENTURE (Child 5 *Gil Brenton*)
2 BOB NORRICE (Child 83 *Child Maurice*)
3 MY LORD DERWATER (Child 208 *Lord Derwentwater*)
4 THE HAWTHORN GREEN
5 WILLIAM AND THE YOUNG COLONEL (Child 88 *Young Johnstone*)
6 FAIR ROSALIND
7 THE CRUEL STEPMOTHER
8 THE GRAZIER'S DOCHTER
9 LORD MEANWELL (Child 93 *Lamkin*)
10 SIR HUGH (Child 155 *Sir Hugh, or, The Jew's Daughter*)
11 THE KING'S DOCHTER JEAN (Child 100 *Willie o Winsbury*)
12 THE CRUEL MOTHER (Child 20 *The Cruel Mother*)
13 LORD GREGORY (Child 76 *The Lass of Roch Royal*)
14 THE WANDERING LOVER
15 THE SQUIRE'S SON OF AIZLING TOWN (Child 105 *The Bailiff's Daughter of Islington*)
16 THE MERRY LYKEWAKE (Child 25 *Willie's Lyke-Wake*)
17 YOUNG BETSY (Laws M 20 *Betsy Is a Beauty Fair*)
18 FAIR ROSANNE
19 WILLIE TAYLOR (Laws N 11 *William Taylor*)
20 LORD LEVEL (Child 75 *Lord Lovel*)
21 THE PENITENT BRIDE (Laws P 31 *The Nobleman's Wedding*)
22 THE THREE JOLLY BUTCHERS (Laws L 4 *The Three Butchers*)
23 WISE WILLIE (Opie 447)
24 THE REEKING HOUSE
25 THE AULD WIFE AND THE PEAT CREEL (Child 281 *The Keach i the Creel*)
26 THE YORKSHIRE RAMBLER
27 THE BUSH OF BROOM
28 MOTHER BUNCH
29 THE HILLS O' GOWRIE
30 THE SHEPHERD'S SON (Child 112 *The Baffled Knight*)
31 THE FAUSE KNICHT (Child 3 *The Fause Knight upon the Road*)

32 THE LAIRD OF OCHILTREE WALLS (Child 217 *The Broom of Cowdenknows*)
33 THE BONNIE BLUE-EYED LASSIE
34 MAY COLYEAN (Child 4 *Lady Isabel and the Elf-Knight*)
35 MALL BOWIE (Laws O 14 *Pretty Polly*)
36 LADY JEAN (Child 52 *The King's Dochter Lady Jean*)
37 EARL RICHARD (Child 68 *Young Hunting*)
38 THE LAIRD O' KELTY
39 THE MASON'S DOCHTER
40 THE THREE RAVENS (Child 26 *The Three Ravens*)
41 THE DEIL'S COURTSHIP
42 POOR GREETING WILSIE
43 SLIGHTED LOVE (Laws P 25 *Love Has Brought Me to Despair*)
44 THE ENSIGN AND THE LADY GAY (Child 69 *Clerk Saunders*)
45 THE UNCO KNICHT'S WOOING (Child 1 *Riddles Wisely Expounded*)
46 ROSIANNE (Child 51 *Lizie Wan*)
47 THE PRINCE OF ORANGE (Laws P 12 *Nancy II*)
48 THE NUT-BROWN BRIDE (Child 73 *Lord Thomas and Fair Annet*)
49 THE LAIRD O' OCHILTREE (Child 217 *The Broom of Cowdenknows*)
50 JAMIE DOUGLAS (Child 204 *Jamie Douglas*)
51 THE FAUGHHILL SHEARING
52 WHEN MY OLD HAT WAS NEW
53 SIR DONALD AND ELIZA LINDSAY (Child 226 *Lizie Lindsay*)
54 THE ROSE SMELLS SAE SWEETLY (Child 11 *The Cruel Brother*)
55 THE SUN SHINES OVER THE VALLEY (Child 25 *Willie's Lyke-Wake*)
56 A YARMOUTH STORY
57 LADY BELTREES
58 LORD THOMAS AND LADY MARGARET (Child 260 *Lord Thomas and Lady Margaret*)
59 JOCK T' LEG AND THE MERRY MERCHANT (Child 282 *Jock the Leg and the Merry Merchant*)
60 THE LAIRD OF JOHNSTONE AND MISS JEAN MACDOWALL
61 THE BRAES OF KILLIECRANKIE
62 LORD EGLINTON'S SONG
63 THE WEE CRAP
64 BONNIE BELLEEN
65 AIRLIE HOUSE (Child 199 *The Bonnie House o Airlie*)
66 YOUNG LOCHINVAR'S COURTSHIP (Child 221 *Katharine Jaffray*)

MARY MACQUEEN

(MRS STORIE)

A

I

LORD BANGWELL'S ADVENTURE

Child 5 *Gil Brenton*

1 Seven ladies liv'd in a bower
  He down and ho down
An ay the youngest was the flower
  He down and ho down

2 They had ae brither amangst them aw
And Sir John they did him caw

3 The seven had to mak him a sark
It was the seven's hale year's wark

4 But whan the sark it was made an dune
They cast lots wha wad with it gang
But the lot fell on the youngest ane

5 As sho was gawn through the leaves o Lyne
Sho met a lord gallant an fine

6 He kept her thare sae lang sae lang
Frae the morning bright to the sun gade doun

7 An frae that again till the next morning
An aw he gade her at their parting
Was a pair o green gloves a gay gold ring

8 An three plaits o his yellow hair
That was a token if air thay shoud meet mair

9 But whan nine months was past an gane
Lord Bangwell buit a courting gang

10 As he was walking through yon green hall
He saw se'en ladies playan at the baw

11 He threw his baw amang them aw
An on the youngest the baw did faw

12 He threw his gloves amang them aw
An on the youngest the gloves did faw

13 He threw his napkin amang them aw
An on the youngest it did faw

14 He cryde whare will I get a man
To come and help my young bride on

15 Tha war nane sae readie as Sir John
To come and help his sister on

16 Than out bespak our foremaist man
I think our bride rides slowlie on

17 Then out bespak our hindmaist man
I think our bride rides weepand on

18 O does the wind blaw on your glove
Or are you bound for sum other love

19 Or ar you weary o your life
Because your made Lord Bangwell's wife

20 The wind does not blow on my glove
Nor I am bound for nae other love

21 But I am weary of my life
Because I am made Lord Bangwell's wife

22 As they at Wedding supper sat
An unco pain come in o her back

23 And as they lay aw in Bride's bed
He put his hand for to hap his bride
An there he fand the young thing leap

24 He tok his fit and he gade her a bang
And out o bed himsel he flang

25 He to the hall amang them aw
An on his mother he gade a caw

26 I thought I got a lily flower
But I hae got sume ither man's hure

27 I thought I got a maid meek an mild
But I got a whore an sho is big wi child

28 O dochter O dochter cum tell me
Wha is the faither o your babee

29 As I was walking the leaves of Lyne
I met a lord gallant and fine

30 He kept me there sae lang sae lang
From the morning bright to the sun gade doun

31 An frae that again till the next morning
An aw he gade me at our parting
Was a pair of green gloves and a gay gold ring

32 An thrie plaits of his yellow hair
That was a token if ere we soud meet mair

33 O dochter O dochter cum tell to me
Where is the green gloves that he gade thee

34 O mother O mother gang to the haw
An there ye'll find them wi my claes aw

35 An whan she fand them she kent her son
For on the gloves was writ her name

36 She to the haw amang them aw
And on her son she gade a caw

37 O son O son cum tell to me
Whaur is the green gloves that I gade thee

38 As I was walking the leaves o Lyne
I met a lady gallant an fine

39 I kept her thare sae lang sae lang
Frae the morning bright till the sun gade doun

40 And frae that again till the next morning
An aw I gade her at our parting
It was thir green gloves a gay gold ring

41 An three plaits of my yellow hair
That was a token if ere we soud meet mair

42 An I wad rather than castles and towers
I had that same lady in my bower

43 I wad rather than my very life
I had that same lady for my wife

44 Ye wad not need rather than castles and towers
For ye hae that same lady in your bower

45 You need not rather than your very life
For ye hae that same lady for your wife

46 Go hap my lady wi quilts o' silk
And feed my young son wi woman's milk

47 These words were written on its breast bane
It was Lord Bangwell's sevent son

48 Thae words wore written on its right hand
It was to be heir of aw Lord Bangwell's land

2

BOB NORRICE

Child 83

1 Bob Norris is to the grein wud gane
He's awa wi the wun
His horse is silver shod afore
In the shynand gowd ahin

2 He said unto his little boy John
I see what ye dinna see
I see the first woman that I eir luvit
Or ever luvit me

3 Gae tack to her this pair o gluves
Thay'r o the sillar grey
An tell her to cum to the merrie grein wud
An speik to Bob Norrise

4 Gae tack to her this gay gowd ring
Its aw gowd but the stane
An tell her to cum to the merrie grein wud
An ask the leive of nane

5 Gae tack to her this gay manteil
It's aw silk but the sleive
An tell her to cum to the merrie grein wud
An ask nae bauld baron's leive

6 I daur na gang to Lord Barnard's haw
I daur na gang for my lyfe
I daur na gang to Lord Barnard's castle
To deprive him o' his wyfe

7 Do I nae pay you gowd he said
Do I nae pay you fee
How daur you staun my bidding Sir
Whan I bid you to flee

8 Gif I maun gang to Lord Barnard's castle
Sae sair agane my wull
I vow a vow an I doublie vow
It sall be dune for ill

9 But whan he cam to Lord Barnard's castle
He tinklit at the ring
Tha war nane sae reddy as Lord Barnard himsel
To let the little boy in

10 What news quhat news my bonnie wee boy
What news hae ye to me
Nae news nae news Lord Barnard he said
But your ladie I fain wad see

11 Here is a pair o gluves to her
Thay'r o' the sillar gray
An tell her to cum to the merrie grein wud
An speik to Bob Norrise

12 Here is a gay gowd ring to her
It's aw gowd but the stane
An sho maun cum to the merrie grein wud
An ask the leive o' nane

13 Here is a gay manteil to her
Its aw silk but the sleive
An she maun cum to the merrie grein wud
An ask nae bauld baron's leive

14 Than out bespak the yellow nurse
Wi the babie on her knie
Sayand gif thay be cum frae Bob Norris
Thay'r welcum unto me

15 O haud your tung ye yellow nurse
Aloud an I heir ye lie
For thay'r to Lord Barnard's ladie
I trew that this be sho

16 Lord Barnard's to a dressing room gane
An buskt him in women's array
An he's awa to the merrie grein wud
To speik to Bob Norris

17 Bob Norris he sits on a trie
He was whistling an singing
Said – merrie merrie may my hart be
I see my mither cumand

18 Bob Norris he cam doun frae the trie
To help his mither off the horse
But alace, alace, says Bob Norris
My mither was neir sae gross

19 Lord Barnard liftit his braid swurd
That hang down by his knie
An he has cut Bob Norris's heid
Aff frae his fair bodie

20 He tock the bluidie heid in his haun
An broucht it to the haw
An flang it into his ladie's lap
Sayand lady thare's a baw

21 Sho tock the bluidie heid in her haun
An kissit it frae cheik to chin
Sayand Better I lyke that weil faurit face
Than aw my royal kin

22 When I was in my faither's bour
Aw in my dignitie
An English Lord a visit cam
Got Bob Norris wi me

23 Than out bespak Lord Barnard than
An a sorrie man was he
Sayand gif I had kennit that he was your son
He wad neir been killit be me.

3

MY LORD DERWATER

Child 208

1 The King he wrote a braid letter
And sealit it wi his hand
An sent it to my Lord Derwater
To come at his comand
To cum at his command

2 The first tway lines that he did read
He seemed to be satisfied
The next tway lines that he did read
He wrang his hands he cryde
He wrang his hands he cryde

3 Then out bespak his gay ladie
As in childbed she lay
Your will your will my Lord Derwater
Before you gang awa
Before ye gang awa

4 I will lea my auldest son
Three thousand pounds a year
And I will lea my youngest son
My houses and my dears
My houses and my dears.

5 And as for you my gay ladie
My sweet and faithfu wife
I will lea you all my lands
To maintain you a lady's life
To maintain you a lady's life

6 The first twa mile he did ryde
His steed tumbled our a stane
And that was a tocken true enough
That he wad na cum hame
That he wad na cum hame

7 And whan he came to merry England
And appeared in Whitehall
A traitor, a traitor, my lord Derwater
And a traitor they all him call
And a traitor they all him call

8 Na I am nae traitor said my lord Derwater
Nor I did na intend such a thing
But I do keep five hunderd men
To fecht for Jamie our King
To fecht for Jamie our King

9 Then up becam a braw auld man
Wi a broad axe in his hand
Your head your head my Lord Derwater
Your head I do demand
Your head I do demand

10 O haud your hand my gude auld man
Till I speak words twa or three
Aw ye lords of merry England
Remember my gay ladie
Remember my gay ladie

11 Here fifty five pound in my pouch
To divide amang the poor
And there as much in the ither side
To divide frae door to door
To divide frae door to door

12 And as for you my gude auld man
For the request you grantit me
The suit of velvet that I wear
I'll bestow it for your fee
I'll bestow it for your fee

4

THE HAWTHORN GREEN

1 A lady as fair as fair could be
Sat marvelling under yon hawthorn tree
She marvelled much how things could be
To see the grein leaves on yon hawthorn tree

2 Then out bespak the hawthorn tree
What makes you marvel sae much at me
The finest dew that ever was seen
Does faw on me and keep me green

3 What if I wud cut you doun
And carry you hence to yonder town
The next year after ye woudna be seen
To spread forth your leaves baith fresh and green

4 To cut me down I put nae doubt
But ye dinna cut me by the root
The neist year after I will be seen
To spread my leaves baith fresh and green

5 But you fair maids you ar not so
When ance that your virginity go
The next year after you may be seen
But never to flourish sae fresh again

6 This fair maid she hearing this
She turned her back to the hawthorn buss
The neist year after she was near seen
To talk onie mair to the hawthorn grein

5

WILLIAM AND THE YOUNG COLONEL

Child 88 *Young Johnstone*

1 As Willie and the young colonel
Was drinkand of the wyne
O will you marry my sister says Will
And I will marry thine

2 No I will not marry your sister
Althou her locks are brown
But I'll make her my leman
As I go through the town

3 Will lifted up his good broad sword
That hang down by his knee
And he has stabbed the young colonel
Out through the bodie

4 And he muntit on his milk white steed
And rode as hard as he coud ride
Untill he came to his sister's bower
In the twilight

5 Light down light down sweet William she says
Light down and stay all night
And you shall have cheer and the charcoal clear
And the candles burning bright

6 I cannot light down nor I will not light down
Nor I cannot light down says he
For I have killed the young colonel
And for it I maun flee

7 If you have killed the young colonel
Alas and woe is me
And I wish that you may be torn at wild horses tails
And from your enemy never flee

8 O wo to you – wild woman he says
And an ill death may you dee
How could I stay with you all night
When you wished such a wish upon me.

9 He set spurs to his milk white steed
And fled as hard as he could flee
Until he came to his true love's bower
Before the clock struck three

10 Light down light down sweet Willie she says
Light down and stay all night
And you shall have cheer and the charcoal clear
And the candle burning bright

11 I cannot light down nor I will not light doun
Nor I will not light down says he
For I have killed the young Colonel
And for it I maun flee

12 If you have killed the young colonel
Alas and woe is me
But the less do I care for that my dear
If your fair bodie be free

13 Light down, light down sweet Willie she says
Light down and take a sleep
And I will wake the Castle round
Your fair body to keep

14 She had not waked the Castle round
A time scercly but three
Till she spied four and twenty armed knights
Come riding owr the lee

15 Good morning to you lady Margaret they said
Good morning unto thee
Did you see a bloody knight
Come riding out this way

16 What colour was his hawk she said
What colour was his hound
What colour was the goodly steed
That bure him from the ground

17 A light brown was his hawk they said
And a dark brown was his hound
And milk white was the goodly steed
That bure him from the ground

18 If light brown was his hawk she said
And dark brown was his hound
And milk white was his goodly steed
He's new rode through the toun

19 They set spurs to their goodly steeds
And rode out ower the lee
And lady Margaret's awa to Willie
As hard as she could flee

20 He lifted up his good broad sword
That hang down by his knee
And he stabbed lady Margaret
Out through the body

21 Hold your tongue lady Margaret he says
For the space of half an hour
And the doctors in fair London town
Shall be within your bower

22 How can I hold my tongue she says
For the space of half an hour
Do you not see my very heart's blood
Come trinkling down the floor

23 Take my Holland shift she says
And tair it from gore to gore
And stop it in my deadly wound
Perhaps it will bleed no more

24 He took her holland shift as she said
And tore it from gore to gore
And stopped it in her deadly wound
But still it bled the more

25 Go and put on a black suit she said
And go whistling out the way
And mourn na more for your true love
When she is laid in clay.

6

FAIR ROSALIND

1 On the banks o a river sae deep
Whaur waters does gently glide on
Fair Rosalind sat down to weep
For sho thought that her lover was gane
The fairest and faithfullest she
O aw that skips owr the plain
But alace the maist fickle was he
Amang the shepherds or swain

2 Bewaur ye bricht maidens bewaur
Lest my fause lover ye meet
Alace he is bewitchingly fair
When he speaks there is nae music sae sweet
Be witness ye powers abuve
Though he is fause bring nae harm on his heid
But crown him wi beautie and luve
Lang after fair Rosalind's dead

7

THE CRUEL STEPMOTHER

1 A noble lord of Exeter
A hunting did ride
An he took wi him aw his train
O gentry by his side

2 He had ane only daughter fair
A beauty bricht was she
She was her father's delight an joy
As ye may after see

3 But woe be to her stepmother
Wha envied her sae much
That day by day she sought her life
Her malice it was such

4 She bargain'd wi the master cook
To tack her life away
An cuming to her daughter deir
This to her did say

5 O daughter ye maun gang hame
The cook for to tell
That he maun dress the dove
The dove he knows full well

6 This lady deir fearand nae harm
Obayed her mother's will
An presently she hastened hame
Her mind for to fulfil

7 She says ye maun dress
This pure and milk white dove
That in the park does shine sae bricht
There's nane so fair doth prove

8 O ye'r the dove that I maun dress
Behold here is my knife
Baith sharp and keen an ready too
To end you o your life

9 Then out bespak the scullion boy
An this began to cry
O maister maister save her life
An mak o me your pye

10 O now I winna save her life
Nor make my pye of thee
But if these words you do declare
Your butcher to I'll be

11 When the good lord cam hame at noon
An at his dinner sat
He called for his daughter deir
That she might carve the meet

12 Then out bespak her stepmother
As by his side she sat
Yer daughter's to some nunnery gane
Your daughter I pray forget

13 The lord he made a solemn vow
Before the company
That he would neither eat nor drink
Till his daughter he would see

14 Then out bespak the scullion boy
And this began to cry
If that your daughter ye maun see
My lord break up the pye

15 Ye'r daughter she is minched sma
An peirsand by the fire
Aw caused by her stepmother
Wha did her life desire

16 The lord he went in mourning then
Aw for his daughter's sake
An caused her cursed stepmother
To be burned at a stake

17 An next he caused the master cook
In boiling lead to stand
An made the little scullion boy
The heir o aw his land

8

THE GRAZIER'S DOCHTER

1 Give ear to these lines I write
As it is reported
A young Squire ruined quite
A damsel he courted

2 She was his fathers servant maid
And dochter to a grazier
Behold how he her heart betrayed
At every time and leisure

3 O noble Squire she replied
Lay aff your fond proceedings
For I am nae ways qualified
For you by birth nor breeding
Ye might have ladies o your ain
O noble birth descended
Therefore dear Squire out o hand
Your friends would be offended

4 My dearest dear then he replied
Fear na my friends' displeasure
While I hae life to take your part;
I love you out of measure

5 Wi these arguments and many more
He strove for to inflame her
She did consent to wed therefore
There's many alive did blame her

6 Onkent to friends or parents dear
She wi the Squire weded
And about the space of half a year
After they baith had beded

This lady proved big with child
Her looks began to shew it;
To his parents were reconciled
He would na have them knaw it

7 Then up to famous Edinburgh town
Immediately he brought her
And jewels fine and silken gowns
He very freely bought her
That she might like a ladie gay
Appear in aw her beauty
And for some time while he did stay
He owned a husband's duty

8 At length his parents came to hear
By private information
That he was lodging near the Strand
Wi a maid of recreation
And having missed a servant maid
They instantly concluded
That she some cunning prank had played
Or certainly deluded

9 They wrote a letter fu of wrath
And threatened her wi ruin
It grieved him so that in truth
While he these lines stood viewing

10 Tears frae his ein they ran amain
She asked him the reason
Quoth he my friends does you disdain;
They baith wept for a season
She read it too as weel as he
And fand them harsh and cruel
Be kind to me my dear she said
Be kind to me my jewel

11 Let me not suffer for your sake
Consider my condition
Or if you do my heart will break;
'Twas not my ambition

To be a lady ye well know,
'Twas lang or I consented
Why do they seem to threaten sae?
We strave for to prevent it

12 He tuke her by the hand and said
My joy my heart and sweeting
Pray in your lodging here abide
Till our neist happy meeting

13 I'll make the matter fair and clear
An in aw cases clear you;
He went but neir returned again
Nor never mair cam near her
In melancholy thought she passed
The time a month and better
An then she travelled doun at last
Having received nae letter

14 But when she came unto the town
She heard that he was married
To a young lady o renown;
Wi grief she then miscarried

15 Thay threatened her with punishment
For talking of the Squire
But fatal death did it prevent
For she did soon expire
That very minute before she died
Her friends and parents hearing
She wrang her hands and bitter cried
Saying is there na appearance

16 Will ye not come and see me now
Ye husband maist fause hearted
Through just vengeance I will hae you
Whan my wranged soul departeth
It came to pass as it was said
The wranged grazier's dochter
Her ghost it cam where he was laid
In bed some minutes after

17 An in the midst o aw their joy
To their amazed wonner
The room was filled wi dreadful noise
Like claps of roaring thunder
About that stately marriage bed
They saw the flash of fire
A voice was heard that often said
You maist deceivand Squire

18 The lady that lies by your syde
She shanna lang enjoy you
It's I that am your lawful bride
Just vengeance shall destroy you

19 Wi arms as cold as ony clay
The spirit did enfald him
An tuke him hence by force awa
His lady could na hauld him

20 She screighed and cryed but aw in vain
The apparition gied him
That very night his fatal doom
Tha were nane alive could save him
His parents they rose up wi haste
Hearing the apparition
An on his body they beheld
These words o lamentation

21 In perfect Roman letters blue:
This wretch was my undoing
And now it's done and proven true
My sad and dismal ruin.

FINIS.

9

LORD MEANWELL

Child 93 *Lamkin*

1 Lamkin was as guid a mason
As eir built a stane
He built Lord Meanwell's castle
An on it payment got nane

2 Said the Lord to the lady
I am gaun abroad
An bewaur of fause Lamkin
That lies be the road

3 I dinna value Lamkin
Nor nane o his kin
For my doors ar aw locked
An my windows are pinnit

4 I dinna value Lamkin
Nor nane o his kin
But the fause nurse had a key
For to let Lamkin in

5 Good morrow, to you Lamkin
Good morrow to thee
Where is the Lord
O this castle I pray

6 Where is the Lord o this castle
Or is he at home
He is awa to merrie England
To see his auld son

7 Whaur is the lady o this castle
Or is she at hame
She is up in her casement
Whaur nae man can win

8 How can we win at her
Said the Lamkin
We'll bluid the bonnie babie
Said the fause nurse to him

9 I think it is a pity
Said the Lamkin
I think it is nae pity
Said the fause nurse to him

10 So Lamkin he stabbed
And the fause nurse she sang
Till the four corners o the cradle
Wi the red bluid it ran

11 The lady was up
In her casement sae high
An she heard her bonnie babie
Aloud as it cryde

12 O still my babie nursie
Still him wi the keys
He'll no be stilled Madam
Let me do what I please

13 Still my babie nursie
O still him wi the knife
He'll no be still Madam
Though I'd lay doun my life

14 O still my babie nurse
O still him wi the bell
He'll no be still Madam
To ye cum yoursel

15 O how can I cum doun
This cauld winter night
For I hae neither coal nor candle
Nor the moon shynan bricht

16 Ye hae three silver manteels
As bricht as the sun
Fling ane o them about you
It'll shew you licht doun

17 She flang ane o them about her
Thinkan na o harm
But wha was sae readie as Lamkin
To embrace her in his arms

18 O Lamkin, O Lamkin,
Pray save my sweet lyfe
And I'll gie you my young dochter
Bedight for your wife

19 If you give me as much gold
As the stanes o the street
I could na keep my lang knife
Aff your lily white neck

20 Then out spak the lady
To the nursie spak she
Since it is ordered
That I am gaun to die

21 Wha'll be my friend she said
Or wha'll be my fae
Or wha'll haud the bason
Till my red bluid does flow

22 I'll no be your friend she said
Nor I'll no be your foe
But I'll haud the bason
Till your red bluid does flow

23 So they killed the fair lady
Without fear or dread
And her gude Lord arrived
Ere she was lang deid

24 Miss Betty was up
In her casement sae high
And she saw her faither's carriage
Cumand ridan hard by

25 She cryde faither, O faither
You need na blame me
'Twas Lamkin and the fause nurse
That killed your babie

26 O faither O faither
Ye need na blame me
It was Lamkin and the fause nurse
That killed your ladie

27 So Lamkin was hanged
On a gallows sae high
And the fause nurse was brunt
In a fire hard by

10

SIR HUGH

Child 155

1 It was in the middle o' the midsimmer time
When the schuil boys played at the baw - baw
Out and cam the Jew's dochter
And on little Sir Hew did caw - caw
And on little Sir Hew did caw

2 She tuke him by the milk white hand
And she led him through the haw - haw
And she led him to a stony chamber
Whaur nane wad heir him to caw caw
Whaur nane wad heir him to caw.

3 She set him in a chair o gold
And she pricked him wi a pin pin
And the first that cam out was thick thick blude
And the next that cam out was thin - thin
And the next that came out was thin
An the next that cam out was his hert's bluid
An there was nae mair within

4 She rowit him in a sheet o lead
Wi mony a plie and mony a fold fold
And she threw him in a deep deep well
An she threw him in a deep draw well
That was baith deep and cauld cauld
That was baith deep and cauld

5 Now lie ye there Sir Hew
And God forbid ye soom soom
To bring my folk to disgrace
Or aw my proud kin kin
Or aw my proud kin

6 Day being dune and nicht cumand on
The schuil boys aw gade hame hame
Every school boy's mammie had her son
But Sir Hew's mammy had nane nane
But Sir Hew's mammy had nane

7 She wanderit up and doun the street
Wi a birk rod in her hand hand
Sayand if I get my little son Sir Hew
I'll whip him for staying sae lang lang
I'll whip him for staying sae lang.

8 She wanderit up and doun the street
Till she cam to the deep draw well well
Whaur he laid in the sheet o lead
That was baith deep and cauld cauld
That was baith deep and cauld

9 If ye be here my little Sir Hew
As God forbid ye be be
Speik ye a word to your mammy who
Is wearied seekand thee thee
Is wearied seekand thee

10 How can I speik mammie he said
And me lays in such pain pain
For the little pen knife has tane my life
And the Jew's dochter has me slain slain
And the Jew's dochter has me slain

11 Go gie my luve to aw the schoolboys
As they play at the kirk kirk
To mak to me a grein coffin
O hazel and o birk birk
O hazel and o birk

12 And make my grave baith lang and wide
And mak it baith lang and deep deep
And lay my bible at my heid
And my testament at my feet feet
And my bow and arrow by my side
And wish me sound to sleep sleep
And wish me sound to sleep

13 They made his grave baith lang and wide
They made it baith lang and deep deep
They fulfilled aw things as he wished
An wished him sound to sleep sleep
And wished him sound to sleep.

11

THE KING'S DOCHTER JEAN

Child 100 *Willie o Winsbury*

1 The king he had but ae dochter
An sho was drest in grein
An sho's awa to yon hie castle wa
For to see her faither's ship sailing

2 What's wrang wi you my dochter Jean
Ye look sae pale and wan
I doubt you hae tane some sair sickness
Or hae lain wi some young man

3 I hae tane nae sair sickness
Nor has line wi nae young man
But aw that grieves or troubles my mind
My love he stays owr lang

4 Qwha is your love my dochter Jean
I'll pray you to tell unto me
For before the morn at twal oclock
Hie hanged he shall be

5 Is he onie o my sailor boys
Or o my courtier men
Or is he ane o my merrie men
But lately cum frae Spain

6 He's na ane o your sailor boys
Nor ane of your courtier men
But he's ane o your merrie men
Thats lately cum frae Spain

7 If that be true my dochter Jean
That ye tell unto me
The morrow before the clock strike twall
Hie hanged will he be

8 O God forbid faither she said
That onie sic thing shoud be
For if that young Willie be hanged
Ye'll near get nae mair good o me

9 He called doun his merry men aw
Be ane be twa be thrie
An the foremaist man was Willie Caldwell
But the hindmaist man was he

10 When he cam before the king
He was drest in silk
His hair hang down like the links o gold
An his skin was white as milk

11 An I think nae wonder quoth the king
My dochter fancies thee
For if I was a woman as I am a man
Your bedfellow I wad be

12 But wul ye marry my dochter Jean
An tack her be the hand
An ye shall dine and drink wi me
An be heir o aw my land

13 I will marry your dochter Jean
And tack her be the hand
An I will dine and drink wi you
But a fig for your land

14 It's my faither is Lord Salisbury
An aw belangs to me
And whaur ye gie your dochter ae penny
I can gie her thirty and three

12

THE CRUEL MOTHER

Child 20

1 Thair was a ladie livit at Newark
   Alane, alane O
An sho fell in luve wi her father's clerk
   Doun be the greinwud syde O

2 Thair luve continued abune five months an mair
Until her apron grew short afore

3 As sho was waulkand throu her father's grein hall
Her belly grew big as sho was lyke to faw

4 She leinit her back on a stane
Thair sho fand her pynes achand on

5 She leinit her back on an aish
Still sho fand her pynes were never the less

6 She leinit her back against a thorn
An thair she had thrie prettie babes born

7 Sho tuke the hair-lace o her hair
Sho tye't thir thrie prettie babes heil an neck there

8 An out o her pocket she tuke a knife
An she robbit thae thrie prettie babes o their sweit lives

9 Sho hid her knife under a stane
An sho waukit awa as a maiden hame

10 She spyit three prettie babes playand at the baw
. . . .

11 O prettie babes O prettie babes if you were myne
I wad cleid you in the silk sae fyne,

12 O mither, deir mither, whan we war thyne
You did na cleid us in the silk sae fyne

13 O mither, O mither deir, we'll tell whan we were thyne
You were a ladie livit at Newark
You fell in luve wi the halie clerk

14 Your luve continued five months an more
Until your apron grew short afore

15 But as you were walkand throu your father's grein hall
Your belly so big you were lyke to fall

16 You leinit your back on a stane
An thare you fand your pains aching on

17 You leaned your back against an aish
But you still fand your pains were never the less

18 You leaned your back against a thorn
An you had us thrie prettie babes born

19 You tuke the hair lace o your hair
And you tyit us heil an neck thair

20 You tuke a knife
And you robbit us thrie prettie babes o our sweit life

21 You hid your knife under a stane
You thought you were walking a maiden hame

22 But for our sake you'll live a miserable life
An you never need think to be any man's wife

23 For our sake seven years you will be a fish in the mud
An for our sake seven years you will be covered with blood

24 For our sakes you will walk unwell
An at seven years end you will fall into hell

13

LORD GREGORY

Child 76 *The Lass of Roch Royal*

1 O wha will shue my bonnie fit
Or wha will gluve my hand
Or wha will father my babie
Till Gregorie cums hame

2 Your faither will shue your bonnie fit
Your brither will gluve your hand
And the best will father your babie
Till Gregorie cums hame

3 Your brother will build a ship
An set her on the main
Sho will be riggit out wi gold
An the tapmast of the same

4 They had na sailed a league on sea
A league but scarcely thrie
Till they met a rank robber
As evir sailed the sea

5 O turn O turn lady Margaret he said
O turn O turn said he
If ye be the lady o Loch Ryan
Seekand Lord Gregory

6 He dwalls within yon bonnie Castle
That's thiekit wi the Tin
An ye stand there to your deeand day
You'r never to win in

7 For in it dwalls an arrant witch
An wiel she knows your case
An ye stand there to your deeand day
Ye'll never him embrace

8 When she cam to yon bonnie castle
That was theikit wi the tin
Arise, Arise Lord Gregory
An let your trew love in

9 Then out bespak the arrant witch
And an arrant witch was she
Sayan quha is that speiks at our gate
Seeking Lord Gregorie

10 O rise O rise Lord Gregorie
O rise O rise said she
It's I the lady of Loch Ryan
That fain wad speik to thee

11 If ye be the lady o' Loch Ryan
As I tak ye no to be
Ye maun tell some love token
That has been between you and me

12 Hae ye mind Lord Gregorie
As we drank of the wine
We changed the rings on our fingers
But still the best was mine

13 Mine was of the gold sae pure
But yours was o the tin
Mine was true and loyal too
But yours was fause within

14 And din na you mind Lord Gregorie
As we sat on yon hill
Twas you got my maidenhead
Fu sair against my will

15 Awa awa wild woman she said
For loud I hear you lea
If you stand there but ae half hour
Hie hangd ye shall be

16 That very minute she left the gate
Her hands she then did wring
And lykewise the locks o her yellow hair
Was frozen to her chin

17 An the first town that she cam to
She sat her doun and cryde
An the next toun that she came to
She laid her doun and died

18 That very minute
Lord Gregorie awoke
A venomed pain had tane his heart
An he thought it wad a broke

19 I dreamd a dream last night he said
I doubt it's for my harm
I thought I saw lady Margaret o Loch Ryan
Wi a babie in her arm

20 Lie doun lie doun foolish man she said
And a soun sleep may you take
For it is not past twa hours
Since that lady left the gate

21 O woe to you, wild woman he said
And an ill death may you die
When my trew love was at the gate
Ye might have waukened me

22 Gae saddle to me the black he said
Gae saddle to me the broun
Gae saddle to me the swiftest steed
That eir rode owr the ground

23 An the first town that he cam to
He heard the sma birds singing
An the next toun that he cam to
He heard the deid bell ringing

24 An next he met lady Margaret's corpse
His hands he than did wring
Sayand Better I liked that weel faured face
Than aw my kith and kin

25 Lady Margaret died that afternoon
And he on Wednesday
And the arrant witch laughs in her coach
Wha did them baith betray

14

THE WANDERING LOVER

1 Here's a health to aw true lovers
To my true love wherere she be
And owr the hill I will rove wi pleasure
Although she's twenty four miles frae me

2 I maun awa I can stay nae langer
For hills and mountains I hae to cross
And owr the hills I will rove wi pleasure
This very nicht to be wi my lass

3 When I cam to my love's window
I leaned me down upon a cauld stane
And whispered saftly through her window
Saying true love art thou alane

4 She lifted her head aff her feather pillow
Stripping the claes aff her milk white breast
Sayand wha's that speaks at my window
Disturbing me o my lang nicht's rest

5 It's I thy lover do not discover
But rise up quickly and let me in
For I am wearied wi my lang journey
Besids I am wet, love, into the skin

6 She threw her coat about her shoulders
She raise up quickly and lute me in
And there we tigged and tyed together
Until bright Phoebus come shining in

15

THE SQUIRE'S SON OF AIZLING TOWN

Child 105 *The Bailiff's Daughter of Islington*

1 There was a youth and a weel beloved youth
And he was a Squire's son
And he fell in love wi the Bailie's dochter
That lived in Aizlan town

2 But when that his father cam to hear
His foolish and frantic mind
He sent him to fair London town
Apprentice for to bind

3 Seven year to study at the law
And seven year o time
Oh and alas will I never see her face
For she ay rins in my mind

4 It happened upon a simmer day
The fields being aw fresh and gay
Aw the maids o Aizling town
Gade out to sport and play

5 Aw the maids o Aizland town
Gade out to sport and play
Aw but the baillie's bonny dochter
An in secret she stole away

6 She cuist aff her gown o green
An drest in page's attire
An she's awa to fair London town
O her lover to enquire

7 But as she was gaun along the road
The feilds was aw fresh and gay
There she saw her ain true love
Coming rydan out the way

8 She catched his horse by the bridal reins
As red as any rose
A penny, a penny kind Sir she said
For to help my troubled woes

9 O whar do you live my bonnie wee page
O whar war ye bred or born
In Aizlan town kind Sir she said
Whar I was held in scorn

10 Do ye know ought my bonnie wee page
Do you know ought or know
It's o' the baillie's bonnie dochter
She's dead Sir lang ago

11 If she is dead and is not alive
And laid in her grave sae low
Tak frae me my milk white steed
My arrow and my bow

12 Take frae me my milk white steed
My arrow and my bow
And I will awa to some foreign land
Quhar nane there dis me know

13 Oh, she is no deid but she is alive
Standing here by your side
Oh she is no dead but she is alive
Waitand to be your bride

14 Hand in hand this couple walked
To kirk and marryed were
And now they live in Aizling town
A sweet and happy pair

16

THE MERRY LYKEWAKE

Child 25

1 O Johnie Dear Johnie what maks you sae sad
  As the sun shines owr the valley
Nae kind o music will mak you glad
  Amang the blue flowers and the yellow

2 I hae courtit a fair maid these seven lang year
And I neir can win her father's consent to gain

3 O Johnie dear Johnie gie the bellman a groat
To invite your trew luve to your merry lichtwauk

4 He has gien the bellman a groat
To invite his trew love to his merry lichtwauk

5 When sho cam to her trew luve's gate
Sho gart deal the white money for his sake

6 When sho cam to her trew love's bed
She strippit doun the claes to look upo the deid

7 But he has grippit her in his airms twa
And he has flung her between him and the wa

8 O Johnie Dear Johnie let me a be
An tomorrow I will marry thee

9 If ye cam here a maid meik and mild
I'll send ye hame baith married an wi child

10 If ye cam here without horse or whip
I'll send you hame in a carriage for to weep

11 If ye cam here without man or boy
I'll send you hame wi a merrie convoy

17

YOUNG BETSY

Laws M 20

1 There was a maid o' beauty clear
And she came out o Stravenshire
A servant maid although she be
Happy is the man that gains Betsy

2 This maid for service she was bound
To a rich merchant in this town
And this rich merchant he had a son
A courting Betty he soon began

3 Oftentimes he did Betty try
But she always did him deny
Saying kind Sir your suit is in vain
For my honour ye shall never stain

4 Ae day as he was in the haw
He loudly on his love did caw
Saying Betty Betty to end aw strife
Next Monday morning ye'll be my wife

5 His auld mother was standing by
And heard these words as she drew nigh
And still she kept her mind
To falsify her son's design

6 Early next morning by break o day
This auld woman went to where Betty lay
Saying dress yoursell and come wi me
Unto the country twa miles or three

7 There was a ship lying in the bay
And she was bound for Virginia
And wi the Captain as a friend
Unto Virginia she did Betty send

8 Then this auld woman returned hame
You're welcome hame mother said her son
But whar is Betty now I pray
That she so lang does behind you stay

9 O son O son I plainly see
How deep your love was to Betty
But all your love is now in vain
For Betty is sailing on the main

10 Now this young man he is gown bad
Nae music will mak him glad
But in his slumber and sleep does he cry
O Betty, O Betty for you I'll die

11 Now this young man he is dead
And his auld mother she is gane mad
Crying if the quick would bring the dead again
I would send for Betty frae our the main

18

FAIR ROSANNE

1 Three noble lords o Salisbury
Was ryding out this way
And aw their talk was of fair ladies
Fair ladies blythe and gay

2 I have a sister young Clifford said
And few do her know
And she's as fair in her colour
As draps o blood in snaw

3 She's lang and smaw complete wi aw
Her body's formed so
I wad na for her weight of gold
King Henry wud her know

4 King Henry was in his bower
As they were riding by
I know nae fitter hand he said
To carry these lines away

5 There is a letter to your sister deir
Be sure you make nae delay
At my will she may cum
At my commands obey

6 Here is a letter sister deir
Maist glorious to behold
Here is a letter sister deir
And it is sealed wi gold.

7 And when she heard him say so
The blude her cheeks forsook
And wi her fingers lang and smaw
The golden seals she brake

8 The first twa lines that she did read
She seemed to be satisfied
And the next twa she did read
She wrang her hands and she cryde

9 Saying deir brother I may curse you
For ye have ruined me
I might have been a gude lords wyfe
But a harlot now I maun be

10 Sayand dear brother I may curse you
For ye have ruined me
Ye might have bragged of your hounds
And no have bragged of me

11 She called for her waiting maid
To dress her in ryding weed
And next her stable groom
To saddle her a milk white steed

12 With thretty slaves to gang before
To convoy her to the king
And when she came to the courts
The bells sweet notes did ring.

13 And when she came before the king
She bowed low on her knee
Saying – what's your will my good liege
Saying what's your will wi me

14 I sent for you my lovely rose
To embrace my princly bed
And when she heard him say so
She blushed like scarlet red

15 Why blush ye my lovely rose
Fear nae unhappy fate
For I hae in my princely power
To grant you a large estate

16 There's no a lady in aw my court
Shall purchase your desert
And when she heard him say so
It gained her very heart

17 She called for her plannet book
And laid it upon her knee
She sees that aw will come to nought
For poisoned she maun be

19

WILLIE TAYLOR

Laws N 11

1 Willie was a loyal lover
Full of pride and youthful air
And his mind he did discover
To a charming lady fair

20

LORD LEVEL

Child 75

1 Lord Leval he stude in his stable door
Caman down his milk white steed
Then by and cam Lady Annobell
She was wishing Lord Level gude speed, gude speed
She was wishing Lord Lovel gude speed

2 O whar ar ye gawn Lord Level she said
O quhar are ye gaun quo she
I'm gaun to merry England
Strange countries for to see, to see
Strange countries for to see

3 How lang will you stay Lord Level she said
How lang will ye stay quo she
A yeir and a day Lord Level did say
Or ere I return to thee, to thee
Or ere I return to thee

4 That's owr lang Lord Level she said
That's owr lang quo she
That's owr lang Lord Level she said
For to stay frae a fair lady, lady
For to stay frae a fair ladie

5 He hadna been a month awa
A month but scarcely three
Till langing thoughts cam till his head
Lady Annobel he wad gae see, gae see
Lady Annobel he wad gae see

6 But when he cam unto the toun
He heard the dead bell toll
And when he cam unto the court
The ladies war mournan all, -an all
The ladies war mournan all

7 Is thar ony ane dead in the toun he said
Or is there any ane unwell
It is the king's dochter they aw did reply
And her name is Lady Annobell, -obell
And her name is Lady Annobell

8 He caused the coffin to be opened up
And the sheets to be fauldit down
And ay as he kissed her cauld, cauld lips
The tears they did faw to the grun, the grun
O the tears they did faw to the grun

9 Lady Annobell died as if it war the day
Lord Level he died the morrow
Lady Annsobel died for pure pure love
Lord Level he died for sorrow, sorrow
Lord Level he died for sorrow

10 He was burried in Sant Mary's kirk
And she in Sant Mary's queir
And out o her grave grew a red red rose
And out o his a lily flower, flower
And out o his a lily flower

11 They grew high, and they grew lang
Till they grew to the kirk tap
And when nae farer they coud na win
They cuist true love's knots, loves knots
Then they cuist true love's knots

21

THE PENITENT BRIDE

Laws P 31 *The Nobleman's Wedding*

1 Here yestrein I was at a wedding
Of a maid that proved unkind
An when she thought on aw her losses
Her former love ran in her mind

2 Wedding dinner being owr
Ilk ane is to sing a sang
When it came to the former lover
Wi these verses he began

3 O how can ye lie on anither man's pillow
You that was my love sae late
An has caused me to wear the willow
Broken hearted for your sake

4 To wear the willow it well becomes me
And I will wear it a month or two
Then I'll throw it aff the waefu willow
And gang a courting again anew

5 The Bride was sitting at the head of the table
A' that was said she mark't weil
An whan nae longer she coud bear it
Doun at the bridegroom's feit she fell

6 Saying these requests that I ask o you
I pray you grant it unto me
Let me lie this nicht wi my mother
To morrow nicht I'll lie wi thee

7 That request it was soon granted
An the bride was stripped an put to bed
An early earlie the neist morning
They raise and fan the young bride dead

THE THREE JOLLY BUTCHERS

Laws L 4

1 There ware three jolly butchours
Rade out on Hallow day
Aw for to pay five hundred pounds
In ready gold away

2 But as they were ryding along the road
As hard as they could hie
Ryde up ryde up said Johnson
I hear a woman's cry

3 Then Johnston he boldly rode up
And viewed the plains all round
And he saw a naked woman
Wi her hair tied to the ground

4 O woman O woman said Johnstoun
Hae ye nae company
O no ten swaggering fellows
Wildly abused me

5 But Johnstoun was a clever man
He bure a valiant mind
He threw his cloak about her
And got her up behind

6 As they were ryding alang the road
As hard as they coud hie
She stopped her fingers in his ears
And gade twa dismal cries

7 And ten swaggering fellows
Wi braid swords in their hands
They cam up to brave Johnstoun
And bauld they bade him stand

8 Its will ye feght O Gibson
Na I would rather die
O will ye fecht then Wilson
Na I woud rather flee

9 But I will fecht quo Johnstoun
For gold or money free
And if the woman stick behind
I'll gain the victory

10 Then Johnstoun's pistols they gade aff
Sae clearly on the plain
Then Johnstoun's pistols they gade aff
Till five of them were slain

11 The rest being fighting
O the woman had nae mind
An she jumped frae behind him
And stabbed him throu behind

12 O woman O woman said Johnstoun
What's this ye hae done to me
Ye hae killed ane of the grandest butchers
That eir set woman free

13 This woman was put in irons
In iron chains so strong
For the killing of brave Johnstoun
A gude and mighty man

23

WISE WILLIE

Opie 447

1 O whar are ye gaun quo Johnie Macpherson
O whare ar ye gaun quo Jamie Macphee
O whar ar ye gaun quo Rabbie Russel
To kill a wee wran quo Wise Willie

2 O whare will ye kill't quo Johnie Macpherson
O whare will ye kill't quo Jamie Macphee
O whare will ye kill't quo Rabbie Russel
In my father's brae face quo Wise Willie

3 What way will ye kill it quo Johnie Macpherson
What way will ye kill it quo Jamie Macphee
What way will ye kill it quo Rabbie Russel
Wi guns and pistols quo Wise Willie

4 What way will ye draw it hame quo Johnie Macpherson
What way will ye draw it hame quo Jamie Macphee
What way will ye draw it hame quo Rabbie Russel
In carts and cars quo Wise Willie

5 What will ye do wi the feathers quo Johnie Macpherson
What will ye do wi the feathers quo Jamie Macphee
What will ye do wi the feathers quo Rabbie Russel
They will make a bed to my sister quo Wise Willie

6 What will ye do wi the ribs quo Johnie Macpherson
What will ye do wi the ribs quo Jamie Macphee
What will ye do wi the ribs quo Rabbie Russel
They will roof my father's house quo Wise Willie

7 What will ye do wi the dung of it quo Johnie Macpherson
What will ye do wi the dung of it quo Jamie Macphee
What will ye do wi the dung of it quo Rabbie Russel
To dung my father's land quo Wise Willie

8 What will ye roast it in quo Johnie Macpherson
What will ye roast it in quo Jamie Macphee
What will ye roast it in quo Rabbie Russel
In pats and pans quo Wise Willie

24

THE REEKING HOUSE

1 Honest neibour, cum and speak
See yonder a house ye'll neir see reek
It's aw co'cred up about the lum
Surely this belangs to some
   To your fill-al-ee til-al-ee

2 O quo they we'll canna tell
But yonder the laird ye maun speir at him himsel,
. . . .
. . . .

3 Weil honest neibour cum an lein
Your back on this dyke it's baith dry and clean
An tell to me gin I may speir
Why your house is standing tume this lang seven yeir

4 The house is mine it's to be free
I want a wife to dwell wi me
But the lasses ar scant an ill to tame
An I dinna chuse to lie my lane

5 Honest neibour, dinna say so
Whare ane'll ser you, ye may get twa
The lasses now are na sae scant
For mony a lass a lad does want

6 But fare ye well, I maun awa
But dinna take ane that gangs owr braw
Nor dinna take ane that has owr muckle sillar
For that is the main thing that takes you to her

7 Sillar it's a cunning bribe,
It mony a fault and famine hides
Beauty is naething but a cheit
That leads mony a young man off his feet

8 But marry ane that's young an duce
An take her hame to your tume house
An then you'll plainly come to know
Beauty's naething but a shew

9 He has married ane wha's young and douce
And tock her hame to his tume house
And he did plainly come to know
Beauty's naething but a shew

25

THE AULD WIFE AND THE PEAT CREEL

Child 281 *The Keach i the Creel*

1 The farmer's daughter gade to the market
Some white fish for to buy
The young squire followed after her
As hard as he could hie, ricadoo
  Tun-un-nay, ricadoo,
  Tun-un-nay, ricadoo a dee a day,
  Raddle, ricadoo
  Tun-un-nay.

2 A gude mornin to you sweet heart she said
For to see you I am richt glad
But my faither he locks the door every nicht
Puts the key below his head, ricadoo

3 But ye maun get a lang leather
That's thirty feet and three
And ye maun gang to the chimney top
And your brither will let you down to me, ricadoo

4 He has got a lang leather
That's thirty feet and three
He has gane to the chimney top
And his brither lute him down in the creel, ricadoo

5 But the auld wyfe she could nae rest
For thoughts ran in her head
I'll lay my life quo the silly auld wyfe
There a man in our dochter's bed, ricadoo

6 The auld man he rose up himsel
To see if it was true
But she tuke the young squire in her arms
An the curtains around him drew, ricadoo

7 Gude morrow to you auld faither she said
Whar are ye gaun sae soon
Ye disturbit me of my prayer
And so did ye last noon, ricadoo

8 O woe to you he said,
And an ill death may you die
It was the braid book she had in her arms
She was prayand for you and me, ricadoo

9 But the auld wyfe she could nae rest
Till she got up hersel
But sumthing or anither tuke the auld wyfe's fit,
And into the creel she fell, ricadoo

10 The man upon the chimney top
He gade the creel a pou
I'll lay my lyfe quo the auld wyfe
The deil will hae us aw jest now, ricadoo

11 The man upon the chimney top
He lute the creel down fa
He brak three of the auld wyfe's ribs
Knock't her agane the wa, ricadoo

12 O the brume and the bonnie bonnie broom
And the broom that I like weel
An every auld wyfe that's jealous o her daughter
May be dangled in the same Peet creel, ricadoo

26

THE YORKSHIRE RAMBLER

1 I'm just new arrived in Lunin town
On a visit, on a visit
I'm just new arrived in Lunon town
Mang heavy rain and thounder

27

THE BUSH OF BROOM

1 As I went out on a May morning
A May morning it happened to be
O there I spied a very bonny lass
She was asking the road to her ain country

2 O where is your country my bonny lass
Or whatna town do ye come frae
Frae London I came kind Sir she says
And for Newcastle I do stray

3 If from London you came my very bonny lass
Wat and weary might you be
I wad hae you sit down by yon bonny buss o Broom
And bear a young man company

4 O fain wad I sit down by yon bony buss o broom
But I'm afraid you wad injure me
The night is dark I am afraid it will be wet
And it's O but I am far frae my ain countrie

5 He's tane her by the green gown sleeve
And by the lily white hand
And he's tane her down to yon bony buss o Broom
To a silent shade whaur no one seen

6 He put his hand into his purse
And then he gied her guineas three
Saying take ye that my very bony lass
It will help ye ham to your ain country

7 He put his hand into his purse
And there he gied her guineas ten
Saying Take ye that my very bony lass
It will fee a nurse aw for your bairn

8 But what will ye say my very bonny lass
When ye gae hame to your ain country
O I'll take a cup and I'll fill it to the top
And I'll drink to the bony buss o broom and thee

9 But nine lang months had scarce been gone
Nine lang months and scarcely three
Till she sent him a bottle of the wine sae red
And a braw lad bairn to divert him wi

10 He took the young thing in his arms
And there he gied it kisses three
Saying weel do I mind o the bonny buss of broom
And the braw faced lass that I sportit wi

11 If I had her here as I had her there
Richt happy happy would I be
I'd make her heir of my houses and lands
And a braw lad bairn to devert her wi

28

MOTHER BUNCH

1 Its doun in yonder glen
There lives auld Bessie Bunch
And she a dochter had
A bonnie blooming wench
  Sing dy-day, atherday, atherday,
  De-day, atherday, O latherday,
  Atherday, atherday, latherday
  Fal da-lel, le-atherday O

2 Scarce seventeen winters auld
And she was much afraid
She wad never married be
But live and die a maid

3 O mother I'll hae a man
Although ye soud gae mad
Dinna ye see Andro Kerr
A blooming bonnie lad

4 He says he lues me weel
An I care nae mair
Sae mother gin ye think fit
The priest maun mak us a pair

5 A pair ye idle jade
And a bonnie pair ye wad be
Gin ye tak Andro Kerr
Ye will neir be the better o me

6 For scarce there's ane of the twa
Has a sark to put on your back
And when you married are
There's mony a thing ye want

7 O mother but ye be cross
As cross as cross can be
Dinna ye see Maggie Spreul
That's twa year younger nor me

8 Gin we hae na muckle geir
We hae as muckle as them
And when they married were
Ye never did them blame

9 But wha then could them blame
When it was out o need
When it was plain to be seen
That young Roger had dune the deed

10 But then gin ye be free
As gude sen ye may be
Gin ye take Andro Kerr
Ye'll near be the better o me

11 It's when I gade to the fair
Wi my bonnie sparklan loun
He wad cum hame wi me
An aw the deed was dune

12 The loun he said to me
When he got my maidenhead
He wad marry me the next day
And gin there was ony need

13 For shame ye idle jade
For shame, for shame, quo she
We'll aw be shamed thegither
An he no buckle to

14 How daur ye now presume
To let him play the fool
And for the deed ye hae dune
Ye maun munt the repenting stool

15 O mither its dinna ye mind
When ye were young and braw
Ye likit the lads yoursel
As weel as ony ane o us aw

16 And though ye wad say it yoursel
I wad na you believe
Gin ye were young again
Ye wad just be lyke the leeve

17 Auld Bessie hang her head
And she could na say nae mair
So aff she quickly ran
To spunkie Andro Kerr

18 The loun he kept his word
And he came there wi speed
And now they married are
And a bonny pair indeed

29

THE HILLS O' GOWRIE

1 Twas on a summer afternoon
A wee before the sun gade doun
A lassie dressed in a braw gown
Gade owr the hills to Gowrie

30

THE SHEPHERD'S SON

Child 112 *The Baffled Knight*

1 Tha was a shepherds son
Kept sheep on yonder hill
He laid his crook and plaid aside
And there he slept his fill
To my fall de ra rel de dair
To my fall de ra rel de rit o day,
Fall de ra rel de dair o

2 He looked east he lookit west
He's tane anither look
And there he spied a fair maid
A sooming in the brook

3 O dinna touch my manteel
And let my claes alane
And ye shall hae a good reward
If ye conduct me hame

4 I winna touch your manteel
And I'll let your claes alane
But I'll take you out o the deep water
For to make you aw my own

5 He sat her on a milk whyte steed
Himsel upon anither
And thay rode alang the green wood syde
Like sister and brither

6 As they war rydan alang the road
They saw some feils o rye
Quo she - isna this a bonnie place
For men and maids to ly

7 As they wer rydan alang the road
They saw some cocks o hay
Quo she is na this a bonnie place
For men and maids to stray

8 Dinna ye see yon bonnie bour
Stands by yon Castle wa
Thare ye may hae your will o me
Amang the sheets sae sma

9 Whan they cam to yon bonnie bower
She tinklit at the ring
Sae ready was the proud porter
To let the lady in

10 Whan the gates war opened
This maid jumpit nimbly in
If ye be a man on the outside
I am a maid within

11 Ye may cast aff your hose and shune
And let your feet gang bare
And if ye meet a bonnie lass
Pray touch her if ye daur.

12 I'll na cast aff my hose and shune
Nor let my feet gang bare
But gin I meet a bonnie lass
Hang me if I her spare

13 Ye ar like a cock my father has
He wears a double kame
He claps his wings an craws fu crouse
I think ye ar the same

14 Ye are like a horse my father has
That feeds in yonder lone
He hings his head abune the sheaf
But daur na prie the corn

15 There is a flower in our garden
They caw it marygold
An he that would na when he could
He should na when he would

31

THE FAUSE KNICHT

Child 3

1 O whar are ye gaun quo the fause knicht upon the road
I'm gawn to the skeul quo the wee boy and still he stood

2 What is that upon your back quo the fause knicht upon the rade
Atweel it is my books quo the wee boy and still he stood

3 What's that ye hae gotten in your arm quo the fause knicht upon the road
Atweel it is my peat quo the wee boy and still he stood

4 Wha's aught they sheep quo the fause knicht upon the road
They are mine an my mother's quo the wee boy and still he stood

5 How money of them are mine quo the fause knicht upon the road
Aw them that hae blue tails quo the wee boy and still he stood

6 O I wish ye were on yon tree quo the fause knicht upon the road
And a guid ladder under me quo the wee boy and still he stood

7 And the ladder for to break quo the fause knicht upon the road
And you for to faw down quo the wee boy and still he stood

8 I wish ye were in yon sea quo the fause knicht upon the road
And a gude bottom under me quo the wee boy and still he stood

9 And the bottom for to break quo the fause knicht upon the road
And you for to be drowned quo the wee boy and still he stood

32

THE LAIRD OF OCHILTREE WALLS

Child 217 *The Broom of Cowdenknows*

1 O May bonnie May is to the Ewe buchts gane
To milk her daddie's yowes
And aye as she sang her voice it rang
Out owr the top o the knows, knows, knows
Out owr the top of the knows

2 Tha came a troup o gentlemen
As thay war rydan by
An ane of them he lichtit down
For to see May milking her kye, kye, kye
For to see May milking her kye

3 Milk on Milk on my bonnie lass
Milk on milk on said he
For owt o the buchts I winna gang
To you shew me owr the lee, lee, lee
To you shew me owr the lee

4 Ryde on ryde on ye rank rydars
Your steeds ar stout and strang
For out o' the yowe buchts I winna gae
For fear that ye do me sum wrang, wrang, wrang
For fear that ye do me sum wrang

5 He tock her by the milk white hand
And by the green gown sleive
An thare he tock his will o her
But o her askit nae leive, leive, leive
But o her askit nae leive

6 But whan he gat his wull o her
He lute her up again
An aw this bonny maid said or did
Was, kind Sir, tell me your name, name, name
Was, kind Sir, tell me your name

7 He pullit out a silver kame
Sayan kame your yellow hair
An if I be na back in thrie quarters of a yeir
It's o me you'll neir see nae mair, mair, mair
It's o me ye'll neir see nae mair

8 He pullit out a pocket Book
An he gae her guineas thrie
Sayen if I be na back in thrie quarters of a yeir
It'll pay the nurse's fee, fee, fee
It'll pay the nurse's fee

9 He put his fit into the stirrup
An rode after his men
An aw that his men said or did
Was, kind maister, you've tarried lang, lang, lang
Was, kind maister, you've tarried lang

10 I have rode east and I have rode wast
An I have rode owr the knows
But the bonniest lass that I ever saw
Was in the ewe buchts milkan her yews, yowes, yewes,
Was in the yewe buchts milkan her yows.

11 Sho put the pale on to her heid
An sho's gane merrilie hame
An aw that her faither said or did
Was, kind dochter you've tarried lang, lang, lang
Was, kind dochter you've tarried lang

12 O wae be to your men faither
And an ill death may thay die
For thay caw't aw the yowes out owr the knows
An thay left nae bodie wi me, me, me
An thay left nae bodie wi me

13 Tha cam a tod unto the bucht
The lyke I never saw
An afore that he tock the ane that he tock
I wad rather he had tane ither twa, twa, twa
I wad rather he had tane ither twa

14 Tha're cam a tod unto the bucht
The lyke I neir did see
An ay as he spak he liftit his hat
And he had a bonnie twinkland ee, ee, ee
And he had a bonnie twinkland ee

15 'Twas on a day an it was a fyne simmer day
She was cawand out her faither's kye
Thare cam a troup o gentlemen
An thay rode ways the lass neir by, by, by
An thay rode ways the lass neir by

16 Who has done to you this ill my deir
Wha has done to you this wrong
An she had na a word to say for hersel
But kind Sir I hae a man of my own, own, own
But kind Sir I hae a man of my own

17 Ye lie ye lie bonnie May he says
Sae loud I hear ye lie
For dinna ye mind yon bonnie simmer nicht
Whan ye war in the yowe buchts wi me, me, me
Whan ye war in the yowe buchts wi me

18 Licht down, licht doun, my foremaist man
Licht doun and let her on
For manie a tyme sho caw't her faither's kye
But she'll neir caw them again, again, again
But she'll neir caw them again

19 For I am the laird o Ochiltree-Walls
I have thirtie plews and thrie
An I have tane awa the bonniest lass
That is in aw the north countrie, countrie, countrie
That is in aw the north countrie

33

THE BONNIE BLUE-EYED LASSIE

1 O gin I were at the tap of yon mountain
Gold in my pocket and money for the counting
I wad gar the guinea gang I wad hae my fancy
I wad marry nane but the bonnie blue eyit Lassie

2 She has tway bonnie blue een her looks are sae tender
Her rosy cheeks and her body lang and sklender
And I wad take her in my arms sae fond I wad embrace her
For how I can love her when all the world hates her

3 For sum folk say she is o a bad station
And ither folks say she is o a bad nation
But let them aw say as they will it never will grieve me
For to the day I die she is my deir girl

4 Though my fause friends they'd revile thee
Here is the hand that never will beguile thee
Here is the hand although in the dark love
The next place ye'll find it will be in the kirk love

5 Sweet sweet swims the swans on yon high streams o Yarrow
Sweet sings the nightingales theire voice is like to an arrow
It's cauld frost and snaw the mune shining clearly
Deep runs the river between me and my dearie

34

MAY COLYEAN

Child 4 *Lady Isabel and the Elf-Knight*

1 Hae ye no heard o fause Sir John
That livit in the north countrie
How he betrayit eight damsels fair
And drownit them in the sea

2 Now he's awa to May Collean
She was her father's heir
The greatest beawtie o the land
I solemnlie declare

3 Thou art the darling o my heart
He said to fair May Collyein
Thou far exceeds the beawties aw
That ever I hae seen

4 And I'm a knicht o wealth an micht
O town-lands twenty three
And ye'se be lady o them aw
Fair May an ye gang wi me

5 Excuse me then she said Sir John
To wad I am owr young
Unless I hae my parents' leave
Wi you I daur na gang

6 But he's tane a charm frae aff his arm
And stack it in hir sleive
And he has gart her follow him
Without her parents' leave

7 O gold and jewels she has tane
Wi her five hundred pound
And the brawest horse her father had
She's tane to ride upon

8 So merrilie they rode alang
Made neither stop nor stay
Until they came to that fatal place
That's callit Benon's Bay

9 Licht down licht doun fair May Colyein
Licht doun and speak to me
For here I hae drounit eight damsels fair
An the nynt ane ye sall be

10 Cast aff cast aff your jewels fine
Sae costlie rich and brave
For they're owr costlie and owr gude
To rot in the sea wave

11 Her jewels fine she then cast aff
And thus she made her moan
Hae mercy on a virgin young
I pray thee sweet Sir John

12 Cast aff cast aff thy gay mantiel
And smock o Holland lawn
For they are owr costlie and owr gude
To rot in the sea saun

13 Weil turn thee round I pray Sir John
And see the leaf flie owr the tree
For it neir befitted a book learned man
A naked lady to see

14 But as fause Sir John did turn him round
To see the leaf flee owr the tree
She gripped him in her arms smaw
And flang him in the sea

15 Now lie you there ye fause Sir John
Whare ye thought to leave me
Ye wad hae drounit me as naked as I was born
But ye hae got my claes frae me

16 Her jewels costlie, rich, and brave
She straught put on again
She lichtlie springs upon her steid
And leads him by the mane

17 Sae aff she rade without fear or dread
As hard as she could hie
And she reached her fathers lofty bower
Before the clock strack three

18 And first she met the stable grume
He was her waiting man
And when he hard his lady's voice
He ran wi cap in hand

19 Where hae ye been fair May Colyein
Wha owes that dapple gray
O that's a fundling she replied
That I got by the way

20 Then out bespack the grein parrot
And said fair May Colyein
O what hae ye dune wi yon braw knicht
That gade wi ye the strein

21 O haud your tung my pretty parrot
And I'se be kind to thee
For whare ye gat ae handful o groats
My parrot ye'se get thrie

22 Then out bespak her father dear
In the chammer where he lay
What is it ails my pretty parrot
He speaks sae lang ere day

23 There cam a cat into my cage
Had nearlie worried me
And I was calland on May Colyein
To cum and set me free

24 And first she telled her father dear
O the deid she had dune
And likewise to her mother dear
Concerning the fause Sir John

25 So aff they gade wi ae consent
By the dawning o the day
Until they cam to the fatal place
And there his corpse it lay

26 His body tall by that grit fall
Was dashed to and fro
And the gold ring that he had own
Was broke in pieces two

27 And they hae taken up his corpse
To yonner pleasant grein
And there they burried fause Sir John
For fear he wad be seen

35

MALL BOWIE

Laws O 14 *Pretty Polly*

1 Noble Sir Arthur a hunting did ride
Wi his hounds at his foot and his sword by his side
And as he was a hunting he happened to spye
A bonny brown girl and her name was Mall Bowie

2 O Mall Bowie O Mall Bowie my butler ye shall be
For to draw the white wine, love, between thee and me
. . . .
. . . .

3 Love, I'll buy thee ribbons, love I'll buy thee rings
Love I'll buy thee jewels and monie braw things
I'll buy thee silk petticoats gilt to your knee
Gin ye can love me my charming Mall Bowie

4 I'll hae nane of your ribbons nor nane of your rings
Or nane of your jewels nor nae sic braw things
And I hae got petticoats suits my degree
And I'll neir love a married man till his wife die

5 O if ye prove wi child and no able for to walk
I'll send you to my friends that are far distant back
At all fairs and markets I'll wait upon thee
Gin ye can love me my charming Mall Bowie

6 O gin I prove wi child and no able for to walk
Ye'll send me to your friends that are far distant a back
Your friends they will frown and look down on me
And I'll love never a married man till his wife die

7 O Mall Bowie O Mall Bowie lend me your penknife
And I will gang hame and kill my ain wife
And I will kill my ain wife mak a lady o thee
Gin ye can love me my charming Mall Bowie

8 O noble Sir Arthur pray dinna ye say so
Gang to your ain wife and let naebody know
For seven lang years I will wait upon thee
But I'll never love any married man till his wife die

9 When seven lang years they were past and gane
This auld woman went unto her lang hame
And I trew a happy man was he
For he's gane a courting his charming Mall Bowie

10 Now Mall Bowie she's married in her coach did ryde
Wi her man to attend her and maid by her side
Come all ye young virgins tak warning by me
And near love a married man till his wife die

36

LADY JEAN

Child 52

1 The King's young dochter was sittan in her window
Sewan at hir fine silken seam
Sho luikit out at her braw bower window
And she saw the leaves growan grein my love
And she saw the leaves growan grein

2 She stack her neidle into her sleive
Her seam down by her tae
And she is awa to the merrie green wud
For to pu the nuts and slaes my love
For to pu the nits and slaes

3 She had na pu't a nit at aw
A nit but scarcely three
Till out and spak a braw young man
Saying how daurst thou bow this tree my love
Sayan how daurst thou bow this tree

4 It's I will pu these nuts she said
An I will bow this tree
An I will come to the merrie grein wud
An no ask leave of thee my love
An no ask leave o thee

5 He tuke her be the middle sae smaw
And laid her on the gerse sae green
An he has tane his will of her
An he luit her up again my love
An he luit her up again

6 Now since you have got your will o me
Pray tell to me your name
For I am the King's young dochter she said
And this nicht I daur na gang hame my love
And this nicht I daur na gang hame

7 If ye be the King's young dochter he said
I am his auldest son
I wish I had died on some distant isle
An never had come hame my love
An never had come hame

8 The first time I came hame Jeinie
Thow was na here nor born
I wish my prettie ship had sunk
An I had neir returned my love
And I had neir returned

9 The neist time I cam hame Jeanie
Thou was sittan on the nurse's knie
An I wiss my pretty ship had sunk
An I had seen neir thee my love
An I had seen near thee

10 An the neist time I came hame Jeinie
I met thee here alane
I wiss I had die't on some distant isle
An never had come hame my love
An never had come hame

11 She put her hand down by her side
Doun into her spare
An she pu't out a wee pen knife
An she woundit hersel fu sair my love
An she woundit hersel fu sair

12 Slowlie, slowlie, rose she up
An slowlie she gade hame
Until she cam to her faither's parlour
And there she did sigh and mane my love
An there she did sich and mane

13 O Sister Sister mak my bed
O' the clean sheets and strae
O Sister sister mak my bed
Down in the parlour below my love
Down in the parlour below

14 And her faither he came trippan down the stairs
His steps they were fu slow
I think, I think, ladie Jean he said
Ye'r lyan far owr low my love
Ye'r lyan far owr low

15 O late last night as I came hame
Down by yon castle wa
O heavy heavy was the stane
That on my breast did faw my love
That on my breast did faw

16 Her mother she came doun the stair
Her steps they were fu slow
I think I think lady Jean she said
Ye'r lyan far owr low my love
Ye'r lyan far owr low

17 O late last night as I came hame
Down by yon castle wa
O heavy heavy was the stane
That on my breast did faw my love
That on my breast did faw

18 Her Sister came tripping doun the stair
Her steps they were fu slow
I think I think lady Jean she said
Ye're lying far ower low, my love
Ye're lying far ower low

19 O late last night as I came hame
Down by yon castle wa
O heavy heavy was the stane
That on my breast did faw my love
That on my breast did faw

20 Her brither he came trippan doun the stair
His steps they were fu slow
He sank into his sister's arms
And they died as white as snow my love
And they died as white as snow

37

EARL RICHARD

Child 68 *Young Hunting*

1 Earl Richard is a hunting gane
As hard as he could ride
His hunting horn about his neck
An his braid sword by his side
An his braid sword by his side

2 But as he was hunting
Down by Charter's hall
He stopped at his trew loves gate
And there he began to call
And there he began to call

3 He stopped at his trew love's gate
And he tinklit at the ring
There was nane sae ready as lady Margaret hersel
For to let Earl Richard in
For to let Earl Richard in

4 Light down, licht doun Earl Richard she said
An cum my bower within
And ye shall have cheer and charcoal clear
An candles for to burn
An candles for to burn

5 I canna licht down Earl Richard he said
Nor I winna licht doun at aw
For a lady fairer than ten o thee
Is to meet me at Richard's haw
Is to meet me at Richard's haw

6 He loutit owr his saddle bow
For to kiss her lips sae sweet
But little thought he o that pen knife
. . . . . .
. . . . . .

7 Why wound you me sae sair lady
Why wound you me sae sair
For there's no a man in aw Scotland
Loves a fause woman mair
Loves a fause woman mair

8 She carried him into her bower
An laid him on a bed
And painfullie she watched him
Until he was dead
Until he was dead

9 She called on her waiting maids
Twa hours ere it was day
Sayand – I hae a dead Squire in my bower
And I wiss he were awa
And I wiss he were awa

10 Silver then shall be your hire
And gold shall be your fee
And I will gang alang wi you
And keep you company
And keep you company

11 They sadled him and bridled him
As he was wont to ride
Wi his hunting horn about his neck
An his braid sword by his side
An his braid sword by his side

12 The tane o them tuke his head
And the ither tuke his feet
Until thay came to yon wan water
An they threw him in the deep
An they threw him in the deep

13 Now lie ye there Earl Richard she said
Till the bluid cums frae your bane
An the lady fairer than ten o me
Will weary till you gang hame
Will weary till you gang hame

14 But as she was walking hame
A wee bird on a tree
Said Gang hame gang hame ye fause lady
An pay your servants' fee
An pay your servants' fee

15 Cum down Cum doun my bonnie wee bird
Cum doun and speak to me
For I hae a cage o beaten gold
Whaurin I will pit thee
Whaurin I will pit thee

16 It's ye maun keep your golden cage
An I will keep my tree
For as ye hae did to your trew luve
So wud you do to me
So wud you do to me

17 Ye wad cut aff my little head
Throw my body in the sea
An as ye said to your trew luve
Sa wad ye say to me
Sa wad ye say to me

18 Gae bring to me my bendit bow
And set it at my ee
And I'll gar this bonnie wee bird
Cum down and speak to me
Cum down and speak to me

19 Before that ye get your bow bent
And right set at your ee
I'll be far far in yon forest
Telland ill tales on thee
Telland ill tales on thee

38

THE LAIRD O' KELTY

1 O whaur are ye gaun, fair maid, whaur are ye gaun sae late
Are ye no afraid o your hard fate
Are ye no afraid of your hard fate
In passing by the young laird o Keltie O

2 She passed on her way by the harrows and plews
'Twas about the gloaming when we are gaun to loose
We said - Stop a little fair maid till we hae our horses housed
An we'll put you by the young laird of Kelty O

3 And the lassie turnd about while sho seemit to gie a smile
She said I hae been here about baith late and air this while
She said I have been here about baith late and air this while
Yet I never saw the young laird of Kelty O

4 But she had na gane into the parks a quarter o a mile
Till she heard a voice behind her saying stop my pretty girl
Till she heard a voice behind her saying Stop my pretty girl
Dinna ye know ye're in the parks o Kelty O

5 The lassie turnd about an the tears stood in her ee
She says I will turn back again if I have offended thee
She says I will turn back again if I have offended thee
For I know you are the laird o Kelty O

6 He tuke her by the milk white hand he gently laid her low
He tuke her by the milk white hand he gently laid her low
Where the gerse growd grein on every side and the apples they
This was into the pretty parks o Kelty O [hung low

7 It's when you gang hame unto your faithers farm
If onie ane shoud ask you wha has dune this harm
If onie ane shoud ask you wha has dune this harm
Dinna deny it was the laird o Kelty O

8 But the lassie being fair its delicate and young
The laird soon repentit the evil he had dune
An he has made her his wife lang ere the child was born
An she is ladie o the pretty park o Kelty O

39

THE MASON'S DOCHTER

1 Doun in Oxford city lived a mason to trade
An he had a dochter a beautiful maid
The fairest o faces but the fausest o hearts
That ever was known in our neighbouring parts

2 She feed wi a lady upon her to wait
She was her companion baith early and late
She had the good will o her mistress therefore
An the finest o garments she commonly wore

3 She had na been there a month or above
Until their young Steward being Isabel's love
He said now come wad I'll mak you my wife
For I vow that I luve you as deir as my life

4 O as for my part I'll no marry yet
I hae nae muckle money and far less wit
An ye hae as little as me for my life
An I laugh when I hear a cloun caw for a wife

5 But this being nane o his cunning design
He was pleased to treat her wi plenty of wine
As muckle as laid her secure fast asleep
That into her arms he might cosily creep

6 Some part of the night in his arms she has lain
Until her senses returned again
Awa frae his arms in a passion she flew
Sayand was I ordained to be ruined by you

7 Ae day he said to her he said to her then
My dearest come wad I'll mak ye my ain
My dearest come wad I'll mak ye my wife
For I vow that I love you as dear as my life
I am no wi bairn I'll no be your wife
I avow I'll never wad you a' the days of my life

8 But nevertheless he kent it was so
And he did watch her wherear she did go
He fixed a net and he fixed it weel
An he fixed a net out owr the draw well

9 Supposing she woud murder or smother there
And he did watch her with abundance of care
When her appointed time began to draw nigh
Ae night at her window a light he did spy

10 Which made him come speedily doun frae the shore
An he saw his true love coming out at the door
Wi something in her hand in the draw well she threw
An when she retired frae it her true lover drew

11 He drew up the nett fand the infant alive
This was an invention that he did contrive
He tuke the babe and he kept it likewyse
Till by good fortune he fand out a nurse
Till by good fortune he fand out a nurse
Till whom he paid money out of his purse

12 He beg'd o the nurse to be tender and free
And for this babie muckle siller he'd gie
An for this babie much siller in store
The like was never paid before

13 In twa years after he said to her then
My dear I am gaun for to visit a friend
Though she wad na wed yet her favour to shaw
A walking wi him did she offer to go

14 An this bonnie babe stood tender and free
As it stands prattling by his mother's knie
She uttered her words an she said wi amaze
I'm sure I near saw as braw a bairn in aw my days

15 He said if it were na for lying your lane
Ye might hae had as braw a bairn o your ain
O that's what I do and I will do that still
An lead my life single let you say what you will

16 But as thay were walking dune by yonder field
He said my dear jewel lang hae I concealed
Your intended murder shall never be known
Rejoice and be thankfu yon babie is your ain

17 O little she said or naething at all
She raise in the next morning wi a heart ful of gaw
She gade to the house cryde the nurse to the door
And she murdered the babie left it lying on the floor

18 O grippit she was and suffered lykewyse
Which made the salt tears to run frae his eyes
For he lued the bairn weel and the mamma for its sake
And just for them baith his heart was readie to break

19 Come all you true lovers o beautiful charms
If ever your true love does fa in your arms
Dinna slight there kind offer or if you do
Perhaps it'll prove a sad ruin unto you

40

THE THREE RAVENS

Child 26

1 Thrie ravens sat upon a tree
  Hey doun hey derrie day
Thrie ravens sat upon a trie
  Hey down
Thrie ravens sat upon a trie
And they were black as black could be
  And sing lay doo-an la doo-an day

2 The middlemaist ane said to its mate
The middlemaist ane said to its mate
The middlemaist ane said to its mate
O quher'll we our dinner get

3 O doun into yon green grass field
O doun into yon grein gerse field
O doun into yon grein gerse field
Thare lies a Squire baith killed and dead

4 His horse was standing by his side
His horse was standing by his side
His horse was standing by his side
An thought he soud get on and ride

5 His hounds war standing by his feet
His hounds war standing by his feet
His hounds were standing by his feet
An lick't his sairs they war so deep

6 Thare cam a lady fu o woe
Thare cam a lady fu o woe
Thare cam a lady fu o woe
As big wi child as she could go

7 Sho streach't hersel doun by his side
She streach't hersel doun by his side
She streach't hersel down by his side
An for the luve o him she died

8 He was burried in Sant Mary's kirk
He was burry't in Sanct Mary's kirk
He was burried in Sanct Mary's kirk
An she was burried in Sanct Mary's quier

9 Out o his grave thare grew a fir
Out o his grave thare grew a fir
Out o his grave thare grew a fir
And out o hers a lily fair

10 They grew till they grew to the kirk top
They grew till they grew to the kirk top
They grew till they grew to the kirk top
And there they cuist a true love knot

11 O dinna ye think but their love was true
O dinna ye think but their love was true
O dinna ye think but their love was true
When out of their graves sic flowers do grow

41

THE DEIL'S COURTSHIP

1 I'll buy you a pennyworth of priens
If that be the way true love begins
If ye'll gang alang wi me my deir
If ye'll gang alang wi me

2 I carena for you nor your pennyworth of preins
If that be the way true love begins
For I'll never gang alang wi you kind Sir
For I'll never gang alang wi you

3 I'll buy you a braw snuff box
Ten tymes it opens and other ten it locks
If ye'll gang alang wi me my deir
If ye'll gang alang wi me

4 I carena for you or your braw snuff box
Ten tymes it opens and other ten it locks
For I'll never gang alang wi you kind Sir
For I'll never gang alang wi you

5 I'll buy you a braw silk gown
Nine stripes up an ither nyne doun
If ye'll gang alang wi me my deir
If ye'll gang alang wi me

6 I carena for you or your braw silk gown
Nyne stripes up and other nyne down
For I'll never gang alang wi you kind Sir
For I'll never gang alang wi you

7 I'll buy you a nine stringed bell
Ye may caw on your servants when you lyke yoursel
If ye'll gang alang wi me my dear
If ye'll gang alang wi me

8 I carena for you or your nine stringed bell
Ye may caw on your servants when ye lyke yoursell
For I'll never gang alang wi you kind Sir
For I'll never gang alang wi you

9 I'll give you a purse of gold
To keep you easy when you grow old
If ye'll gang alang wi me my deir
If ye'll gang alang wi me

10 Mount up Jack ye hae won the day
And wi you I'll gang away
And I'll gang alang wi you my dear
An I'll gang alang wi you

11 They had na gane a mile atweel
Till she saw his fit cloven to the heel
Sayand, I rue I cam wi you kind Sir
Sayand I rue I cam wi you

12 I have gat you now I'll haud you fast
Gowd wan your virgin heart at last
An I'll no part wi you my dear
An I'll no part wi you

13 Nae mair she said but went alang
At every mile that dulefu sang
I rue that I cam wi you kind Sir
I rue that I cam wi you

42

POOR GREETING WILSIE

1 O wha will gang to the wood wi me quo Wilsie quo Wilzie
O wha will gang to the wood wi me quo poor greetand Wilzie
O I will gang to the wood wi thee quo Nansie quo Nansie
O I will gang to the wood wi thee quo bonnie blythe Nansy

2 O what an I wad lay thee down quo Wilsie quo Wilsie
O what an I wad lay thee down quo poor greetand Wilsie
O can I no rise again quo Nansy quo Nansy
O can I no rise again quo bonnie blythe Nansy

3 O quhat an I wad fyle thy goun quo Wilsie quo Wilsie
O quhat an I wad fyle thy goun quo poor greetand Wilsie
Can I no wash it again quo Nansy quo Nansy
Can I no wash it again quo bonnie blythe Nansy

4 O what an I wad get thee wi bairn quo Wilsie quo Wilsie
O what an I wad get thee wi bairn quo poor greetand Wilsie
I'm able enough to bear it aw quo Nansy quo Nansy
I'm able enough to bear it aw quo bonnie blythe Nansy

5 O what'll we do for a cradle till't quo Wilsie quo Wilsie
O what'll we do for a cradle till't quo poor greetand Wilsie
There ar trees in my father's land quo Nansy quo Nansy
There ar trees in my father's land quo bonnie blythe Nansy

6 What way will we cut them doun quo Wilsie quo Wilsie
What way will we cut them doun quo poor greetand Wilsie
We'll tak an axe an hag them down quo Nansy quo Nansy
We'll tak an axe an hag them down quo bonnie blythe Nansy

7 O what way'll we get them hame quo Wilsie quo Wilsie
O what way'll we get them hame quo poor greetand Wilsie
We'll take a horse and draw them hame quo Nansy quo Nansy
We'll take a horse and draw them hame quo bonnie blythe Nansy

8 O what'll we tye him to quo Wilsie quo Wilsie
O what'll we tye him to quo poor greetand Wilsie
Ye maun tye him to your muckle tae quo Nansy quo Nansy
Ye maun tye him to your muckle tae quo bonnie blythe Nansy

9 What if the horse rin awa quo Wilsie quo Wilsie
What if the horse rin awa quo poor greetand Wilsie
Deil tak the horse and you and aw quo Nansy quo Nansy
Deil tak the horse and you and aw quo bonnie blythe Nansy

43

SLIGHTED LOVE

Laws P 25 *Love Has Brought Me to Despair*

1 Tha're a flower the folk did say
Tha'r a flower they caw it heartease
And if that I could but find
It would ease my heart and it would ease my troubled mind

2 To the meadow she is gane
And pu't the flowers just as they sprang
And every flower she will them pu
Until she does get her apron fu

3 She laid them down and she made her bed
On a soft down pillow she laid her head
She laid her down and nae mair she spake
Crying alas for love my poor heart it break

4 But when they saw that this maid was cold
They went to her fause love and him they told
If that be's true that you do me tell
I am glad to hear that she is sae well

5 What a foolish young woman must she be
To think I could love nane but she
A man is not bound for ane alone
And I tak great delight for to hear her mane

6 Gae dig her grave baith large and deep
And a merval stane lay at head and feet
And write there on that it may stand
That love has gained the upper hand

44

THE ENSIGN AND THE LADY GAY

Child 69 *Clerk Saunders*

1 An Ensign and a lady gay
As they were walking on the green
The ensign said to the lady gay
Will you let me come to your bower at een

2 O gude forbid Ensign she said
That sic a thing should eir be seen
Until I be your wedded wife
Ye maunna come to my bower at een

3 For I hae seven bludy brethren
And they hae to you nae good will
And if they catch you in bed wi me
They wad na value your blude to spill

4 O ye may take me on your back
And ye may carry me to your bed
That ye may swear wi a voice sae clear
That your chamber floor I never tread

5 Ye may tak the napkin aff your neck
And ye may blindfauld baith your een
That ye may swear wi a voice sae clear
That ye did na see your luve sin the strein

6 O she has tane him on her back
And she has carryit him to her bed
That she might swear wi a voice sae cleir
That her chamber floor he never tread

7 O she has tane the napkin aff her neck
O she has blindfaulded baith her een
That she might swear wi a voice sae clear
That she did na see her love sin the strein

8 But when these lovers gade to bed
They slept as though they had been dead
Till in and cam her seven breither
Sayand there's a naked man in our sister's bed

9 Then out and spak the youngest of them
Sayand I think the ensign shoud be killed
Then out and spak the second o' them
Sayand tha'll no a drap of his blude be spilled

10 Then out and spak the third of them
It is a pity to kill him sleeping here
Than out and spak the fourt o them
I wad rather fecht him in battle fair

11 Then out and spak the fifth o' them
True love is better worth than gold
Then out and spak the sixt of them
Sayand our het luve does soon turn cold

12 Then out and spak the sevent o' them
O but he had an angry ee
Sayand an he war aw the men in ane
The ensign's butcher I will be

13 Then instantly he drew his sword
And plunged it in the ensign's breast
But he lay in his true luve's arms
And slept awa to endless rest

14 But in the morning she awoke
Saying true love ye maun awa
The sun is shynand in the room
An it'll na be lang till the cock does craw

15 She tossed him and she tumbled him
Sayand O but thou art a weary man
But whan she stripped down the claes
She saw his face baith pale and wan

16 O wae be to my seven breither
They killed him sleeping in his bed
In they had foucht him in battle fair
There wad mony a drap o' blude been shed

17 She tock the napkin aff her head
And ay she dichtit his bludy wounds
But ay the mair that she dichtit them
The mair the blude it did rin doun

18 Then in and cam her aged father
Sayand dochter dinna mourn sae sair
But ryse and put on your gown o black
And ryse and kame your yellow hair

19 And I will get a lord for you
That's willing to make you his bride
O haud your tong faither she said
For they'll neir a man ly by my syde

20 For I will do for my true luve
What other maidens wad neglect
For seven years will come and go
Before I fling aff my gown o black

21 And I will do for my true luve
What other maidens wad na do
For seven years will come and gang
Before I change stocking or shoe

22 And I will do for my true luve
What other maidens wad na care
For seven years will come and gang
Before I kame my yellow hair

11 O what is whiter than the milk
Or what is safter than the silk

12 Or what is sharper than a thorn
Or what is louder than a horn

13 Or what is greener than the grass
Or what is waur than a woman's wuss

14 O Heav'n is heigher than the tree
An' Hell is deeper than the sea

15 O sin is heavier than the lead
The blessing's better than the bread

16 The snaw is whiter than the milk
An' the down is safter than the silk

17 Hunger's sharper than a thorn
An' shame is louder than a horn

18 The Peas are greener than the grass
An' the Fiend is waur than a woman's wuss

19 As sune as she the Fiend did name
He flew awa in a fierie flame

46

ROSIANNE

Child 51 *Lizie Wan*

1 Rosie she sat in her simmer bour
Weeping an makand grit mane
Whan doun by cam her faither
Sayand what ails thee Rosianne

2 A deal a deal deir father she said
Grit reason hae I to mane
For thare lyes a little babe in my syde
Between me an my brither John

3 Rosie she sat in her simmer bour
Weeping an makand a grit mane
Wha cam by but her mither deir
Sayand what ails thee Rosianne

4 A deal a deal deir mither she said
Grit reason hae I to mane
For thare lyes a little babe in my side
Between me an my brither John

5 Rosie she sat in her simmer bour
Weeping an makan grit mane
Wha cam doun but her sister deir
Sayand what ails thee Rosiann

6 A deal a deal deir sister she said
Grit reason hae I to mane
For there lies a little babe in my syde
Between me and my brither John

7 Rosie she sat in her simmer bowr
Weeping an makand grit mane
Wha cam by but her fause fause brither
Sayand what ails thee Rosianne

8 A deal a deal deir brither she said
Grit reason hae I to mane
For there lies a little babe in my side
Between me an thee, deir brither John.

9 Weil ye hae tauld faither an ye hae tauld mither
And ye hae tauld sister aw thrie
Syne he pou't out his wee penknyfe
An gae her deep wounds three

10 What blude is that on the point of your knyfe
Deir son cum tell to me
It is my horse's that I hae killit
Deir mither and fair ladie

11 The blude o your horse was neir sae red
Deir son cum tell to me
It is my grandfather's that I hae killit
Dear mither and fair ladie

12 The blude o your grandfather was neir sae free
Dear son cum tell to me
It is my sister's that I hae killit
Dear mither and fair ladie

13 What will ye do whan your father cums hame
Dear son cum tell to me
I'll set my fit on yon ship bord
An I howp she'll sail wi me

14 What will ye do wi your bonnie wife
Deir son cum tell to me
I'll set her in anither ship
And I howp she'll fallow me

15 An' what will ye do wi' your little son
Dear son come tell tae me
I'll lea' him wi' you my dearest mither
Tae keep ye in mind o' me

16 What will ye do wi' your houses an' lan'
Dear son com tell tae me
I'll lea' them wi' you dear mither
Tae maintain my wee babie

17 An whan will you return again
Dear son come tell tae me
Whan the Sun an' Moon meet on yon hill
An' I hope that will never be

47

THE PRINCE OF ORANGE

Laws P 12 *Nancy II*

1 Ae nicht as my luve and I was wauking
I offerit to her a marriage ring
But she gade me sic a scornfu answer
I neir thought on sic a foolish thing

2 Begone thou proud and thou prattling fellow
How daur ye tauk to sic as me
Go put on a suit o' green willow
For my true love ye sall na be

3 I gade up to her auld mither
Thinking that she wad hear my mane
But she was far waur than the other
She scornfullie bade me begone

4 I said ye blame me to wrang your dochter
An for her sake I hae suffered sair
I am confined in jail upon bread and water
Abune these six weeks and mair

5 But now she is married to the Prince o Orange
An like a beau he walks up the town
An for his wife he does not regard
Her loftie pryde he will soon pu doun

MEG WALKER

(MRS CALDWELL)

48

THE NUT-BROWN BRIDE

Child 73 *Lord Thomas and Fair Annet*

1 Sweet Wille & fare Anni
Sat a day on yon hill O
When they had sat the lang simmer day
They cou'd na talke there fill O

2 Sweet Wille said a word in jest
Fair Anie took it ill O
Ill never marrey a tocherless bride
Against my ain friends will O

3 If you will never wed a bride
A bride will never wed thee O
And for my blessing Wille she says
Let the broun bride abee O

4 Wille awa to his father gain
As fast as he coul'd hee O
O will I marry the nut brown bride
Or bring hame fair Anie O

5 The nut brown bride has houses and lands
Fair Anie she has nean O
And for my blessing Willie he says
Bring me the broun bride hame O

6 And Willie awa to his mother gain
As fast as he could hee O
O will I marrey the nut broun bride
Or bring hame fair Anie O

7 The nut broun bride has houses & lands
Fair Anie she has nane O
And for my blessing Wille she says
Bring me the brown bride hame O

8 Wille awa to his sister gain
As fas as he could hee O
O will I marrey the nut broun bride
Or bring hame fair Anie O

9 The nut broun bride has houses & lands
Fair Anie she has nane O
But for my blessing Wille she says
Bring fair Anie hame O

10 He has ridden throu yone green sha
And throu yon sha sa broun O
And he was at fair Anie yet
A couple o hours or day O

11 What nues What nues sweet Wille she says
What nues What nues to me O
I am come for to bide thee to my wedding
And that a nues to thee O

12 Come riddle come riddle us mother she says
Come riddle us both in ane O
Whether will I gan to sweet Wille wedding
Or will I stay at hame O

13 There is few to be your friends Anie
There mony to be your faes O
Betide the death betide the life
To Wille wedding dina gan O

14 There few to be my friends mother
There mony to be my faes O
Betide me death betide me life
To Wille wedding Ill gan O

15 She calld on her waiting maid
To dress her ridding tweed O
Likewise on her stable groom
To dress her ridding steed O

16 When four and twenty siller bells
Shall hing at my Horse mane O
And the first muir that she rade o'er
Sa loudly as they did ring O

17 Anie Horse was shod we siller before
With burning goud behin O
And every town that she road throu
They took her for some Queen O

18 When she came to St Marey Kirk
She lat her claiths fall side O
Sa meekly and sa modestly
She kis'd the nut broun bride O

19 When she came in to St Mary Kirk eard
She sat doun on a stane O
Your Wellcome Wellcom fare Anie
Into this unco lan O

20 Sweet Wille had a red rose in his han
He gead it kisses three O
He rached it by the nut broun bride
And laid it on fair Anie knee O

21 The nut broun bride had a we pen knife
Hung low doun by her gair O
She stabb fair Anie to the heart
A deep wound & a sair O

22 What ails what ailes fair Anie he says
Thou looks sa pale and wan O
For ance thou had as bonie a face
As ever the sun shine'd on O

23 What need's thou spere sweet Wille she says
What need's thou speir at me O
O distna see my heart blood rinning
Fast doon by my knee O

24 Fair Anie she died or the middle o the night
Sweet Wille on the morrow O
Fair Anie she died with sare sickness
Sweet Wille we greef and sorrow O

25 The tean was buried at St Mary Kirk
The other at St Marey Queer O
The tain sprang up a bonie birk
The tider a bonee brier O

26 Ay the grew and ay they threw
Till on the kirk tope did meet O
And every one that passed by
Says they ben lovers sweet O

49

THE LAIRD O' OCHILTREE

Child 217 *The Broom of Cowdenknows*

1 Meys bonnie Meys to the ewe bughts gain
To milk her dady ewe's
And ay as she sang her vioce it rang
It rang out owr the nows nows
It rang out owr the nows

2 There was a shipard ya daughter
Gaed to milk her dady ewe's
And there she espied a troup of fine Gentelmen
Road merrely out owr the nows nows
Road merrely out owr the nows

3 Good morrow good morrow fair made he says
This night has been some rain
Which causes a dark and a mistey morning
I am afraid that I have road wrang wrang
I am afraid that I have road wrang

4 You are not far wrang kind sir she says
The road is a little near by
I'll have you beware of Ocheltrey watters
For they run wonderous hiegh hiegh
For they run wonderous hiegh

5 He lighted aff his milk white steed
And tyd him till a tree
Willt thou na pity me fair made
Willt thou na pity me me
Willt thou na pity me

6 Willt thou na pity me fair made
Will't thou na pity me
Willt thou na pity my poor steed
Stands trembling at yon tree tree
Stands trembling at yon tree

7 What pity would you have from me kind sir
What pity would you have from me
There corn and hay at your command
And the grass liys at liberty liberty
And the grass liys at liberty

8 Milk on Milk on my bonnie Lass
Milk on milk on said he
For out o the ewe bughts I winna gae
Till thou show me out oe'r the lee lee
Till thou show me out oe'r the lee

9 Ride on Ride on thou rank rider
They steed beath stout and strang
For out o the ewe bughts I winna gae
For fear that thou do me some wrang wrang
For fear that thou do me some wrang

10 He took her by the milk white hand
And by the green goun sleeve
And there hes tain his will of her
At neabody speard his leave leave
At neabody speard his leave

11 When he had gat his will of hir
He lift her up again
If I come na back or three quarters o a year
Thou'l get na mair of me me
Thou'l get na mair of me

12 He took out a siller came
Cam'd back her yellow hair
Ga thou east or ga thou west
Of thee I'll ask na mair mair
Of thee I'll ask na mair

13 He put his han in his pocket
And he's gein her guines three
Take that take that my bonie lass
It will pay the nurish fee fee
It will pay the nurish fee

14 Well I ken by they hiegh coket Hat
And by thy gay goud string
That thou is the laird of Ocheltrey
That beguiles all fair wemen wemen
That beguiles all fair wemen

15 You are mistaking with me fair maid
You are mistaken with me
But I am one of his bright gentelmen
That rides aften in his company companey
That rides aften in his company

16 Well I ken by they red rosey cheeks
And by they dimpled chin
That thou is the Lady of Cowden nows
And sa well as it seems to me me
And sa well as it seems to me

17 You are mistaken with me kind Sir
You are mistaken with me
But I am one of the fair Ladees bright
That rides aften in her companey companie
That rides aften in her companey

18 He sat his fit in his stirup
And he road after his men
And all that his merreman said to him
Was kind master you have tarried lang lang
Was kind master you have tarried lang

19 I ha road east and I hae road west
And I hae road oe'r the nows
And the boniest lassey that e're I sa
Was in the ewe bughts milking her ewes ewes
Was in the ewe bughts milking her ewes

20 She took her nappey on her head
And she gaed merrily hame
And a that her father said to her
Was kind daughter you have tarried lang lang
Was kind daughter you have tarried lang

21 Wo be to your men father
And an ill death may they dee
The scattered the ewe's out o'er the knowes
And they wa'd na bught in for me me
And they wa'd na bught in for me

22 But there came a Tod amang your ewes
The like I near did see
Before he took the one that he took
You had better hae gien him three three
You had better hae gien him three

23 The Tod came in into your bought
The like I ne'er did see
And ay as he spake he lifted up his hat
And he had a bonie twinkling eye eye
And he had a bonie twinkling eye

24 When ninteen week's was past and gain
And ninteen week's and three
This lassey began for to think lang
For to think lang for his bonie twinkling ee ee
For to think lang for his bonie twinkling ee

25 It happened on a bonie simmer day
She was c'aing out her father key
And there she spied a troop of fine gentelmen
Sa merrily come riding by by
Sa merrily come riding by

26 Thou's roun about the waist a we fair maide
Thou's roon about the waist a wee
Thou's roon about the waist a we fair maid
Im afraid that with child thou be be
Im afraid that with child thou be

27 The lasse turnd her round about
And O but she thought shame
And a that she had to sa for hersel
Was I hae a goodman at hame hame
Was I hae a goodman at hame

28 Had they toung thou dirty slut
Sa loud as I hear thee lie
Distna mind o the misty morning
That I was in the ewe bughts wi thee thee
That I was in the ewe bughts wi thee

29 He jumped aff his milk white steed
To set this Lady on
C'a out your kine guidfather he says
For she winna c'a them out again again
For she winna c'a them out again

30 He caus'd one of the formest o his men
To jump aff and set her on
And he has taen her to Ocheltrey
Mad her lady of all his lands lands
Mad her lady of all his lands

31 When the babie he was born
And sat on the nourish knee
And ay sa well as he father'd himsel
For he had a bonnie twinkling ee ee
For he had a bonnie twinkling ee

50

JAMIE DOUGLAS

Child 204

1 O I am sike and very sike
A Frind of mind came to visit me
The Blackemore whisperd in my Lords ears
That he was too lang in my Companey

2 In the morning when he arase
As well a pleas'd Lord as ear could be
But when that he came back again
Never a word he woud speak to me

3 In the morning when I arase
A my pretty palace's for to vew
I whisper'd in at my Lord window
But the never a word he wou'd ansure me

4 When my father heard of the dispute
That was between my good Lord and me
He sent five score of his soilders brave
To conduct me hame to my own Country

5 Come doun the stairs my Jimie Duglas
Come doun the stairs and drink tea with me
Ill set thee in a chair of gold
And not one farthing it will cost thee

6 When cockel shells grows siller bells
And mussals grows on every tree
When frost and snow turns red bolts of Iron
Then will I come doun and drink tea we thee

7 When I sat in my coach and six
Its no delight that ilded me
. . . . . .
I wish I was in my own countrey

8 Of a the Birds flee's in the air
The Hawk flee's farest frea its nest
And a the world may plainly see
Its Jimie Duglas I like best

9 Fare you well my Jeamie Duglas
And fare ye well my childreen three
May a that's new still attend you
Till I see you a safe in my ain cuntrey

10 She looked out at her father window
To take a view of the countrey
Wha did she see but Jemie Duglas
And alang with him her childreen threee

11 There cam a soilder to the gate
And he did knock right Hasteley
If Lady Duglas be within
Bid her come and speak to me

12 Come away my Lady fair
Come away now alang with me
For I have hanged the Blackemoor
The verey place where he tald the lie

51

THE FAUGHHILL SHEARING

1 I am a young plowman I live at Fahill
Where money brave shearers has gotten there fill
Of beith meat and drink and there wage after all
To make amens for the tiol o the shearing ot

2 The master he cries pray shear legh and clean
And let not the corn be abused O
And let us be guid friends till the harvest be done
But aft times his passion was rising O

3 And all to the kempting like furey the go
And wha to be formest the do what the dow
Wha hates to be hinmost it is a fine show
To see who the play wi the sheering o t

4 Some cries o there backs some cries o there arms
Some has Cutted fingres which does them great harm
And some cries drough for the weather is warm
Well a be undone wi the sheering ot

5 When the Harvest is o'er and they corn is cut doon
The plentyful crop a there labour does crown
We will all rejoice as lang as it lasts
For to mak amens for the tiol sheering ot

6 The barnman says hame to my barn I will ga
And all the hale winter Ill burrey ont
Althou I work hard Ill stan drieh and warm
Ill rest me whan that I am werit o't

7 The smith he saiys hame to my study Ill ga
My Horses to shoe an the irns to lay
For another new crop we maun a gae prepare
For to make amanes for the sheering ot

8 The wright says hame to my Fil an my ax I will go
The plows are to make and the Harrows also
And for anuther new crop we must a be prepare'd
For to make amans o the tiol o the sheering ot

9 The Tylor says hame to my needles Ill go
To shap and shew claise to bear ut frost an snow
And for anuther new crop we must a be prepar'd
For to make amans o the tiol o the shearing ot

52

WHEN MY OLD HAT WAS NEW

1 When my oll Hat was new
It was about four score of years
But now it is both oll and torn
Falling doun about my ears
It was made of the silk sa fine
And stood aboun my brow
O what a strappen youth was I
When my old hat was new

2 But now the times are altred much
And what mair can I say
O What great alterations
Been in mine aged day
My old wife she a Toy did wear
A corse claith on her brow
And he himsel a guid gray coat
When my old hat was new

3 The guidman sat at the board head
And did the table grace
The servents sat doun as the came
A ranked in there place
The goodwife serv'd we modesty
Gie'd every one there due
Humility did then abound
When my old hat was new

4 When the corn was a cut doun
And built into a mow
The sheerers gat a ranting kirn
When my oll hat was new

53

SIR DONALD AND ELIZA LINDSAY

Child 226

1 There was an assembly at Edinburgh
An money bra Ladies was there
But there was nane at a the assembly
Wi bonnie Eliza Lindsay cou'd compare

2 At lenght there came Sir Donald
And a bra young man was he
He wadna ge muckel co Donald
To take this young lady wi me

3 Will ye ga to the Hielands bonnie Eliza
Will ye ga to the Hielands wi me
Will ye ga to the Helands bonnie Eliza
The Lands of Glen Coshe to see

4 Out and spack Elise mother
And a jolley o'll Lady was she
If you take ony mair to my daughter
Hiegh hanged Ill cause thee to be

5 Donald he turned him roon
And a lou'd loud laugh gied he
The laws is no in your City
This day that dare hang me

6 Will ye ga to the Helings bonie Elize
Will yo ga to the Helings we me
Will you ga to the Heling bonie Elize
The Lands of Glen Coshen to see

7 In I would ga to the Helings wi theee
My frinds they wad me blame
I would need to ken some mair about thee
And wha I was ganing wi

8 My father he is an ol'd cooper
My mother an ol'd derre
And I am his eldest son
And sa bravly as I can herd the kind

9 Here is ten guinis I ge thee
For one hour o thee in my room
That I may hae they fair bodey painted
To keep me fra thinking lang

10 I valew not they ten guines
As little as thou can valew mine
If thou wad my person enjoy
Ga with me if thou incline

11 She packt up her claiths in small bundles
Throw aff her fine silk goun
She packt up her shoes en a bundle
And awa wi Sir Donald she's gaen

12 The road it was hard and wery
The braes the were stuborn an stay
Elize Lindsay not used with travel
Brought mony salt tears fra her eye

13 O Had they toung Elize Lindsay
O Had they toung said he
Or Ill ha thee hame at they mother
And that right speedley

14 O Had they toung Sir Donald
O Had they toung said she
Thou I ware at hame we my mother
Now wha wad care for me

15 When they came in sight o the sheillings
He left her a little thereby
Till he wad gan into the sheillings
To take wi the old Derre Dei

16 Ye are wellcom hame Sir Donald
Ye are wellcom hame said she
Ye are wellcom hame Sir Donald
For lang I ha weared for thee

17 O c'a me na mair Sir Donald
But c'a me Donald your son
And Ill c'a you my mother
If you'l just c'a me Donald your son

18 Ga mak for my Lady that comming
A bed o green rushes to lie
Make up the best bed in the shieling
For a bra young Lady is she

19 Elize Lindsay came into the sheillings
She looke'd just like oney fool
They warna a sate for to sit on
But ya we three fitted stool

20 Elize Lindsay being weared we travel
She lay till nine the next day
Ye might a been helping my mother
To milk a her ewes and her kind

21 Had they toung Sir Donald
And dina talk say to me
I might a stayd at hame we my mother
I can neither milk ewes nor kind

22 He took her by the white han
And he led her a little thereby
He led her out o' the sheillings
To view a his ewes and his kind

23 When the came in sight of Glen Coshe
His mother was out on the green
Wi four and twenty Ga Ladys
To welcome hame her son

24 Your wellcome hame Sir Donald
Ye are Welcome hame to me
Ye are Welcome hame Sir Donald
For lang ha I weared for thee

25 Ye are welcome hame Elize Lindsay
The flour of a your kin
For ye's be Lady Glen Coshen
Young Donald the Laird my son

54

THE ROSE SMELLS SAE SWEETLY

Child 11 *The Cruel Brother*

1 There was three Ladies at the wa
With a hey and a lilley ga
There came three Kings and court them a
And the rose it smells sa sweetly

2 The first o them was clad in green
And he has courted her for to be his Queen

3 The second o them was clad in yellow
He's courted her for to be his marrow

4 The youngest o them was clad in white
And he's courted her for to be his bride

5 Ye man ask at my father the King
And sa man you my mother the Queen

6 I have asked your father the King
And sa have I your mother the Queen

7 Her father the King led her throu the Ha
Her mother the Queen led her doun the stair

8 Her sister An led her throu the closs
Her brother John set her on the Horse

9 You are hiegh and I am low
And we man kiss before we go

10 She louted doun to ge him a kiss
He stabd a penknife in her breast

11 Out and spack the bonney bridegroom
I think our bride comes but Hooly on

12 Ride back ride back said the formest man
I think our bride looks pale and wan

13 She had not ridden throu the close
Till the bonnie bride fell af her Horse

14 What will you leave to your mother the Queen
The bloody rob that I am in

15 What will you leave to your sister Ane
My gilded Bible & silver fan

16 What will you leave to your brother John
The Gallows Tree for to hing him on

17 What will you leave to your brothers waens
The warld is wide the may beg therein

18 What will you leave to the bonnie Bridegroom
Ill leave Havens gates to let him in

19 She had not these words sooner spock
Then he went aff in a flash of smock

55

THE SUN SHINES OVER THE VALLEY

Child 25 *Willie's Lyke-Wake*

1 I loved a lady this seven years and mare
As the sun shines over the valley
For her has my heart been mony a time sare
Doun amang the blew flowers and the yellow

2 O Willie Willie I'll learn thee a wile
Who that thou this fair Lady should beguile

3 Its ley thee doun as thou were dead
And sen for this Lady to a merry night wake

4 Ge the bellman his belling groat
To ring they dead bell at this ladies bour door

5 He has rung his buriel bell
Just now at this ladiest bour door

6 Oh how is this I hear is dead
Its sweet Willie they trew love

7 You are bidden take your horse and your boy
You must gan to your trew lovers best convoy

8 Ill take neither horse nor boy
But Ill ga alang and Ill mourn & criy

9 She went weeping all alang
Weeping to her father she came

10 To sweet Willie late wake I man gan
His dead bell was rung at my bour door

11 To sweet Willie late wak thou mana gan
For swiet Willie was a slim young man

12 If to sweit Willie wake thou does gan
They seven briedering must gan wi thee alang

13 She went weeping all alang
Weeping to sweet Willie she came

14 When his bed side she began to come neer
This dead corp began for to steer

15 He took her by the middle sa sma
He flang her between him and the wa

16 Oh Willie O Willie now let me gan
For my seven breedren is come wi me alang

17 Thou a they friends were at they feet
Before thou ga fra me thou sall lose they maidenhead

18 Thou came to me a maiden meek and mild
But Ill send thee hame a married wife with child

19 He gave her a ga gold ring
To night well bed and tomorrow well wed

56

A YARMOUTH STORY

1 She from her master received five pound
She put in a box wi her necklace and her Gown
She put in a box wi the rest of her cloths
And away from her master & mustress she goes

2 As she was a walking alang the heigh way
She espied a tinkler sitting on the style
Good morrow good morrow the tinkler he said
And where art thou going this morning fair maid

3 I am gan to Yarmoth wher my parants dewell
Your hame said the tinker I know very well
If you would be rulled and take my advice
For you shurly shall be robbed upon the heighways

4 The tinker and the fair maid togeither did walk
A till the cam to a very lanesome place
For the tinker he stared the fair maid on the face

5 He took of the box and demanded the key
She told him it was lost wi the teer in her ee
As he was about for to oppen the lock
With his lang pickstaff she gave him a nock

6 She gave him a strock which laid him to the ground
She gave him another which laid him in a swoon
She gave him annother which killd him quit dead
With a lang streem of blood running doun fra his head

7 She took ove the box and was walking on the road
She met with a Gentelman did her intorogate
Demanding that she should oppen the yet

8 ·O fair maid to whome does that box belong
O fair maid some murder thou has done
O kind Sir in crime I hea done ill
For I do beleeve that a roge I hea killd

9 If you would walk wi me alang the Hiegh road
I will show thee the place where the tinkley lies dead
With a lang streem of blood running down fra his head

10 They search'd his bundles and in them they found
Four loaded pistols with pouder and ball
A knife and a whistle the roges for to call

11 The Gentelman gave the fair maid one in her han
Demanding that she on her gard should stand
O kind Sir I will surly play my part
And in time of danger I never shall start

12 He sat the whistle to his mouth and gave a loud call
Till three of the rogues came running doun the hill
The gentelman he shot one threw the head
The fair maid killd another clean dead

13 The other one seeing then what was done
He took to his heels and away he did run
Thy soon overtook him before he came to Toun
And brought him to justices the truth to be known

14 Now these Lawyers was all in a strief
Which of them was to have this fair maid to wife
But this young gentelman did them all outstrip
And has made her a lady of honour sa great

57

LADY BELTREES

1 The ladie lukit owr the Castle wa
She saw mariners mae nor twa
It was then she thocht on gaun awa
She is muntit and gane wi her Laddie

58

LORD THOMAS AND LADY MARGARET

Child 260

1 Lord Thomas he was an Erl's son
Lady Margaret she luet him well
And she's awa to the guid green woods
To see her love hunting

2 He caw't on his merrie men aw
By ane by twa and by three
Gar hunt awa this vyle woman
For her face I dow na see

3 They huntit her heich an huntit her law
Ladie Margaret ran owr the plain
The petticotts of scarlet that Lady Margaret wore
Neir coud be mendit again

4 She ran est and she ran west
And she ran alang the way
Until she met wi a gay grand lord
Unto him she did say

5 Sum help sum help thou gay grand Lord
Sum help give unto me
For I am a Ladie deep deep in love
Banishit frae my ain country

6 Nae help no help fair ladie he says
Nae help will I gie unto thee
Excep thou forsake aw the men in the warld
And my own weddit Lady thow be

7 He muntit her on his milk whyte steed
Himsel went along the way
Until he came to yon fair castle
And he made her his ladie gae

8 Ladie Margaret was sittand in her bour window
Sewand her silken seim
Wha did she see but Lord Thomas
Cumand beggand her luve again

9 Cum doun Ladie Margaret he says
Cum doun and speik with me
And with my braid swurd I will kill thy weddit lord
And I'll make thee my fair ladie

10 O no O no fair Thomas she says
O no that maun na be
But I hae gat wine in my cellar
And ye'll drink along wi me

11 She cawit on her butler boy
To bring her a bottle o wine
And wi her fingers lang and smaw
She steirit the poison in

12 She pat it to her red rosie cheiks
And to her dimplit chin
She put it to her pale cherrie lips
But neir a drap gade in

13 He pat it to his red rosie cheiks
And to his dimplit chin
He pat it to his pale cherrie lips
And he drank the poishon in

14 Awa awa Ladie Margaret he says
For I am weiryit o thee
And sae was I lord Thomas she says
When ye huntit your hounds at me

15 But I will burrie thee Lord Thomas she says
Amang the chief o aw my kin
And I will tell my own weddit lord
That thou is my sister's sin.

59

JOCK T' LEG AND THE MERRY MERCHANT

Child 282

1 Jock the Leg and the merry merchant
Are up to England gane
He had a Pack upon his back
And it was well buckled on, on, on,
And it was well bucklit on

2 As they came in by yon tavern house
Where quarterers were wont to dine
Make readie a supper said Jock t' Leg
Gae ready it gude ane fine, fine, fine,
Gae readie it gude ane fine,

3 For the merrie merchant will pay for it
Altho it were crowns three
Never a bit quoth the merry merchant
For hauffers thou sal be, be, be
For hauffers thou sal be.

4 At night when they went to their bed
Thinking upon a sleep
Up and starts muckle lang Jock to Leg
At the merry merchant's bed feet, feet, feet,
At the merrie merchant's bed feet.

5 Rise up rise up thou merrie merchant
Thou might a been miles three
Ne'er a bit quoth the merrie merchant
Till day light come that I see, see, see,
Till day light come that I see

6 Never a bit quo the merrie merchant
Till day light come that I see
For Jockteleg is a rank robber
He'll take my pack frae me, me, me,
He'll take my pack frae me

7 As they came in by Nottingham
And down by yon green bay tree
Repent repent thou merrie merchant
For what thou said of me, me, me,
For what thou said of me

8 Never a bit quo the merrie merchant
For a rank robber thou be
Jockteleg set a whistle to his mouth
And he gave whistles three, three, three
And he gave whistles three,

9 Till four and twenty well armed men
Came linking owr the lee
O what is yon quo the merry merchant
O what is yon that I see, see, see,
O what is yon that I see

10 It's four and twentie well armed men
That'll tak thy pack frae thee
Tak eleven o thy well armed men
Thy sell the twelfth to be, be, be,
Thysell the twelfth to be

11 . . . .
. . . .
And put me but one inch from my pack
And all sall go wi thee, thee, thee,
And all shall go with thee

12 He took eleven o his well armed men
Himsell the twelfth to be
And to put him but one inch frae his Pack
Was a thing they coudna do, do, do,
Was a thing they coudna do

13 Will thou gie me as muckle of thy light links
As clead my men and me
And when we come to Nottingham
Gude billy bairns we sall be, be, be,
Gude billy bairns we sall be

14 I'll no gie thee as muckle of my light links
As clead thy men and thee
And when we come to Nottingham
Neir a farthing care I thee, thee, thee,
Neir a farthing care I thee

60

THE LAIRD OF JOHNSTONE AND MISS JEAN MACDOWALL.

1 The Collier gains a saxpence a day
And I can spend it brawlie
I'll mak my bed on the heich coal hill
And lie down wi my Collier ladie

2 Where's aw your towirs and lands
That you said you'd make me ladie
And now you're seeking money to borrow
Frae Jean and her collier laddie

61

THE BRAES OF KILLIECRANKIE

1 Bonnie lassie wilt thou go
Wiltu go wiltu go
Bonnie lassie wilt thou go
To the Braes of Killiecrankie
And I'll buy thee a gown o silk
A gown o silk a goun o silk
And I'll buy thee a goun o silk
And a coat o Killiemankie

2 Bonnie lad I daur na go
I daur na go I daur na go
Bonnie lad I daur na go
My minnie will be angrie
My father he will fallow fast
Fallow fast, fallow fast
My father he will fallow fast
Seekand his bonnie Nancie

3 Let the soger lie his lane
Lie his lane, lie his lane
Let the sodger lie his lane
And bear his ain pockmankie.

62

LORD EGLINTON'S SONG

1 A sweet country life is bonny and charming
O to go abroad on a fine summer's morning
Your towns and cities and lofty high towers
Can never be compared to our sun-shined bowers

2 I dont much admire your follisome dresses
Your velvets and laces and other excesses
My own country-clothing is far more endearing
My little fresh mantle—our home-spun wearing

3 As I was walking out along yon mountain
A feeding of my flocks beneath the fountain
Our flocks a feeding and each dewy morning
Bright Phoebus the sun all the fields adorning

4 No fiddle nor fife no hautboy nor spinnet
Can never be compared to the lark and sweet linnet
Abroad as I am aroving in each dewy morning
Bright Phoebus the sun all the fields adorning

5 Jockie the plowboy was walking all alone
A feeding his flocks right early in the morn
He spied lovely Nancy among the green bushes
Who was charmed with the notes of the black-bird and thrushes

6 Now, to conclude, and make an end of this ditty
Here is a health to all maidens that are fair and pretty
Never to leave off your own country employment
No city can afford so great enjoyment

63

THE WEE CRAP

1 I rise in the morning and gangs my wa and gangs my wa down
To crack my crack wi wee Jamie Daisie in the next neighbour
To crack about our wee crap upon yon stanie land [town
Whether it was gude or bad, I fain wad understand

2 I never had a waur crap sin ever I was born
I never had a waur crap o neither grass nor corn
The year I had but seven stacks instead of nine and twa
Which gars me gang about the dykes and my auld head to claw

3 I sew a pickle barley doun upon yon holm
It was na worth the shearing scarce five lengths o my thumb
And when it was made in groats man it wadna sair our kale
The malt it will be dear the year to the brewsters o our ale

4 The lint it was na gude and spinning it is dear
And for to fee a lassie it pits me in a fear
She'll eat a rug of meat the worth o her yarn
Ten bows o meal and baken bread she'll eat every grain

5 I rise me in the morning I caws out my kye
When I think on my wee crap I dow na easy lie
When I think on my wee crap my heart is like to break
I wring my hands and tear my hair and lean me owr the dyke

6 My auld man Wattie Crawfurd that I had last year
I fed him on potatoes or else I am a liar
The year I am resolved to keep na man at aw
But thrash in the barn wi candle light and clean the horses staw.

64

BONNIE BELLEEN

1 O did ye e'er hear of Bonnie Belleen
The flower o' Avonwood lee
And did ye e'er hear o' her brothers brave
Wha fought by the Warlock tree
And did ye e'er hear o Todecliff Tower
That frowns o'er the dashing tide
Or of gallant Ross, its statly Lord
The Lothian's boast and pride

2 The bonnie Bellien sat in her bower
And O she was fair to see
For her skin was white and her een was bright
As the stars in the lift sae hie
The gallant Ross was a hunting then
And he stepp'd her bower within
And he daff'd his cap and he bent his knee
Her heart's trew love to win

3 And they ha'e met by the moon yellow light
And he's kiss'd below the tree
O come wi me my bonnie Belleen
And Lady Ross thou shalt be
He blew a blast, till glen and shaw
Powr'd out his merry men bold
And they plac'd her on a milk white steed
And borr her to Todecliff hold

4 O she has sat in Todecliff Tower
And a weary wife was she
For the Ross was proud and her friends were gane
And there faces she dar'd na see

And the seamaw skreigh'd o'er the Castel wa
And the waves dash'd wearilee
And she thought o her hame and her brothers brave
And the bonnie braes o Avonwood lee

5 A Lady gay came doun frae the south
Wi riches and jewels most precious to see
O leeze me she said on the gallant Ross
For I love the glance o his bright black ee
And he's te'an her east and he's tean her west
And he's seated her in ha and bower
But little he thought on his bonnie dame
That mournd in gloomy Todecliff Tower

6 The merry bells did ring and the tapers did blaze
When he wedded the Southern Lady gay
But a weird voice was heard boon the revelrie
Saying wo to the Ross for the deid done this day

7 O mirk was the night and fearfu the storm
When the pud Belleen frae her lanley bed
And percingly she shriek'd and the watter spirit laugh'd
As the green sie swirled o'er her bonnie head
For they ha'e dround the bonnie Belleen
And nae mair she'll chant by Avonwood lee
And her brother's hae slain they cruel Ross
Where his ghost still howls by the Warlock Tree

WILLIAM GEMMEL

65

AIRLIE HOUSE

Child 199

1 It was about the simmer time
When feilds grow green and rarly
When great Locheal wi a his men
Came to plunder the Bonnie house Earlie

2 The Lady looked o'er her Castle wa
And O but she look'd wailly
Say's gin my guid Lord had been at hame
As he is at the crowning o King Charle
Great Lochisle nor na Scoth Lord
Durst set a fit on the green of Earlie

3 But come doon stairs madam Said he
Come doon Stairs and Ill kiss you fairley
O Ill no kiss you great Lochael
Thou you shoudna lea one stanand stain in Earlie

4 But he taen her by the milk white han
And O but she look'd Wailley
And he tean her up to the tap o' yon tour
Bad her look to the burning of Early

66

YOUNG LOCHINVAR'S COURTSHIP

Child 221 *Katharine Jaffray*

1 Low doun on yon bordor bar
There leav't a galant May
And she has lov'd young Lochinvar
And that's c'ad fair play
She has lov'd him well and favour well
Which mony a an doth say
And this night she's another man's bride
And that c'ad fool play

2 But She wrot a lang letter
And seal'd it carefully
And Sent it to young Lochinvar
There wedding to come see
The first line he did read
A lou'd lou'd laugh lout he
And the nix line that he did read
The salt tear blind his ee

3 But he has wrot a lang letter
And sent it throu the lan
To fourscore o his best traind men
To be at his command
He ranked them and reaied them
All on the Kylen green
And he's into the wedden house
There weddeng to ha'ee seen

4 The plac'd him at the table head
Amang the gentelmen
Where he began to speak some words
But fuie that the coul'd ken

Says there lives a man in our countrey
He courted a galant may
And this night she is another man's bride
And that's no fair play

5 But if she were mine as she is his
I wou'dna count a pin
To take her on her wedding day
Fra a the gentelmen
In she were mine as She is his
I wadna count a fley
To take her on her wedding day
Fra a them I do see

6 Up then gat the bold bridgroom
And an angre man was he
Gin ye be come to fight kind Sir
Its me ye man fight we
Na I am na come to fight guid Sir
But to bear guid companey
Ill drink the wine wi you kind Sir
And then Ill ga my way

7 Then a bowl o' guid red wine
Was drunk between the twa
Ill speak ye word wi your bride bridegroom
And then Ill ga my wa
He's taen her by the milk white han
And by the grass green sleev
And he's mounted her on a galant steed
And at her bridegroom speart na leave

8 But four and twenty belted knights
Was a clad o'er we gray
Was sent for to bring back the bride
We a the hast they may
But the blood ran doun the Kylen bank
And doun the Kylen brea
And that will learn a bride again
To gie her love fair play

9 So ye lusty Lairds of Lanerdale
That be in England born
Ga na man to Scotland to seek wives
For fear yee get the scorn
For fear ye get the scorn the scorn
All on your wedding day
For the'll ge you frogs instead o fish
And that is fair play

67

THERE WAS AN OLD MAN WAS SMOKING HIS PIPE

1 There was an old man was smocking his pipe
Beneith a greenwood tree
And there was an old womin sat doon for to sh-t
As ne'er as ne'er coul'd be

2 But the sparks from her arse flew in to his eee
That the divel a stiem he could see
Ye old damnd dirty bitch shite farder away from me
Shite farder away from me

68

AS I WAS A-WALKING BY YON GREEN GARDEN

As I was a walking by yon green garding
I espied an auld wife she was clawing her hole
I said you old bitchie what makes it so itchey
Begone you young Rogue I will claw it my fill

69

BLACK JOKE

1 A wee black thing sat on a cushon
Was hairy without and toothless within
  We her black Jock and her belley so white

2 A piper and twa little drummers came there
To play wi the wee thing well covered o'er wi hair

3 The piper went in and he jiged about
The twa little drummers stood ruffling without

4 But when he came out he hang doon his head
He look'd like a snail that was trodden to dead

5 Say's he thay wa'd need to hae something to spare
That meddle we you or your wee pickle hair

70

JOHNIE MILLER OF GLENLEE

1 My name Johnie Miller I carna wha know's it
And sometimes I live at the Mill o Glenlee
And I am the man that can parich and brose it
And drink six bottle gin ye'll keep me free
O Johnnie Miller was there ere such another
As the laird o Glenlee and the Justices Clarks brother
For twenty fat weather like rabbets Ill smother
And eat them my lane at the Mill o Glenlee

2 Religion a whim I know nathing about it
Its princepals never was stuided by me
My belley my God and if that you dout it
Its alter's in state at the Mill o Glenlee
For thousands o victoms I yearly do offer
To no other being devotion I proffer
Except twise a year to the gold in my coffer
When I lift the rents o the lands o Glenlee

3 Its many lang years since my trunk was deformd
And handsomeness now is a stranger to me
My head's like a Buls if it was as well hornd
Wad fright a the cows in the bogs o Glenlee
My belley so big wi the weight o my penches
The greas o' my sides it hings over my henches
Which mak'es me unable to kiss the bresk wenches
For which I lament at the Mill o Glenlee

4 Thus Im rendred unfit for the pleasure of Venous
And nathing like that is expected from me
But with eating and drinking Ill nourish my genies
And leave like a beast at the Mill o Glenlee
And when I am dead the'll say here ly's a fat an
And some they will add to it a drunkard & Glutton
But let them say what they will Ill devore my lord mutton
With greed while I live at the Mill o Glenlee

71

LINTON RACE

1 Where hea ye been my bonnie may
And bounding so fast
From Linton race couth She I win
What pleasure there was past
It seems thou has been in a gast
Come tell us what thou saw
And who the game it gaid at last
And who the ended a'

2 I canna tell thee the twentth part
But I can tell thee some
What mirth and skilfu art was there
Playing on pip and drum
There was saxteen drummers a in a ra
And twenty pipers ean
And sike a raerd I never heard
No ne'er since I hea mine

3 The soon ran doun throu a the Lan
Till a the hills the heard
The silley plover sweetly sang
The Leverocks took the sky
The maves and the shirping chat
There nots they war so shill
The eacho ansurd under the crag
Was like to rend the hills

4 Of a the men that I saw there
Earl of Wigton I loo best
And if he's gane I vow an swear
And solomly protest

I solomly protest
And likewise vow and swear
My mind with him is gane to rest
Till he again appear

5 It was a pleasent sight to see
The silver cup was there
Neathing but run an'd won in heast
Set out by the Lord Traquair
O may he still grow mair and mair
He is of a noble kine
He is the bravest of his clan
Born wi a loyal mine

6 But it was a bonnie sight to see
The munted steeds outbrought
There cleiding of the tapestray
O silver they were wrought
All kind of colours wante'd nought
Blue yellow red and green
And sadly to the score the sought
To the number of hale fifteen

7 Lord Lou'den boy he was na blate
He bore it well to the end
He didna wait to rin but flew
Wi money a sturdy sten
He rade five miles ere he was kent
Na langer might he stay
He wan the race at Linto hills
And took the gree away

8 Fair fa my walley hakie
Wi they glazen ee
He wan the race at Linton hills
And took awa the gree

72

THE WEE WEE MAN

Child 38

1 As I was walking mine alan
Between the watter and the wa
And There I espied a little we man
He was the least that er'e I sa

2 His leg was scarsly half inch lang
And thick and trusty was his thiey
Atwen his en it was a span
Atween his shoulders ells was three

3 He lifted a stane up frea his fit
And throw'd as far as I could see
Had I been as strang as Wallace wight
I coud na lifted to my knee

4 O little we man thou semes to be strang
Come show me where they dwelling may be
Its oe'r ayont yon bonnie green
O come away and Ill let you see

5 Then we lap on and we rid on
Till we came to yon bonnie green
We lighted doun to baet our horse
And up then started a galant Queen

6 We four and twenty at her han
And the were a clade oe'r in green
Had he been the King of fair Scotland
The warst o them might have been his Queen

7 Then we lap on and we came on
Till we came to yon bonnie ha
Wher minstralls was playing at every stair fit
And Ladies dancing jimp and sma
But in the quinkling of an eye
The little we man was far awa

JOHN SMITH

73

THE OLD BACHELOR

1 I am a man unmarried
And has been all my life
Now I am resolved
For to go seek a wife

2 Such a wife I must have
Is scarce for to be found
And such a wife I must have
Scarce walks upon the ground

3 A bonnie a braw wife
A wife with meikle gear
If I dinna get a bonnie wife
I'll want another year

4 A bonnie wife if she be na gude
She is gude companie
And if she be gude
Sho is pleasant to the ee

5 If I marry a tall one
I am sure she'll crack my crown
And little women is peevish
They'll pull a strong man doun

6 If I marry a black one
The lads will laugh at me
And if I marry a fair one
A cuckle I am sure to be

7 If I marry a young one
She'll ruin me with pride
And if I marry an old one
They'll say she has been tryde

8 But as I was musing
Mark what came to pass
In my sight appeared
A handsome tall young lass

9 The first question that I speired at her
What was her name
The answer she gave to me
Was modesty and fame

10 The next question that I asked her
If she was a maid
And the answer that she gave to me
I was once what you said

11 The next question that I asked her
If she was one just now
And the answer she gave to me
And I may be one for you

12 The next question that I asked her
If she wad take a man
The answer she gave to me
A little now and then

13 The next question that I asked her
If she wad marry me
And the answer that she gave to me
It's no be what may be

14 The green it is a bonny thing
Till ance it gets a dip
And he that courts a bonnie lass
Is sure to get the slip

74

THE BLACKBIRD

1 As up the wild meadow brave boys
And doun the wild forrest I ran
My bonnie blackbird has taken the flight
And there's naebodie kens where she's gane brave boys
And there's naebodie kens where she's gane

2 As up the wild meadow brave boys
And doun the wild forrest I ran
There I spyet my bonnie blackbird
Tyet fast to another man's hand brave boys
Tyet fast to another man's hand

3 O he that gat her I wish may keep her
And make the best of her he can
For I vow and swear she is my dear
And alake! with her now and then brave boys
And alake! with her now and then

75

MOSSGROVE

Child 81

1 There is four & twenty ga ladies
Dancing at yon ball
Doun an came Lord Bangwill fair Lady
She is the flower amangst them all all all
She is the flower amangst them all

2 She fixt her eys on Lord Bangwill
He was comely black and grim
She fixt her eys on little Mosgrove
As bright as the morning Sun Sun Sun
As bright as the morning Sun

3 What must I give you little Misgrove
For one hour of your company
O ga ye wicked woman
Ye are the begginin of strief
I know by the Ring on your finger
That you are Lord Bangwell wife wife wife
That you are Lord Bangwell wife

4 Allthou I be Lord Bangwill wife
What is that to theee
But what must I give you little Misgrove
For one night of your company -y -y
For one night of your company

5 Gold shall be they hire fit Page
Bright money shall be they fee
If thou dont tell to Lord Bangwell
That little Misgrove withe me me me
That little Misgrove withe me

6 I'll have nane of your gold he says
Nor nane of your bright money
But I will tell Bangwell
That little Misgrove with theee theee theee
That little Misgrove with theee

7 But when he came to the brocken Bridge
He bent his breast and swam
And when he came to the dry ground
He took up his coats and ran ran ran
He took up his coats and ran

8 And when he came to Lord Bangwell gate
He tinkled at the pin
And nane so rady as my Lord
To let his foot page in in in
To let his foot page in

9 What neues what nues my little fit page
Wat nues does thou carrey to me
Bad nues bad nues my lord he says
Bad nues I carrey to thee thee thee
Bad nues I carrey to thee

10 Is there any of my Bridges brock
Or any of my towers win
Or is my fair Lady brought to bed
Of a daugher or a son son son
Of a daugher or a son

11 There nane of your Bridges brock
Nor nane of your Towers win
But your fair Lady and lettle Misgrove
To merrey bed they are gone gone gone
To merrey bed they are gone

12 Ga saddle to me the bonnie Black
Ga saddle to me the Brown
Ga saddle to me the swiftest steed
That ever set feet on ground ground ground
That ever set feet on ground

13 The saddled to him the bonnie Black
The saddled to him the brown
The saddled to him the swiftest steed
That ever sat fit on ground ground ground
That ever sat fit on ground

14 He took his horn upon his side
He blew bath loud and shill
And a at the turning o his tune
Misgrove Ill do you no ill ill ill
Misgrove Ill do you no ill

15 He took his horn from aff his side
He blew baith pale and wan
And a' at the turning o his tune
Misgrove I wish you begone -gone -gone
Misgrove I bide you begone

16 They lay in each othir arms so close
Till the bath ded fall asleep
And long before the break of day
Lord Bangwill stood at there bedfeet -feet -feet
Lord Bangwill stood at there bedfeet

17 How do you like my blankquets you little Misgrove
Or how do you like my sheets
Or how do you like my wedded Lady
That in o your arms do sleep sleep sleep
That in o your arms do sleep

18 Well I like your blankquets my Lord
Far better I like your sheets
But wo be to your wedded Lady
That in of my arms do sleep sleep sleep
That in of my arms do sleep

19 Rise up Rise up you lettle Misgrove
Your claths each one put on
It ne'er shall be said in Buckelstonberry
That I fought we a naked man man man
That I fought we a naked man

20 The first strock Misgrove he struck
Lord Bangwill he wounded sare
The nex strock Bangwill struck
Misgrove he never struck mare mare mare
Misgrove he never struck mare

21 Wo be too my merrey man all
That did not hold my hand
For I hea kill'd one of the fairest creaturs
That ever the sun shin'd on on on
That ever the sun shin'd on

76

THE WIDOW'S DOCHTER

1 There livit a widow woman in the West Mure land
She had never a daughter but ane
And she was telland her day and nicht
Neer to gie her maidenhead to nane

2 It happened on a day on a bonnie simmer's day
As she sat by her mother's knie
Thare is a jolly jinker in the King's life Guards
That has tane the maidenhead frae me

3 She took up the airn tangs
And gied her lunders thrie
Get out my house ye base like jade
Get out my house said she

4 O she's awa to the jolly jinker gane
As fast as she may hie
Sayand you maun gie me back what ye got last night
For my mammy has banished me

5 Or will ye hae it in your hand
Or will ye have it on your knee
Or will ye have it in the dark corner
Where there is no one will not see

6 I'll have it not in my hand she says
Nor have it on my knei
But I will have it in the dark corner
Where no one will us see

7 He tuke her by the milk white hand
Led her away to the jolly jinker's bed
And laid her head where her heels was before
And gied her back her maidenhead

8 She's awa to her mother gane
As fast as she micht hie
I'm as leil a maid now deir mother she said
As the first nicht ye bore me

9 It happened on a day on a bonnie summer's day
This jolly jinker's ganeng to be wed
. . . .
. . . .

10 And she drest herself as braw as braw could be
With a fan in every hand
And she's awa to the green wud gane
And so merrilie as she sang

11 Wha is yonder the bride she says
That sings sae fine and braw
That is a widow woman's daughter in the West Mure land
But she tells her mammie aw

12 How could she do it for I could na do it
Or how could she do it for shame
I have lyne nine summer nichts wi my ain true love
And I neer telled that to nane

13 If you've lyin nine summer nichts with your an true love
Ye sall neer ly an wi me
And he's tane the widow woman's daughter in the West Mure
And let his ain bride be [Land

77

THE MAILIN

1 The first wha cam to court me
Was the farmer's auld son
If I ever marry onie
It'll surely be him
For he's neat for he's handsome
He is charming and young
The colour of his mounting
Was a high claret brown
  Still abiding still providing
  Still abiding for me
  There is a braw lad and mailen
  Still abiding for me

2 The neist ane cam to court me
Wore a bonnet and plaid
It's a wonner I refusit him
For he was a bonnie lad
He was neat and he was handsum
He was charming and yung
And the colour of his mounting
Was the high claret broun

3 The neist ane cam to court me
Wure a fether and hat
And the sailar cam to court me
Did ye neir heer of that
But he that soud have me
Provit waur than thae three
Sen he is my fortune
I can na let him be

4 You may tell my auld sweathearts
If you find them in lyfe
That I ance was their sweatheart
But I'll neir be their wife

Their faces and manners
I wish them mair grace
But I found a far better
And a far better place

Far better far neater
Far better for me
And their looks wont be linings
To the braw lad luves me

78

THE WEAVER'S DOCHTER

1 One day as I was walking
To view my father's land
And having all things ready
I went to see a friend
I went to see a friend
And a young man I spyed
Unto my misfortune
He proved my delight

79

JOCKIE AND THE FAIR MAID

Laws O 9 *Branded Lambs*

1 As young Jockie was a walking one fine summer's morning
He carelessly sat down beneath a thorn
He had not been there long till a pretty maid cam by
And upon her young Jockie cast a longing eye

2 Did you see any yows she said as like a Goat she ran
Or two young things new strayed from their dame
O yes pretty fair maid I saw them pass by
Going into yon green wud but that was a lie

3 She searched the wud all over but her sheep she could not find
She heartily cursed the young swain in her mind
And how she was betrayed though a poor silly maid
By the schemes of this young man so artfully laid

4 . . . .
He tuke his pretty Polly down to the shade below
Where he kissed her oer and o'er again her joys for to renew
While the lambs played round them all on the morning dew

80

THE WOOER CAME TO THE WIDOW'S DOOR

1 The wooer cam to the widow's dore
And fain was he was he
The wooer came to the widow's dore
And fain was he I's warran

2 Wooer, wooer, would ye be in
O aye quo he quo he I's warran
She opened and let him in
And fain was he I's warran

3 So wooer wooer wad ye hae a seat
O aye quo he quo he I's warran
She gied him a seat and he sat down
And fain was he I's warran

4 It's wooar wooar wad ye hae meat
O aye quo he quo he I's warran
She gied him bread and cheese to eat
And fain and fain was he I's warran

5 Sae wooar wooar wad ye hae a bed
O aye quo he quo he I's warran
She gied him a bed and he lay doun
And fain and fain was he I's warran

6 She jumpit behind him on the wa
And squeek cryed he I's warran
So woor woor wad ye be out
O aye quo he quho he I's warrant

7 She openit the dore and let him out
And fain was he I's warran
There being a hole afore the dore
In fell he I's warran

8 Woor woor I doubt ye are faun
O aye quo he quo he I's warran
Deil may care if ye cum out
Amen cryed he cryed he I's warran

81

THE MAID'S COMPLAINT TO HER MOTHER

1 O mother let me marry, I long to be a bride,
To have some jolly young man to dawnle by my side:
For my maidenhead I swear, doth fill my heart with care,
It is a burden every morning more than I can bear.

2 O dochter, hold your toungue [young
And make no mention of marriage, for you're seven years too
Dear mother, what do you mean, am not I above fifteen,
Let gallants try me, do not deny me; thousands I have seen
Married before my age,
Therefore if you longer tarry you'll put me in a rage.

3 O dochter, I was nyneteen before that I was wed,
And was not overburdened with my maidenhead
Loving mother, that may be, but it's otherwise with me
I am brisk and airy, therefore I'm weary of virginity.

4 O dochter, if you be presumptuous, I'll pull your courage doun
With hard and painful labour, strip off your silken gown
With your loup knots sae gay; to the feilds this very day
I'll send you, in cloth of sack, and then perhaps you may

5 O mother, if you send me to labour in the fields,
Young batchellors will tempt me, and I perhaps may yield,
To the thing I will not name; so mother never lay the blame,
Upon your dochter, if thereafter I should play the game:

NOTES

THE MUSIC that appears in this volume is reproduced from the first edition of Motherwell's *Minstrelsy*, and is as Blaikie engraved it, except that it has been very slightly reduced in size. In the text of 32 1.2 I have altered 'For to' as found in both Blaikie and Crawfurd to 'To' to fit the music. If the 'For to' in the text is accepted, then the slur should be ignored. In 25, the first line of the refrain is not represented in Blaikie although the air requires it, and it seems to have been omitted accidentally, possibly by the printer.

In the opening verses of ballads recorded by Blaikie as well as by Crawfurd, there are two instances where the Blaikie wording suggests an emendation: 10 1.5, 6 where the 'only' written by Crawfurd seems likely to be a mishearing of 'on little', and 16 1.1 where the 'sae' that occurs in Blaikie's text but not in Crawfurd's seems likely to have been accidentally omitted by Crawfurd, *cf.* Child B 1.1 'what makes you sae sad'. In other cases, slight differences between the texts may reflect differences in the ballads as sung by Mary Macqueen on different occasions. I have printed the Crawfurd text except where there is a different number of syllables in the two texts, and at these points, nine in all, I have given the Blaikie wording which fits the music. I have also given two Blaikie spellings in 1 and 36 which make the syllabic treatment of the words quite clear. The following are the materially different readings in the two texts of which the one printed here is given first: 1 1.1 'liv'd' B, 'lived' C; 1.2, 4 'and' B,—C; 2 1.2 'He's' B, 'He is' C; 1.4 'shynand' C, 'burning' B; 5 1.2 'Was', 'of' C; 'Were', 'at' B; 1.3 'O' B,—C; 10 1.1 'o' the midsimmer' B, 'of the summer' C; 1.2 'boys' C, 'weans' B; 16 1.3 'Nae kind o' C, 'I think nae' B; 25 1.4 'hard' C, 'fast' B; r.2, 4 'Tun-un-nay' C; 'Tunaway' B; r.2 'dee' C, 'doo' B; 36 1.2 'fine' B,—C; 1.3 'luikit', 'at her braw bower' B; 'looked', 'o the bow' C; 37 1.1 'a hunting' B, 'to the hunting' C; 1.3 'about' B, 'hung about' C; 40 1.4 'were black' B, 'were as black' C.

The texts are given here with only occasional punctuation in addition to that supplied by the original writers, and all additions have been noted. Normally the verse lines and verse divisions seem to be adequate to signal pauses, and I have felt that in these texts it was preferable to keep as close to the manuscript as possible so long as there is no obscurity. It did seem advisable, however, to reduce the very various ways of representing repeats to a norm, but I have given full information on how they are set out in the manuscript in the notes to individual songs. I show in full the entire repeats in those cases where the repeats vary from verse to verse but print choruses and interlineary refrains with the first verse of the song only as inset lines.

All other lines of the songs are printed here from a left-hand margin, but the practice in the manuscript is irregular. Macqueen and Orr write the lines without insetting. Crawfurd more often than not insets the rhyming lines where there is alternate rhyming, but he is not consistent and sometimes fails to do this, as in 28 *Mother Bunch*, or insets alternate lines where the verse does not have alternate rhymes, as in 17 *Young Betsy*. Occasionally also he will inset the opposite lines from the expected ones, as in 6 *Fair Rosalind* where lines 5 and 7 of the second verse are inset instead of 6 and 8.

The practice as regards the numbering of verses is also various. Macqueen does not number verses, but Orr usually does, though his numbering is rarely complete. Items 55 and 69 are numbered throughout and 51, 53, 54, 66 and 70 from 2 to the end (in 66 the deleted figure 2 additionally occurs at 1.5). In 48, verses 2-5 are numbered correctly, the next verse is not marked, and verses 7-10 are incorrectly numbered 6-9. In the case of 50, the last verses, 10-12, are numbered, but a binding strip covers where the numbering of earlier verses may have been. There are also the following numbers: in 49 2-8, in 52 1-3, in 56 2 only, in 64 2-4, in 65 2 only, and in 71 2-6. There is no numbering in 67, 68, 72 or 75. Crawfurd does not normally number verses, but he does have centre-page numbering in 36, 60 and 61. In 36 *Lady Jean*, which has a direction that an additional verse is to be inserted 'Between the 12 and 13 and between the 14 and 15' all fifteen verses originally given are numbered. Crawfurd has also completed the numbering of 48, not continuing from Orr's wrong verse number 9 for the tenth verse, but correctly numbering from verse 11 onwards. In 12 *The Cruel Mother*, faced by some irregularities, he has put line numbers at each fourth line (see notes to this ballad). Often division into verses is quite clearly indicated by the leaving of a space but, where this is not so, Crawfurd has sometimes shown the divisions by small lines between verses in Orr's texts as well as his own. These divisions are recorded in the notes to individual songs in cases where there is some doubt created by irregular numbers of lines.

Crawfurd's lineation has variations from the lineation as printed here, sometimes because of possible alternative treatments of the lines or difficulty in knowing how to divide when there is some irregularity in the verse, but quite often Crawfurd has a line or two set down which are not in accordance with the scheme of the rest of the song. In the following cases two printed lines are written as a single line of verse: 2 8.3-4; 7 1.1-2; 9 11.4-12.1, 20.3-4; 13 18.1-2; 17 9.1-2; 22 12.1-2; 25 8.1-2; 30 1.1-2; 37 2.1-2; 73 4.3-4, 12.1-2; 76 2.1-2, 3.1-2, 5.1-2. There are the following instances where one printed line has been written as two, the second line beginning with the word quoted: 3 8.1 'said'; 5 4.3 'to'; 24 3.2 'it's', 3.4 'this', 4.1-4 'it's', 'to', 'an', 'to'; 32 7.3 'in'; 36 3.4 'bow'; 37 3.3 'as'; 38 1.1 second 'whaur', 2.2-3 'when', 'till'; 3.1-3 'while', 'baith', 'baith'; 4.1-3 'a', 'saying', 'saying'; 5.1-3 'an' ('when' in MS.), 'if', 'if', 6.1-3 second 'he', second 'he', 'and', 7.2 'wha', 8.1-3 'its', second 'the', 'lang'; 39 10.1 'doun', 10.3 second 'in'; 43 1.4 'and', 2.2 'just'; 76 1.1 'in', 11.3 'in', 13.3 'in'; 79 1.1 'one', 1.3-4 'till', 'cast', 2.4 'but', 3.1 'but', 3.3-4 'though', 'so', 4.2-4 'down', 'her' ('he' in MS.), 'all'; 81 1.2 'to', r.1-2 'doth', 'more', 2.2-4 'for', 'am' ('I' in MS.), 'thousands', 2.6 'you'll', 3.1 'before', 3.3-4 'but', 'of', 4.1-4 'I'll', 'strip', 'to', 'and', 5.1-4 'to', 'and', 'so', 'I'. Two lines in print and writing are differently divided at the following points: 2 9.3-4 'reddy/As' ('Is' in MS.), 20.1-2 'heid/An in', 5 20.3-4 'through/The', 8 20.1-2 'cryed/But', 17 5.3-4 'falsify/Her', 32 1.2-3 'sang/Her', 14.3-4 'spak/He', 39 15.1-2 'had/As'. Three lines in print and writing are differently divided at 27 7.1-3: 'her/Guineas ten saying Take ye that/My'; and three lines as printed are written as two at 27 6.1-3 'her/Guineas'. Two printed lines are written as three at 12 20.1-2 'thrie/prettie babes/O our' and 43 3.2-3 'pillow/She laid her head she laid her down/And'. Orr generally gives the lines as printed but 75 17.1 is written as two, the second line beginning with the second 'you'.

The words 'never the less' (12 5.2, 17.2), 'be lyke' (28 16.4), 'a we' and 'a wee' (49 26.1, 2) are printed with divisions though written as single words; and the following are printed as one word though written as two: 3 3.2 'child bed', 11 11.4 'bed fellow', 13 15.1 'wom an', 28 13.3 'the gither', 44 5.2 'blind fauld', 48 14.1 'a wa', 51 9.3 'a nuther', 52 3.1 'guid man', 54 11.1 'bride groom', and 75 2.3 'Mos grove', 3.1, 5.4, 6.4, 14.4, 15.4, 17.1, 20.1. 'Mis-grove' and 15.5 'Mis grove'.

Crawfurd's writing, though untidy, is generally legible but there is sometimes doubt about whether a letter is 'i' or 'e', and there is the possibility of confusion between 'a' and 'u' as 'a' is sometimes written with an open top, as in 'candle' at 5 10.4, 'cat' at 34 23.1 and 'tak' at 35 10.3. Occasionally 'd' is written as a curved stroke only as in the case of 'said' at 38 3.2, and similarly the 'e' of 'the' is sometimes merely a curve going back towards the 't' as if to cross it. At 18 1.1 the 'l' of 'Salisbury' is stroked like a 't'. In several cases, Crawfurd has written an extra minim so that 'n' has the appearance of 'm' at 8 5.1 'many', 24 2.2 'yonder', 34 15.1 'John' and 35 4.1 'nane' and 'r' the appearance of 'rr' in 'far' at 35 6.2 and the first 'far' at 37 19.3, and conversely sometimes a minim is omitted so that the 'm' of 'my' at 11 5.3 is like 'n' and the 'nn' of 'bonnie' at 30 6.3 is like 'm'. Sometimes the apostrophe is wrongly given and the following corrections have been made: 8 4.2 'friends' ', for 'friend's' and 11.4, 11.6 ' 'Twas' for 'T'was', 10 3.6 'hert's' for 'herts' ', and 37 14.5 'servants' ' for 'servant's' and 16.1 'It's' for ' 'Its'. As a rule Crawfurd gives the capital letter at the beginning of a line of verse but, in the few cases where he does not, I have altered to the capital, and I have also made the necessary adjustments between upper and lower case letters where emendations have caused lines to start at different points.

Orr generally begins each line of verse with a capital but now and then he uses a lower case letter. I alter to capitals in these instances and also at several proper names where Orr has not supplied capitals. A large 'k' used by Orr does not seem to be necessarily intended as a capital since it occurs in mid-word in 'twinkling' (49 31.4) and it has been treated as a lower case letter except at 48 25.1 'St Mary Kirk' (parallel to 'St Marey Queer'), at 54 1.2 'Kings' (parallel to 'Ladies'), 54 5.1, 6.1, and 7.1 'King' (parallel to 'Queen'), 65 2.4 'King Charle' and 66 3.6, 8.5, 6 'Kylen'. The letter 'o' as the abbreviation of 'of' is sometimes written large as if it were a capital letter, but in these instances it is printed as a lower case letter. Conversely, the exclamation 'O' which appears in 64 as 'o' ' has been printed as 'O'. Orr has underlined words here and there but I have not indicated this in the texts as printed. Underlined words are: 48 11.1 'Sweet Wille she says', 50 6.3 'Iron', 51 2.1 'legh', 6.2

'burrey', 6.3 'drieh', 6.4 'werit', 9.2 'claise', 53 4.1 'Out', 'Elise', 5.1 'roon', 8.4 'kind', 11.3 'shoes', 18.2 'lie', 20.4 'kind', 21.4 'kind', 71 3.7 'eacho' and 75 4.1 'Lord Bangwill'.

Quite frequently, Orr uses a minim more or less than a letter requires. He sometimes writes 'n' and 'u' with one minim, like 'i', as in 'mony' at 48 13.2 and 'Thus' at 70 4.1, and 'm' and 'w' with two minims, like 'n' and 'u', as in 'my' at 56 3.1 and 'twa' at 69 2.1. He also writes 'i' or 'e' with two minims like 'u' as in 'like' and 'they' at 51 3.1, 53 13.2, and 'n', 'u' and 'v' with three minims, like 'm' and 'w', as in 'ten' at 53 10.1, 'justices' at 56 13.4 and 'five' at 56 1.1. Since two-minim and three-minim letters appear interchangeably as 'w' and 'u' there is sometimes doubt about which of these letters should be given. In these cases I have aimed at the consistent use of the spelling I have adopted for a word, as 'doun' and 'ewe'.

The letters 'i' and 'e' do not seem to have been distinguished very clearly by the writer, but I have generally printed an open letter as 'e' and a dotted stroke as 'i', while an undotted stroke is given as either letter. Exceptionally, however, I have read 'e' where there is a dotted letter in the word 'well' at 56 3.2 and elsewhere. The letters 'o' and 'a' cannot, I think, be distinguished by their form, *e.g.* the first 'o' of 'bloody' at 54 14.2 is like 'a' and the 'a' of 'make' at 51 1.4 is like 'o', and so when a letter looks like 'o/a' either of these letters is read. Often the choice of letter is related to the question of pronunciation, and *e.g.* spellings like 'mair' (49 11.4) suggest that 'mare' should be given in preference to 'more', but quite probably Orr was not consistent in conveying pronunciation, and in 51 I have used both 'ga' and 'go' in view of the rhyme 'lay' and the spelling 'gae' at 7.2, 3 and the rhymes 'also' and 'snow' at 8.2 and 9.2. The letters 'o' and 'a' can be open at the top like 'u' as at 50 9.1 'you' ('yuu') and 75 7.2 where the rhyme 'ran' indicates that the word that has the appearance of 'swum' should be read as 'swam', and the 'a' of 'company' at 75 4.4, 5. An 'o' is sometimes incompletely formed and looks like 'e', *e.g.* the second vowel in 'convoy' 55 7.2 which rhymes with 'boy' and 56 1.2 'box'.

The letter 'h' can be crossed like a 't' as at 65 4.3. A doubtful 'e' at 48 4.3 'marr[e]y', 49 4.3 'watter[e]s', 55 2.2 'Lad[e]y', and a doubtful 's' at 65 1.1 'time[s]' have not been read. A few letters are written small above the line to indicate abbreviation or the apostrophe: 48 18.1 and 19.1 the 't' of 'St'; 49 5.3, 4 and 6.1 the 't' of 'willt'; 49 1.1 the 's' of 'Meys' in the first case is a little above the other letters and in the second case is below them. At 65 4.2 the downstroke of 'y' in the previous line seems to be allowed to stand for the apostrophe in 'look'd'.

Crawfurd has made a small number of revisions and additions in the texts and notes written by Orr. In 48 at 13.4 and 14.4 he has added 'g' at the end of 'gan', at 16.3 he has deleted 'forest' and written in 'first' twice, deleting it once, at 20.3 he gives 'reatched' above 'rached', at 20.4 'laid' above 'laid' which is difficult to read, and similarly at 26.1 he has written 'threw' beside Orr's 'threw' which is not easily read. In 54 he has deleted 'wa' and added 'baw' at 1.1 and in 55 he gives 'been many times sair' above 'been may time sare'. In 66 he has written in additional readings in the first two verses without deleting the original: 'luit' for 'lov'd' (1.3 and 1.5), 'foul' for 'fool' (1.8), 'wrate' for 'wrot' (2.1), 'lute' for 'lout' (2.6). At 1.6 he has added an 'e' to 'an' and also given 'or yin' above, and at 2.3 he has corrected the final letter of 'yound' to 'g'. In 71 he has written 'she I ween' for 'She I win' at 1.3 and altered 'the', meaning 'they', to 'she' at 6.7. In the accompanying prose he has added 'or ringle't' after the first mention of 'wall eyd' as well as adding the note about the informant. In 48 and 49 he has added titles and end-notes and also written 'Meg Walker' on pages 322-3, 326-7 and 329-33. At the end of 54 at page 349 he has added 'or Meg Walker' after Orr's ascription 'Mrs Caldwell'.

Crawfurd also made a number of small adaptations to the texts he wrote himself, with a view, in the main, to thickening the Scots. He wrote his preferred words, sometimes more than once, near the words he intended them to replace and often, but not always, deleted the originals; sometimes the alternatives are introduced with 'or'. At 9 27.4 his substitution 'tandle' has evidently been written into the text while he adds as a gloss the word 'fire' which seems fairly certain to be the word sung and which is printed here as part of the text. This raises the possibility that the songs which appear in Crawfurd's handwriting may include words he has substituted. This does not appear to be common but there are instances where it is quite conceivable that Crawfurd has been making adjustments as, for example, in 8 where the word 'Onkent' appears at 6.1 where the chapbook text in the appendix has 'Unknown' and where 'gied him' at 20.2 fails to rhyme with 'save him' as 'gave him' would have done. The substitutions made by Crawfurd in the texts he wrote out himself are shown below in brackets.

1 4.2 lots (kevils) *and* cast lots (drew cuts)
4.3 lot (cast)
11.1, 12.1, 13.1 threw (cuist)
16.2 slowlie (huily)
17.2 weepand (greitand)
27.1 meek (mim)
27.2 child (bairn)
2 5.4 askit (speir)
6.4 deprive (twine)
9.4 boy (callan)
12.4 ask (speir)
16.1 dressing (busking)
21.4 Than (Nor)
23.1 than (Syne)
23.2 sorrie (wae wae)
23.3 kennit (wat)
5 5.4, 10.4 burning (lowand)
7.3 I wish (I'll bid)
7.4 enemy (fae)
9.1 sets (clappit)
12.3 But the less, care (Littil, am redd)
19.1 set (clappit)
23.2 tair (ryve)
23.4 Perhaps (Aiblins)
24.2 tore (ryvit)
7 1.1 Exeter (Eglinton)
1.3 train (menyie)
9 11.4 cryde (grat)
17.4 embrace (kep)
25.2, 26.2 blame (wyte)
27.4 fire (tandle)
10 2.2, 3 led (wysit)
4.3, 4 threw (flang)
7.2 rod (wand)
7.5 staying (byding)
8.1 wanderit (danderit), street (gate)
10.3 tane (twynit o)
11 11.1 wonder (ferlie)
13 4.3 robber (reiver)
20 1.5 wishing (bidding)
2.4 Strange (Frem)
3.4 returned (cam back)
5.3 langing (wearying)

20 6.2 toll (jaw)
8.1 caused (garrit), coffin (kist)
21 2.3 former (forlorn)
3.3 caused (gart)
4.4 courting (wooing)
25 1.3, 6.3 squire (laird)
2.1 sweet heart (my jo)
2.3, 12.3 every (ilka)
3.3 chimney top (divat lum)
4.3, 10.1, 11.1 chimney top (strae rape lum)
7.3 disturbit (yesterit)
9.1 could nae (duchtna)
12.3 that's jealous o (wha yarks at)
12.4 dangled (shuc't)
30 7.2 cocks (quyles)
10.1 gates (yetts)
10.2 jumpit (jinkit), nimbly (eithlie)
14.2 yonder lone (yon sweit garth)
31 6.1, 8.1 wish (bid)
6.2 ladder (trap)
36 7.3, 10.3 distant (frem)
8.4 returned (cam back)
15.1 last night (yestrein)
37 8.3 painfully (eidentlie)
9.3 Squire (lord)
10.1 then (syne)
12.4 threw (cuist)
17.1 cut (sned)
17.2 Throw (Fling), body (wee wee bouk)
18.1 bring (fesh)
40 3.4 Squire (laird)
6.4 child (bairn)
7.1 streach't (streikit)
42 1.2 greetand (sillie)
63 5.2 easy (eithly)
6.1 last (fern)
6.2 potatoes (grey lang kale), else (anse)
6.3 at aw (avaw)
6.4 horses (aivers)

Occasionally, Crawfurd's manuscripts show him revising the traditional texts a little more radically than this, as where in 5 *William and the Young Colonel* Crawfurd has overwritten the fourth verse, incidentally obscuring the letters shown in brackets:

(An)d he muntit on a (mi)l(k) white steid
And (as hard as he) coud r(i)de
(Until)l he cam(e) till he came
To (his) siste(r's) bower
In the twilight

with the words:

An he muntit his milk-quhyte steid
An as hard as he coud hie
Untill he cam till he cam to his sister's bour
In the gloming frae skaith he did flee

Perhaps he wanted to avoid the very short line 'In the twilight'. A comment in his *Eik to Jamieson's Dictionary* (3.179) on 'gloming' says, 'This term has no equivalent in English for tenderness and beauty. A fine and melodious word'. Similarly, a rewriting by Crawfurd of 30 *The Shepherd's Son* (which cannot have been set down before 1835 as the paper on which it is written bears this date in its watermark) includes the revision of a verse with rhyme change from:

He looked east he lookit west
He's tane anither look
And there he spied a fair maid
A sooming in the brook

to:

He luikit eist, he luikit wast
He saw a cozie glen
And whar he keikit a fair maid
As soumand in a lin

Most of the changes made by Crawfurd, however, are simple substitutions of preferred words, as 'braw propyne' for 'good reward' (3.3), 'mird wi' for 'touch' (4.1), 'gait' for 'road' (6.1), 'tirlit' for 'tinklit' (9.2), 'sonsie' for 'bonnie' (11.3), 'I'se' for 'I'll' (12.1), 'Foul fa me' for 'Hang me' (12.4) and 'trew' for 'think' (13.4).

In the case of 23 *Wise Willie*, Crawfurd's manuscripts include what appears to be a satirical adaptation of the song. The names are local ones but I have not discovered what group of people is being treated. As there have been partial attempts to destroy the two copies of the satire (see notes to 23), it must, I suppose, have been considered that it could be hurtful. The letters in brackets are conjectural.

Wyse Johnie and his Session

1 Whare are ye gaun quo Tammie Brydine
To slay a wee wran quo wyse Johnie

2 Whare wil ye slay it quo eller Aitkine
At Cloke brae face quo wyse Johnnie

3 Wi quhat wil ye kill at quo Macdonallie
Wi a gritt gun of the evangyl quo wyse Johnnie

4 Be quhat wil ye leade it hame quo eller Stewart
Be aivers and carrs quo wyse Johnie

5 What will ye do wi the fethers quo Yardfit Caldwell
They will mak a bed to my wife quo wyse Johnie

6 What will ye do wi the ribs quo eller Fultoune
They will (th)auk (the) manse quo wyse Johnie

7 What will ye do wi the muck quo Langyard Orrie
To muck my gleib quo wyse Johnie

8 Wh(at) will (ye) sey(th it in) quo eller Joh(nshill)
In basins and pans quo wyse Johnie

9 Wha will eat it quo Barfod Jamie
It is I mysel quo wyse Johnie

10 What will be the upshot o't quo Robin Barclay
A gude three days banning quo wys Johnie

Crawfurd made a great many deletions in his texts, a few of which are mentioned in the notes to the individual songs. The rest are listed here, with the deletion shown within brackets and the position of the deletion in the line indicated by the context. Very often the redundant words occur again in the immediate context or in a line above or below the one quoted. Usually the words or letters intended to be read follow the deleted words or letters but sometimes they are written above or superimposed.

1 4.2 (An cast lots) They cast lots
7.2 (he) aw he
9.1 (the) nine
10.1 (the) yon
14.1 (wil I) will I
14.2 (help) come and help
19.1 (weary) you weary
23.1 (on?) aw
31.2 (he ga) aw he gade
40.3 (an) a gay
47.1 (as?) its
2 1.4 (b) ahin
2.1 (li) wee
5.2 (silk b) aw silk but
5.3 (And) An
6.1 (g not) na gang, (hall) haw
6.2 (not) na, (lyfe) lyfe
7.1 (him) you
8.1 (If) Gif
8.2 (wil) wull
8.3-4 (sall) doublie vow/It sall
10.2 (to me) hae ye to me
10.4 (wad) fain wad
11.1 (Here is) Here is
12.2 aw (of) o
14.4 (u) unto
15.2 (I loud) Aloud (and) an
15.4 (be sho a) that this be sho
17.1 (was) sits
17.3-4 (I) my hart be/I
18.2 (her) his
18.3 (said) says
18.4 (sae) was neir sae
19.4 (And) an aff
21.3 (lik) lyke (it) that
21.4 (kine) kin
22.1 (bower) bour
3 3.1 (gay) gay
8.1 (am) I am
8.4 (our) for (our) Jamie our
9.1 (out) up
9.2 (an) a
10.1 O haud (O), (good) gude
10.3 (And) Aw
11.1 (pound) five pound
12.2 For the request (for)
12.3 (I) of velvet that I
4 3.1 (What) What
5.2 (that) ance that
5 3.1 (Willie) Will lifted
6.2 (says he) light down says he
6.4 (an) I
7.3 (tal) tails
8.3 (I) could I
10.2 (st) and stay
11.4 (For) And for
13.2 (int?) and
14.2 (And) A time (but) scercly but
18.1 (a) light
18.4 (Has) He's
19.3 (lad) lady
21.1 (Out?) Hold
23.3 (m) in my
23.4 (bled) bleed
25.1 (as) she said
25.3 (nor?) na
6 2.3 (bel?) bewitchingly
2.4 (On) When
7 7.2 (ay) and
7.3 (this) does
8.1 (I that) that I
8.4 To end you(r life are) o your life
10.2 (me a) my (thy) pye
11.1 (An) When
11.2-3 (he) sat/He
14.2 (did) began
14.3 (ye maun see) your daughter ye maun see

14.4 (th) up the
17.4 (h) aw his
8 3.5 Ye might have (ye)
4.4 (Ye luve) I love you
5.2 (her) for to inflame her
6.2 (weded) wi the Squire weded
6.7 (pat) parents
10.1 his ein (his)
15.8 (the) is there
16.1 (Wh?) Will
19.3 (Unto) An tuke
9 2.1 (So the Lord) Said the Lord
3.2 (name) nane
7.3 (her) up in her
12.1 (lies) O still
13.3-4 (though) Madam/Though
13.4 I'd (may leave) lay
15.4 (Nother) Nor the
16.3 (about you) ane o them about you
25.3 (the) Lamkin and the
27.4 (the) a
10 4.5 (And) That
8.3 (lay) laid
9.4 (weary) wearied, (me) thee
10.2 (lays in) lays in
11.1 (the) aw the
11.2 (to?) at
11 12.1 (William) wul ye
12.4 (my) heir (to my) o aw my
12 10.1 (spieit) spyit
12.2 (O mither) You
13.1 O mither, (deir) O mither deir
17.2 you(r)
13 1.1 (shall) will
3.4 tap(maist)mast
14.3 (mine) my
15.4 (Hie hang) Hie hangd, be (be)
16.2 (did) then did (ring) wring
18.3 (venom) venomed
20.2 (soon) soun
24.3 (did) I liked
14 1.2 (lover?) love
1.3 (wander) rove
4.2 (aff) the claes aff
15 1.4 (Aizlin) Aizlan
3.3 (wh?) will
4.2 (and) fresh and
8.2 As (she)
16 2r.1 (shines) sun shines
2.2 (can) neir can
5.1 (his) her
6.2 (the) doun the
7.2 (the) and the
8.2 (Unto) An tomorrow, (thee) marry thee
17 1.3 (she) maid although she
2.1 This maid (this)
4.4 Next Monday (next)
11.4 (out) our
18 2.1 (Lord) young Clifford
2.3 she (has) 's
2.4 (snaw) blood (and) in snaw
9.1 (may) I may
12.4 (we) sweet
17.3 (to nought) to nought
19 1.1-2 (fu)/Full
20 5.1 (awa a) a month awa
8.3 (he) as he
21 1.1 (wad) was at a wedding
23 1.2 (John) Jamie
6.1 (make) do
24 1.3 (cur) co'ered
2.2 (the) yonder the
7.1-2 (it)/It
8.1 marry ane (and)
8.4 Beauty (is) 's
9.3 (to) come to
25 2.4 the key below (the)
3.1 (get) maun get
3.4 (me) you down to me
4.4 (He) And
9.4 into (the) the
27 3.1 (you came) from London you came
6.3 (her) ye
7.4 (ill) will (feee) fee
28 2.3 (would not) wad never
3.4 (lad) bonnie lad
4.3 (my) mother
6.3 (marry) married
7.2 (ye) can be
9.2 (out) it was out
9.4 (But) That
10.2 (be) may be

28 10.4 Ye'll near ('ll will) be
12.1 (said) he said
17.2 (na) na
18.3 (wer) married are
30 12.2 (An) Nor
14.2 (It) That
15.2 (marygoud) marygold
32 1.2 (a) yowes
1.4–5 (ou)/Out
7.3 (na I) na
7.4 (you sall) you'll
9.3 (his) aw that his
12.2 (thay) ill death may thay
12.3 (ow) out owr
14.2 (ever) neir
14.3 (he) as he
14.5 (eee) ee
16.1 (How was) Who has
16.2 (this) done to you this
16.3 (for) for
19.4 (in in the?) in aw the
33 4.3 (o the dark) although in the dark
5.4 (my) me and my
34 9.4 (ye'se be) ye sall be
10.1 (off) aff *1st*
11.1 aff (and thus she made)
13.2 (the) owr the
13.3 (be) neir befitted
19.3 that (is) 's
22.2 (And) In
22.3 (al) ails
35 5.1 (to) no able for to
36 1.2 (seam) silken seam
6.4 (ha) hame
9.5 (the) seen near thee
14.2 (it) they
15.1 (O latelie O latel) O late last
37 4.3 ye('ll) shall
5.3 (o ten o) fairer than ten o
5.4 (As) Is
10.1 (your) shall be your
16.4 (I?) wud
17.1 (aff) cut aff
19.1 (you) ye
38 3.1 (While the tears) while sho seemit
7.2 (th) dune this
39 10.1 (sch?) shore
10.3 (h) she
16.3 (be) never be
40 1.2 (Hay) Thrie
2.4 (get) our dinner get
4.1 (aside) his side
6.4 (go) could go
10.4 (cuist?) cuist
1r.3 lay doo-an-(day) la doo-an day
6r.1 (Th) Hey
41 3.4 wi me (my deir)
4.3 (ga) never gang
6.2 other (the?)
7.2 (when) on your servants when
7.3 (For I'll) If ye'll
8.3 (ga) never gang
9.3 (ki) my deir
10.2 (I'll) wi you I'll
10.3 (wi you) I'll gang alang wi you
11.4 (cam) rue I cam
42 1.1 wha(t)
2.1 (will) wad
43 *title* (Sighted) Slighted
3.3 and (she) she
4.1 they saw that (they saw)
5.3 (An) A man
6.2 (feet) head and feet
44 2.2 (be) eir be
5.1 tak (me)
5.3 ye may swear (ye)
8.3 in (the)
11.2 (than) worth than
46 11.3 It('s) is
47 2.1 Begone (ye)
48 1.1 (Sh?) Sweet
4.1 awa(a)
5.3 (s)he
19.2 (st) sat
49 1.4 (at) out owr the(re)
4.1 (fair) kind
8.2 (s)he
11.3 (in) or
19.1 ha(ve)
28.3 o(f)
29.3 (ewes) kine
50 3.4 (he w ansur? me) ansure me
8.1 (are) air

11.2 (sp) Hasteley
51 7.3 (be) a gae prepare
9.4 (for) o the tiol
52 2.6 (my) her
2.7 (cloat?) coat
3.5 (with) we
53 10.2 (thine) mine
13.3 (F)or
14.3 (at) we
15.1 o(f)
21.2 (take) talk
54 9.1 (W) You
55 15.1 sma(ll)
17.2 thou('l) sall
59 2.5 fine, (fine)
4.4, 5 bed('s)
8.1 (Neever) Never
60 2.2 (me) me
61 1.3 (wiltu) wilt thou
3.1 so(l)ger
62 6.1 (and) an
63 5.4 (owr) owr
64 1.3 (of) hear o'
5.4 glance(s)
7.8 (gost) ghost
65 2.5 Loch(l)isle
66 2.8 (did) blind
5.4 the(se)
8.6 (bea) brea
68 1 (yon) yon (gran) green
2 (oll) auld
71 2.6 (in?) ean
3.7 crag(e)
4.1 (that) men that
6.8 (N) number
7.1 bl(e)ate
8.1 (ha) hakie
8.4 awa(y)
72 1.1 alan(g)
73 3.2 (of?) with
6.1 (may) marry
10.3 (she) that she
11.2 (that) one
75 5.3 (litt) tell
9.1 (nu) neues *1st*
15.5 (gone) bide you begone
76 3.3 (j) base like jade
3.4 (she) said she
4.2 (As she f) As fast as she (micht) may
5.1 (ha?) ye hae
5.4 (What) Where
7.3 (head heels) head where her heels
8.3 as leil (as I am) a maid
77 2.2 (W W) Wore
2.4 he(s) was
79 2.2 (thing) young things
4.2 (Polly) pretty Polly
4.4 all (along) on
80 1.1, 3 wi(n)dow's
2.2 quo he (quh) quo
4.1 (h?) ye hae
4.2 quo he (quh) quo
5.3 (jum) gied
81 2.6 (Therefore) Therefore
3.3 (al?) with
5.1 to labour (to lab)
5.3 (la) never lay

It is not surprising to find that, when Crawfurd required to make so many deletions, there are a number of points where he has failed to delete material which should evidently not have been included in a final text and I have felt it necessary to make a number of omissions. Editorial omissions from the texts as written (with the exception of some mentioned in the notes to individual songs) are shown below within brackets.

2 2.3 I eir (I)
4.2 (An) its
8.2 Sae (sae)
11.1 (Thare) here
19.4 (an) aff
20.1 (An) in his haun
3 4.1 (Will) I will
5.3 (And) I

4 3.3 be(en) seen
5 4.3 Untill he came (till he came)
5 12.3 for that (for)
25.2-3 whistling out the way/ And mourn(ing)
7 4.4 (An) this
8 3.7 out o hand(s)
6.4 they baith (they)
6.7 (He) To
7.2 (He) immediately he
16.4 depart(t)eth
21.1 In perfect (in)
9 25.3 'Twas (was)
26.3 (Twas) it was
10 4.2 and (o) mony
6.1 Day being (day) dune
8.1 the (the)
8.3 in (in)
12.2 (an) baith lang and
11 3.4 he('s) stays
4.4 (He) hie hanged he
6.4 (But) Thats
12 14.1 months (months)
24.2 end (and)
13 20.4 that lady (that)
21.4 (When) ye
15 14.4 A(nd) sweet and
17 3.1 (Often he) oftentimes he
3.4 (And) for
8.4 she (is) so lang does behind you (she) stay
18 16.4 (And) it gained (to)
3.4 return(ed)
22 2.2 (they) hard as they
25 5.3 lay m(a)y
30 7.2 (As) they
32 1.5 (o) the top of
33 1.3 (And) I
4.4 it (it)
34 11.4 (And) I
13.1 (and) I
37 6.2 (He) for
39 7.4 (have) love, dear(est) as
11.4 (he) by good fortune he
13.4 (An awa awa) a walking
44 15.3 stripped (him) down
17.3 the(y)
17.4 The(y), the(y)
21.4 change(d)
51 2.1 (l) legh
52 2.3 Wh(t)at
53 16.1 (Ye ar)/Ye are
73 8.2 (As) mark
75 18.1 (I well) well I
77 r.3 mailen (for me)
80 7.4 (And) in
81 2.3 (I) am not I
5.2 I('ll)

Crawfurd, besides making many deletions in his texts, also made a considerable number of insertions, but very often it seems that he has neglected to repair an omission. James Dobie, writing to David Laing (21 February 1845, Edinburgh University Library La.IV.17) notes as a disability of Crawfurd's related to his semi-paralysis that 'he occasionally omits small words in his sentences'. This kind of omission can be demonstrated in three instances in 1 where he first omits and later inserts small words. 4.1 read 'But whan the sark it was and dune' and had 'made' inserted, 4.3 read 'But the lot fell the youngest ane' and had 'on' inserted and 35.2 read 'For on the gloves was her name' and had 'writ' inserted. In the circumstances, a quite exceptional number of small additions seemed called for and I list below the editorial insertions that are not mentioned in the notes to individual songs. Where part of the word is in square brackets only the enclosed letters have been added; in other cases the whole word is an addition.

1 4.2 with
14.1 wha[re]
22.1 th[e]y
40.1 again
44.2 hae
45.1 rather

45.2 ye hae
3 2.3 lines that
2.4 c[r]yde
3.1 The[n]
6.1 first
8.2 na
12.1 for
4 1.2 ma[r]velling
1.3 ma[r]velled
2.2 makes
3.1 cut
5 2.3 I['ll]
4.2 rode
5.3 shall
7.4 And
9.2 fled
11.1 *2nd* light
17.1 th[e]y
7 3.1 be
7.4 There['s], fair
15.3 caused
16.3 cause[d]
8 2.3 heart
5.1 these
5.4 There['s]
6.5 big
6.7 were
8.3 lodging
8.6 The[y]
9.4 he
10.2 ask[e]d
11.1 not
11.4 not
14.1 when
15.1 her
15.7 [w]rang
16.1 not
16.2 hu[s]band
17.4 roaring
9 1.4 got
6.2 he
7.3 in
8.1 can
8.2 the
21.1 be
23.4 was
24.3 saw
10 2.5 heir
3.2 p[r]icked
11 6.4 lately
12.4 be
12 2.1 continued
8.2 the[ir]
17.2 fand
22.1 for, you['ll]
23.1 be a
23.2 will
24.2 at
13 1.2 wha
6.3 there
8.2 the
12.3 o[n]
15.2 loud
17.2 doun
18.4 it
21.4 might have
14 1.1 Here['s]
1.2 where[re]
15 3.3 see
9.2 war
16 2.2 consent
5.2 deal
17 3.2 did
4.4 be
6.2 where
18 6.4 is
7.4 golden
8.2 to
9.2 have
17.3 will come
20 4.2 That['s]
11.3 th[e]y
21 4.3 I['ll]
6.4 I['ll]
22 5.4 up
12.2 this
13.1 was
13.4 and
23 5.4 will
24 6.4 take[s]
25 3.4 down
4.4 down
6.2 if
9.4 And
27 4.4 far
5.3 her

27 8.1 what
11.1 here, *2nd* her
11.3 I['d]
28 1.4 bonnie
2.2 was
4.4 mak
5.4 be
6.1 there['s]
6.4 There['s]
18.3 now
33 2.1 are
3.2 is
3.3 *2nd* will
5.2 nightingale[s], like
5.3 clear[ly]
34 6.2 it
9.4 ane
11.1 then
35 4.4 love
5.1 able for
6.1 able
6.3 down
9.2 went
37 5.1 lich[t]
14.3 *1st* hame
18.3 I['ll]
38 1.1 *1st* are
2.2 lo[o]se
2.3 hae
7.1 you
39 6.1 has
6.2 return[ed]
7.2 I['ll]
7.3 I['ll]
8.3 *2nd* fix[ed]
10.2 out
11.6 of
13.4 she offer
14.2 stand[s]
15.1 if
17.3 c[r]yde
17.4 murder[ed], lying
42 9.3, 4 *2nd* and
44 1.4 at een
3.2 th[e]y, to
7.2 blindfauld[ed]
8.4 there['s]
14.4 na
16.4 a
17.3 dicht[it]
18.1 in
18.3 on
19.2 That['s]
46 10.3 I
15.3 deares[t]
16.3 them
47 2.3 on
48 22.1 say[s]
49 11.3 o
24.4, 5 to
50 3.2 my
8.3 m[a]y
51 6.1 say[s]
7.1 Th[e]
8.2 Th[e]
54 14.1 you[r]
55 1.2 mo[n]y a
2.1 I['ll]
56 3.1 parant[s]
4.1 Th[e]
4.3 tinke[r]
13.2 to
14.2 was
58 6.3 war[l]d
63 2.4 and
69 3.2 ruff[l]ing
70 4.1 Im
71 3.3 p[l]over
72 3.3 [s]trang
4.3 yon
73 4.3 if
5.3 little
12.1 that I asked her
74 1.4, 5 she['s]
75 10.1 of
19.3 in
76 13.1 you['ve]
77 4.3 was
4.4 I['ll], be
79 1.3 long
4.2 to
80 8.3 if
81 2.3 what
2.4 do
3.2 not
5.1 if

I have given standard spelling forms of the titles in the body of this work but the manuscript titles are shown below in the notes to the individual songs. The Crawfurd heading title is shown before the oblique and the list of contents title following it; where the two coincide the title is given only once, without an oblique. Dates that accompany the songs are listed in the introduction and are not normally included in the notes to the individual songs.

1 1.21-6 SEVEN LADIES AND THE BOWER / LORD BANGWEIL'S ADVENTURE

Head-note: 'Mrs Storie from her great grandmother'. 6.2 the 'F' of 'Frae' is altered from 'Th'; 8.2 'thay' deleted and 'air' added above; both words are given here with 'air' first as in 32.2 and 41.2; 9.2 'buit a courting gang' = had to go courting; the idea of compulsion may have been mistakenly attached to Lord Bangwell instead of the youngest sister, *cf.* Child C 7.1 'And to the greenwood I bud gae'. 10.2 'se'en': 'seen'; 40.2 'I', written above 'he' which is deleted; 32.2, 41.2 'we': 'they'; these emendations are parallel to the alterations made by Crawfurd at 40.2, but the singer may possibly have sung 'he' and 'they' at all three points. Between verses 43 and 44 the following lines are deleted:

Ye needna rather than your very life	*cf.* 45.1
For that same lady in your bower	*cf.* 44.2
Ye needna rather than your very life	*cf.* 45.1
I wad rather than	*cf.* 43.1 (42.1)

This passage seems to show the singer losing the narrative line and then picking it up again. It brings forward 45.1 to be the first line of verse 44, which then closes with 44.2. This gives an unrhyming couplet and the singer begins again in the same way. Then it seems that she casts back to 43.1 (or possibly 42.1) and may have sung through the intervening lines as already noted by Crawfurd until she reached 44.1 in the shape given in the text. The groups of three lines given here as verses 23, 31 and 40 are marked off as separate verses by short lines in the manuscript. The refrain is indicated only in the first three verses. At the end of 1.1 '- he down ho down' is written out and the repetition of these sounds is indicated by 'Do' after 1.2, 2.1, 2, and by 'D' after 3.1, 2.

2 1.8-12 BOB NORRIS / BOB NORRICE

Head-note: 'From her grannie'; 3.1 only the 'e' of 'Gae' in the line of verse is visible but 'Gae' has been written separately at the edge of the paper apparently to replace the faded word; 4.4 'ask': 'ask' with 'it' added; 5.4 'ask': 'askit'; 9.3 'as': 'Is' followed by faint letters, perhaps 'it'. This ballad occurs also in Motherwell's *Ballad Book*, pp. 510-13, and the following words from M have been taken into the present text: 2.3 'first', 4.3 'merrie', 5.1 'to', 6.4 'o' ', 8.3 'a vow', 16.1 'room', 18.1 'doun', 19.2 'down', 19.4 'fair', 20.3 the 'in' of 'into', 20.4 'lady' and the ' 's' of 'thare's', 21.4 'royal' and 23.3 'son'. The following M readings have been accepted into the text: 12.2 'aw gowd' for 'aw o gowd', *cf.* 4.2; 15.3 'Barnards' for 'Barnard' and 23.4 'been' for 'be'. Other M variations, shown in brackets, have not been accepted: 14.4 'Thay'r welcum unto me' ('They are welcum to me'), 16.2 'women's' (woman's'), 17.2 'was' ('is'), 17.3 'Said' ('Says'), 20.3 'broucht' ('he brocht'), 9.3 'Barnard' ('B'). Motherwell made a number of alterations to the text as written by him in his *Ballad Book* when Mary Macqueen sang the ballad to him and three classes of alteration can be distinguished.

(*a*) Where Crawfurd has deliberately made changes and Motherwell restores the words as originally sung, as in the following cases:

	C text	C substitution	M text	M revised readings
5.4	askit	speir	speir	ax
13.1	gay		braw	gay
16.1	dressing	busking	busking	dressing
19.3	cut		sneddit	cut
23.3	kennit	wat	wat	kent

At 10.1 where Motherwell alters 'lad' to 'boy', Crawfurd had probably made his substitution straight into his manuscript and 'boy' is read here. Motherwell has not apparently paid close attention throughout or he would also have had to alter other words which were deliberate substitutions of Crawfurd's, *e.g.*

	C text	C substitution	M text
6.4	deprive	twine	twyne
9.4	boy	callan	calland
12.4	ask	speir	speir
21.4	Than	Nor	nor

(*b*) Where there were probably omissions and mistakes in the text as first written by Motherwell from Crawfurd's copy which are rectified by this check; for example Motherwell has restored words that were in C but not in M, 12.1 'gay' and 18.1 'doun', and at 19.4 where M originally had 'And aff frae his bodie' Motherwell has deleted 'And', which Crawfurd had apparently caught up from the beginning of the previous line, and inserted 'fair' before 'bodie'.

(*c*) Where Motherwell's alterations indicate that the ballad is being sung differently on this second occasion as at 8.3 where C has 'I vow an I doublie vow' and M has 'I vow a vow and doubly vow', Motherwell has altered 'doubly vow' to 'I do protest'. He does not alter the first part of the line and this tends to authenticate 'I vow a vow'. 'I do protest' seems alternative to 'I doublie vow'. At 19.1, C has 'liftit (his braid) sword' with 'his braid' deleted and 'his' written above. M apparently had in the first place a space before 'sword', and Motherwell has a side-note, 'the epithet applied to the sword not remembered by the reciter; but I afterwards saw her & she mentioned it was 'nutbrown' the corrections are noted from her recitation'. Besides writing 'nutbrown' in the space, Motherwell also altered 'liftit his' to 'had a', which suggests that Mary Macqueen had worded the line differently.

3 1.108-11 MY LORD DERWATER / LORD DERNWATER

The heading title has an extra minim before 'w' in 'Derwater' which may have given rise to the 'n' in the title in the list of contents; *head-note:* 'Her mother - and her grannie'; 5.4, 5 *cf.* Child H 5.4 'To maintain you a lady's life'; 6.2 'His': 'He'; 'tumbled' should possibly be 'stumbled' but *cf.* Child A 8.2 'his horse fell owre a stane'; 8.3 'keep': 'intend', probably caught from 8.2; 9.2 'broad axe': 'project'. The first four verses have the repeat written out in full as printed. In the remaining verses, the repeat is indicated by the first word as 'To, &c' (5.5) except at 8.5 where there is no indication given. This absence of indication seems to be related to the fact that this verse, as written, already had five lines since 8.1 was split into two: 'Na I am nae traitor / Said my lord Derwater'.

4 1.27-8 THE HAWTHORN GREIN / THE HAWTHORN GREEN

Head-note: 'Her mother'; 4.1 'To cut me down I put nae doubt' = I have no hesitation about being cut down; 4.2 'But' = So long as; 5.1 second 'you': 'that', probably caught from 5.2.

5 1.29-34 WILLIAM AND THE YOUNG COLONEL / WILLIAM AND THE YUNG CORNAL

Head-note: 'Her mother'; 2.2 'are': 'as'; 4.1-4 this verse was written over by Crawfurd and not all the original letters are clearly decipherable, see general notes above; at 4.2 in the revised form Crawfurd deleted 'he' before 'as hard as he'; 5.3 'clear': 'cheer'; 7.3 'And I wish that you may be torn at wild horses tails': 'And I wish that at wild horses tails', *cf.* Child B 8.3 'But I wish ye may be hanged on a hie gallows' and D 13.3-4 'To be torn at the tail o wild horses / Is the death I weet ye'll die'; 13.3, 14.1 'wake(d)' = walk(ed); 18.4 'new rode': 'rode' written first, and then 'rode' deleted and 'new' superimposed, this 'new' deleted and 'new rode' written below; 25.1 'Go and put on a black suit': 'Go (and) put on a black suit' with 'and' deleted and 'of' inserted before 'suit'; possibly sung as 'Go and put on a black suit', with Crawfurd modifying to 'Go put on a suit of black' but failing to reverse the order of 'black' and 'suit'.

6 1.38 FAIR ROSALIND /

Head-note: 'Her mother'; 2.4 'sweet': 'swee' with binding strip covering the end of the word; 2.8 'Lang': 'Lang, lang' with the second word deleted; Crawfurd's comma has been omitted. The song is written in four-line verses.

7 1.39-42 THE CRUEL STEPMOTHER / THE CREWEL MITHER

Head-note: 'Her mother'; 2.3-4 'She was her father's delight an joy / As ye may after see': 'She was her father's delight / An joy(ous) and ye may see'; line division has been changed, 'and' altered to 'As' and 'after' added on analogy with the broadside text (*RB* 6.651) 'She was her father's only joy, as you shall after see'; 5.2 'for': 'to her'; 5.3 'dress': 'drest'; 7.2 'pure': 'puir'; 7.3 'shine': 'she'; 10.4 'your': 'Ye('ll)' with 'your' written above deletion; 12.3 'daughter's': 'daughter (she)' with 'she' deleted; 15.2 'peirsand' = parching, roasting; Crawfurd gives the gloss 'stewing' at the side; 16.1 'mourning': 'mournings'.

8 1.46–53 THE GRAZOUR'S DOCHTER / THE GRAZIOUR'S DOCHTER

Cf. Appendix No 1 *The Unfortunate Grazier's Daughter; head-note:* 'She got from her mother'; 1.3 'A': 'O'; 2.3 'Behold how he': 'Behold he who'; 4.3 semi-colon added; 6.4 'they baith had': 'they baith they'; 6.8 'na have them': 'na' with 'them' added above; 7.3 'And': 'Wi'; 7.6 'Appear in aw': 'Appearing in'; 7.7 'for': 'first'; 8.7 'had': 'he'; 9.3 'so that in truth': 'sincere and truth'; 10.3, 11.3 semi-colons added as in appendix text; 11.5 'well': 'will'; comma added as in appendix text; 11.7 'they': 'I'; question mark added as in appendix text; 12.1 'and': 'he'; 12.3 'your': 'her'; 13.5 'In': 'An'; 15.6 'friends and parents': 'parents and friends', *cf.* 6.1; 16.8 'In': 'An'; 17.2 'amazed': 'amazement'; 17.4 'of': 'or'; 17.5 'About': 'And'; 18.3 'I that am': 'that I am'; 20.3 'That': 'The'; 'his': 'he'; 21.1 the colon is added, *cf.* the semi-colon in the appendix text; 21.2 'was my undoing': 'is my ain doing'. The ballad has been divided into stanzas equivalent to those in the appendix text; it is written in four-line verses.

9 1.59–65 LORD MEANWELL / LAMKIN OR LORD MEINWEIL

Head-note: 'Her mother's' 7.3, 11.2, 24.2 'casement': 'cagement'; possibly Crawfurd thought of 'cagement' as an inner fortified place but there is no such word, and it seems fairly probable that the word sung was 'casement'; 6.4 'auld' = eldest; 8.1 'How': 'Who'; 12.3 'no' was deleted before 'Madam' and inserted before 'stilled' by Crawfurd; I have inserted it before 'be', *cf.* 13.3, 14.3; 17.2 'na': 'onie'; this emendation throws the stress on to the 'an' of 'thinkan'; 18.4 'Bedight': 'Bedit'; another possible sense is 'bedded'; 19.3 'knife': 'life'.

10 1.71–5 SIR HEW

Head-note: 'Her mother'; 2.4 'heir': 'neir'; 3.6 as this line is at the top of a page it is possible that 3.6–7 should be given as an independent verse; 4.2 'a plie': 'o plie'; 'o' is an insertion by Crawfurd; 5.2 'soom soom': 'soon soon'; *cf.* Child N 10.2 'And God forbid ye to swim'; 5.4–5 There is only a single line written 'Or my proud kin or o myne proud kin kin'. I take it that 'o' (of) is a mishearing of 'aw' (all), that the 'n' sound in 'myne' has been caught from 'kin', and that the beginning of the line was made redundant when words were repeated with 'o' included, *i.e.* '(Or my proud kin) or o my(ne) proud kin kin', and that Crawfurd perhaps did not have time to write the repeat in the fifth line of the stanza as a result of the delay caused by this alteration; 6.3–5 'Every school boy's mammie had her son / But Sir Hew's mammy had nane nane / But Sir Hew's mammy had nane' has been adapted from the confused form

'Every schuil boy's mammie had nane nane (with "Sir Hew's" written above to be inserted before "mammie") / Every school boy's, Sir Hew's mammy had nane'; 12.2 'lang and deep': 'lang and wide' is deleted and 'wide and deep' written above; the added 'wide' is deleted and 'lang' written beside it. Repeats are shown at the end of the second line of each verse except 6 where I have supplied the repeat of 'hame'; in verse 12 there is also a repeat shown in the fourth line. The repeating lines at the end of the verses are written out in full as printed except in the case of verses 5 and 6 (see notes above).

11 1.76, 78-9 THE KING'S DOCHTER JEAN / THE KING'S DOCHTER JEIN

The folio containing the end of the ballad has been erroneously placed in the middle and has been bound in upside down. The distribution of the verses of the ballad is as follows, with Crawfurd's page numbering in brackets: 1-5 on 76 (68), 6-11.2 on 79 (69), 11.3-14 on 78 (70) reversed; page 77 (71) reversed is blank. *Head-note:* 'Her mother'. The date 'St. Andrew's Day' is deleted. 1.4 'sailing' should possibly be 'sail in', *cf.* Child J 1.4; 7.3 'strike': 'struck'; 14.1-4 The way in which this verse is set down suggests that it was being recollected by the singer as Crawfurd wrote. Its first form runs:

For ye gie your dochter ae penny
An gie her pounds thirty
For ye give your dochter ae penny
I can gie her

Its my faither is Lord Salisbury

These lines are deleted. 14.1 'It's my faither is Lord Salisbury' is written below the first of them, 14.2 'An aw belangs to me' below the second, and lines 14.3-4 'And whaur ye gie your dochter ae penny / I can gie her thirty and three' follow after the deleted passage.

12 1.91-5 THE CRUEL MOTHER / THE CREWEL MITHER

Head-note: 'John'shill. From her mother'. 13.1 'O prettie babes O prettie babes' is written and deleted on a separate line above this one. The refrains are given in full in the first five verses 'Alane, alane (alone) O' and 'Doun (Down) be the grein wud (greinwud) syde (side) O'. They are indicated in verses 6-13 by 'Alane, &c.' and 'Doun, &c.' In the three-line verse 13, the second and third lines are both followed by the 'Doun, &c.' refrain. There are no indications of the refrain with the rest of the verses, except for a 'Doun, &c.' following 21.2. In verse 3, the words 'An by the Sea O' (or possibly 'Lea O') occur where they might be meant as alternative to either of the normal refrain lines which appear there. Crawfurd has put line-numbers before the following lines: 2.2 (4), 4.2 (8), 6.2 (12?), 8.2 (16), 10.2 (20), 12.2 (24), 13.3 (28), 15.2 (32), 17.2 (36), 19.2 (40), 21.2 (44), 23.2 (48), and has bracketed together the two lines of verses 6, 7, 8 and 9.

13 1.102-7 LORD GREGORIE

Head-note: 'Her mother'; 2.3 'the best' = God; 5.2 'said he': 'he said'; 6.2, 8.2 'thiekit' = roofed; 7.1 'an': 'a'; 11.1 'If awa awa' is written on a separate line before this one, *cf.* 15.1; 20.3 'p' is inserted and deleted between 'twa' and 'hours', and the full word 'past' is inserted between 'not' and 'twa'; 22.4 'rode': 'ride'; 25.3 'coach', perhaps = funeral coach. From 10.2 to 17.2 breaks are wrongly indicated by spaces and division lines at mid-verse instead of at the end of verses. There is a copy of the opening verses as far as 'but' in 4.2 at 3.16-17, but there are no verbal differences apart from the addition of 'be' in 3.3, which is read in the present text.

14 1.117-18 THE WANDERING LOVER

Head-note: 'her mother - Hogmanay, 1826'.

15 1.119-22 THE SQUIRE'S SON OF AIZLING TOWN / THE SQUIRE'S SON OF AIZLINGTOWN

Head-note: 'her mother Hogmanay, 1826'.

16 1.169-70 THE MERRIE LYKEWAKE / THE MERRIE LICHTWAUK

Head-note: 'her mother'; 2.2 'win' : 'maun'; 5.2 'gart deal the white money' = caused silver to be distributed. The refrain lines are given in full in the first two verses and are indicated in the third by 'As &c' and 'Among &c'. Thereafter the continued use of the refrain is indicated by '&c.' written at the end of each line except 6.2 where there is no space at the edge of the page.

17 1.171-3 YOUNG BETSY / YOUNG BETSIE

Head-note: 'Her mother'.

18 1.175-9 FAIR ROSANNE

Cf. Appendix No 2 *Fair Rosamond*; *head-note:* 'Her mother'; in the date, '12' appears to have been altered from '10'; 3.4 'wud her': 'her wud'; 9.1 'may' deleted before and inserted after 'I' by Crawfurd; 13.3 'liege': the manuscript does not have this word but gives 'sage' and 'vage' bracketed as alternatives; 16.1 'And w' is written and deleted on a separate line before this one, *cf.* 16.3; 16.2 'purchase your desert' = obtain what you deserve; 17.1 'plannet book' = book of fortunes told by the planets. The end-note is quoted in the introduction, p. xxxiii.

19 1.191 WILLIE TAYLOR /

Head-note: 'her mother'; *side-note:* 'modern, English murder in a ship'; 1.4 ends 'fair, &c'.

20 1.196-8 LORD LEVEL

Head-note: 'Her mother'; 1.2 'his': apparently 'withis', but the 't' is uncrossed; I have presumed that this represents 'his' with a false start; 1.3 'Then by and cam': 'By and then cam'; 11.3 'nae': 'thy', probably caught from later in the line where there is a 'thy' I have emended to 'they'. The shape of the stanza is made clear by verse 11 which is written out in full; in all other cases there is some abbreviation. The following do not have a fifth line but end the fourth line as shown: 5.4 'gae see gae see &c' 6.4 'mournan all, an all &c' 7.4 'Annobell, -obell, &c' 8.4 'the grun, the grun, O &c', 9.4 'sorrow, sorrow' 10.4 'flower, flower'. In the first verse the pattern has not yet been established and the ending runs: 'She was wishing Lord Level gude speed / Gude speed, (Gude s) She was wishing Lord Lovel' (1.4-5). In verses 2-4 the ending is given as follows: 2.4-5 'to see, to see / to see, &c', 3.4-5 'to thee, to thee / To thee, &c.' 4.4-5 'lady, lady / Ladie, &c'. I have taken it that this is a way of writing what could be more clearly expressed in abbreviated form as *e.g.* 'to see, to see / . . . to see'.

21 1.199-200 THE PENITENT BRIDE

Cf. Appendix No 3 *The Wedding*; *head-note:* 'Her mother'; 4.1 'well': 'will', probably caught from 'willow' earlier in the line; 6.1 'these': 'there she'.

22 1.211-13 THE THREE JOLLY BUTCHERS / THE THREE JOLLY BUTCHEOURS

Head-note: 'Her mother'; 1.3 'Aw': 'O'; 2.1 'As they were ryding' is written and deleted on a separate line following this one; 5.1 'clever' = sturdy; 9.3 'stick': 'stuck'; 12.3 'ane of the grandest butchers': 'ane the grandest of butchers'.

23 1.217-18 WISE WILLIE

Head-note: 'Her mother'; 3.1 'ye' is inserted and deleted before 'will' and inserted after 'will'; at 3.1 and 4.1 the manuscript has only 'What will ye kill it' and 'What will ye draw it hame'; I have added 'way' as in 'What way will ye kill it' although Crawfurd, in adapting these verses, says 'Wi what' or 'Be what'. The opening verse is written out in full, but thereafter the first three lines are represented only by the varying half-line (as 'O whare will ye kill't' in 2) followed by a number of ditto signs. The last line is generally written in full, but all or part of 'quo Wise Willie' is omitted in 2, 5 and 6. Crawfurd's adaptation in ten verses which is printed in the general notes above, was written out twice. A, at 1.219 immediately following *Wise Willie*, has been partially rubbed out and most of the verses have been overwritten. The entry in the list of contents has been obliterated but it appears to end with the word 'modern'. This copy is written in long lines as printed. B, at 2.320-1, is headed No 129 *Wyse Johnie and his Session* and the same title appears in the list of contents where it has been scored through. The first four verses, each of which is written in four lines with new lines beginning at 'Quo', can be read clearly although they have been scored through, but the remaining six verses were on page 2.321 and the folio containing them has been torn out so that only the opening letters at the inner margin remain. Verses 5–10 of the text quoted above are therefore from A, with the exception of the first two letters of 7.2 and 8.1. For verses 1–4 I have followed B since parts of A cannot be made out, but when a verbal difference can be distinguished I have given the A reading: 1.2 'wee' (B 'little'), 3.1, 2 'Wi' (B 'Be') and 4.1 'eller' (B 'John'). I have inserted 'be' at 10.1. In the A text there is a deletion after 'Be' in 4.2 and 'kirk' is deleted before 'manse' in 6.1. It seems possible that at least the first of the two additional verses in the adaptation may have had a traditional basis.

24 1.43–5 The Reekan House / The Reikand House

Cf. Appendix No 4 *Neighbour Hark*; *head-note:* 'She suspects this is modern. She got it from her brother Hamilton. She supposes he got it about Edinburgh'; 3.4 'Why': 'Gin', probably caught from 3.3; 8.1 'that is young an duce': 'that she (is) young an duce' with the 'young an' added above the deleted 'is'; I suppose that Crawfurd intended the deletion of 'she'; 8.3 'plainly come': 'plainly' is inserted after 'come'; I insert it before 'come', *cf.* 9.3. The refrain is given at the end and is followed by a note: 'To your fill al eer / Til-al-ee - (ea) every after 4 lines'.

25 1.182–5 The auld wyfe and the Peet Creel / The auld Wyfe & the Peet Creil

Head-note: 'Her mother' is deleted and followed by 'Her brother Tam'; 3.1, 4.1 'leather' = ladder; 4.2 'That's': 'That is' with the 'i' deleted; 8.1 'And an ill death may' has been written and deleted on a separate line after this one; 8.3 'braid book' = Bible; 10.4 'just': this word is deleted and 'e' added above, and there is also an 'e' inserted between 'just' and 'now'; 12.2 'the': 'thy'. The refrain is written in full only after verse 1. Other verses have at the end of the fourth line either 'ricadoo, &c.' (2, 5–8, 10–11), 'ricadoo' (4, 9) or '&c.' (3, 12).

26 1.191 The Yorkshire Rambler /

Head-note: 'from Tam'; *side-note:* 'modern'; 1.4 ends 'thounder, &c.'

27 1.35–7 The buss of Broom / The Buss o Brume

Cf. Appendix No 5 *Bonny Bush of Broom*; *head-note:* 'Her brother'; 3.2 'Wat and weary': 'What or where it's', *cf.* appendix text 4.2 'For wet and weary may I be'; 8.4 'and': written '&' to fit this exceptionally long line into the width of the page.

28 1.186–90 Mother Bunch

A deleted heading at 1.13 gives the title as *Bessie Bunch*; *head-note:* 'Her mother' deleted and then 'a lad in Galloway - Samuel Gardener'; 4.3 'Sae': 'Say'; 9.1 'then': 'them', probably caught from later in the line; 13.4 'buckle to' = marry; 16.4 'leeve' = lave, rest; 17.3 'she': 'the'.

All the verses close with a comma and '&c' but in the last verse the '&c' is deleted and the refrain written out in four lines as printed; r.1 'dy-day': 'dy day' with the 'y' of 'dy' altered from 'e'; r.4 'atherday, O' is written on a separate line above this one and deleted, and 'dadel' is deleted before 'da-lel'.

29 1.191 THE HILLS O GOWRIE

Head-note: 'by the same lad, &c.' *i.e.* Samuel Gardener, from whom Mary Macqueen learnt 28 *Mother Bunch*, the song which precedes this one in the manuscript; 1.4 ends 'Gowrie, &c.'

30 1.149-50, 147-8, 155 THE SHEPHERD'S SON / THE SAFT SHEPHERD'S SON

Head-note: 'A lass in Galloway - Girzy Connel'. The first six verses, on pages 149-50, have been written over in ink with the recomposed version mentioned in the general notes, and some of the original words are not completely legible. These are listed below; where part of a word is shown in brackets, only the enclosed sections are indecipherable: 1.1 'Tha was a'; 2.1 'He', 'west', 2.2 '(t)an(e)', 2.3 'th(e)re', 2.4 '(A so)oming', 'the', 3.1 'di(nna)', 3.3 '(An)d', 3.4 'If', 4.1 'your', 5.3 'th(a)y', 6.1 'th(e)y', 'war', 6.2 '(r)ye', 6.3 'Q(u)o'. At 2.4 the word read as 'A sooming' begins with a deleted 'And' which has 'As' written above. The rest of the revision is not written over the original on pages 147-8 and 155 but is on added pages, 151-3, which bear a watermark which includes the date 1835. 1.2 'hill': 'hi' at edge of page; 2.2 'look': the first letter is like 'b'; 3.4 'me': 'my'; 4.3 'out o': 'to'; 4.4 I have inserted 'you aw' in this line following the revision which has 'For to make ye aw my ain'; 7.2 'cocks': the first letter is like an 'r'; 10.3 'on': 'and'. The refrain occurs after the first verse only. As originally written it appears as, 'To my fall de ra rel de dair (my) To my / fell de ra rel (th) the rit o day, / fell de ra rell the dayro', and in the revised form as, 'To my fal de ra rel de dair / To my fal de ra rel the rit o day / Fal de ra rel the day ro'.

31 1.209-10 THE FAUSE KNICHT, OR THE DEIL / THE FAUSE KNICHT

Head-note: 'a Galloway woman named Mrs Dole or Doll'; 1.2 'stood' runs off the edge of the page, only 'sto' and the back loop of the 'd' being present; 2.1 the 'a' of 'rade' is doubtful and should possibly be 'o'; 3.2 the word 'peat' is marked with an asterisk and there is the following side-note: 'It was a custom in many parts of Scotland where coals are scarce, and perhaps it is continued to this day, as Galloway; for the parents of the wee scholars to send (sand) by every callan and lassie a peat or more to eik the common fire or ingle, to the master, every day'; 4.1 'Wha's aught' = Who owns; 4.2 'an': 'are', probably caught from earlier in the line; 6.2 'guid': 'guide'. The first two verses are written in two long lines as given in the present text. Verse 3 is written in four lines with new lines beginning at 'Quo', and the rest of the verses are in abbreviated form and indicate the repeating words in separate lines by 'Quo the &c.' (4) or 'Quo &c.' (5-9). Motherwell printed this ballad in his *Minstrelsy*, introduction pp. lxxiv–v, and Crawfurd gives a copy of the first three verses in a gloss on 'peits' in his *Eik to Jamieson's Dictionary* (4.207–8). All the verses in these texts are written in four lines with the extra divisions coming before 'Quo', and there is some abbreviation of the repeating words in M. I have inserted into the text the M readings 'are' in 1.1, the 'up' of 'upon' in 2.1 and 'for to' in 7.2; the first two are also present in the *Eik* text. M also has the following variations, shown in brackets, from the Crawfurd manuscript text: 3.1 'ye hae gotten' ('ye've got'); 4.1 'they' ('the'); 5.1 'of'('o' '); 5.2 'them' ('they'); 6.1 'were' ('are'); 7.1 'the ladder' ('a lather'); 9.2 'you for to be drowned' ('ye to be'). The *Eik* copy has 'I's' for 'I'm' (1.2) and 'ye've gat' for 'ye hae gotten' (3.1).

32 1.13–19 THE LAIRD OF OCHILTREE WALLS / THE LAIRD OF OCHILTREE-WALLS

Head-note: 'St John's Hill From a lass Mary Douglas in Ayr'; 4.1 'Ryde on ryde on said she' is written and deleted on a separate line below this one; 7.3, 8.3 'be na back': 'may na back', 'may back'; 7.4 'It's o me you'll neir see nae mair': 'It's aw o me you'll neir see me mair'; I have taken it that 'aw' is an anticipation of 'o' and the second 'me' a mishearing of 'nae'; 7.5 'It's o me ye'll neir see nae mair'; I have added 'o' and 'neir' and altered 'me' to 'nae' to make this line a repeat of the preceding one; 10.1 before this line occur the deleted lines, 'She put the pale unto her head / An sho gane merrilie hame', *cf.* 11.1–2; 11.1 'on to': 'unto'; 11.4 'you've': Crawfurd wrote 'you you've' and deleted the first 'you' and the ' 've'; 12.3 'knows': 'know', at edge of page; 13.1, 14.1 'tod' = fox; 13.3 'An afore that he tock the ane that he tock': 'An afore ance he took the ane he took'; 14.4, 5 'twinkland': 'ing' deleted and 'and' added; 15.4, 5 'ways': 'was'; 16.3 'to say for': 'for to say (for) for'; apparently Crawfurd has deleted the wrong 'for' and then replaced it above; 17.2 'Sae loud as': 'Aloud as'; 19.2 'plews' = ploughgates (measures of land of varying extent); 19.4 'is in the': 'is (the) in', with 'in' written twice above deleted 'the', *cf.* 19.5 'is in aw the'. This ballad is in Motherwell's *Ballad Book*, pp. 517–21. At the points where I have made the above alterations M has: 7.3 'be na back' and 8.3 'may na be back'; 7.4 'Its o' me ye'll ne'er see nae mair', with 'ne'er' inserted, and 7.5 'Its ye'll see me nae mair'; 11.1 'upon'; 11.4 'ye've'; 12.3 'knowes'; 13.3 'An afore that he took the ane that he took', with a 'd' deleted at the end of the first word and 'that he took' and 'that' inserted; 14.4 'twinkland'; 15.4, 5 'ways'; 16.3 'to say for'; 17.2 'Sae loud's', altered from 'Aloud's'; 19.4 'is in a' the'. I have also made the following insertions of words present in M but not in the Crawfurd manuscript: 3.3 'o', 9.3 'that', 12.2 'And', 16.1 'to you'. At 5.1 and 6.3 M has ' "milkwhite" hand' and ' "bonny" lass' and obviously the words in inverted commas, which are not in the Crawfurd text, were added at some point in the manuscript transmission; it is quite likely, however, that they were accidentally omitted when the words were first taken down and I include them here as 'milk white' and 'bonny'. There are also the following other variations between the Crawfurd manuscript text and M, shown in brackets: 2.1 'Tha' ('There'); 2.4, 5 'For to' ('To'); 3.4, 5 'To' ('Till'); 3.4 'owr' ('out owr' with 'out' inserted); 7.1 'pullit'; 'silver' ('pou't', 'sillar'); 7.3 'if' ('gin'); 8.1 'pocket Book' ('silken purse purse string' with the last two words deleted and first 'purse' inserted); 8.2 'gae' ('gied'); 8.4 'It'll' ('It will'); 8.5 'It'll' ('I will'); 8.4, 5 'nurse's' ('nourice'); 9.4, 5, 11.4, 5 'tarried' ('taiglit'); 10.3 'lass' ('lassie'); 13.4, 5 'rather' ('leifar'); 15.1 ' 'Twas' ('It was'), 'it was a fyne simmer day' ('a bonnie simmer day' with 'it was a fine' deleted before 'simmer' and 'a bonnie' written above). The fifth-line repeat is written out except in verses 15, 18 and 19, where it is omitted. The double repeat of the last word in the fourth line (as 'Lang, lang' in verse 11) is written on a separate line following the fourth except in verses 15 and 18, where it is omitted, and verses 1 and 3, where 'Knows, Knows, Knows' and 'Lee, Lee, lee' are given on separate lines after the fourth lines.

33 1.180-1 THE BONNIE BLUE EYED LASSIE / THE BLUE-EE'T LASS

Head-note: 'old Mrs Smith of Ayr - I was servant to her'; 1.4 'blue': there is an insertion with 'bl' deleted and followed by 'bue'; 4.2 'that never': 'of the ever' with 'the' deleted.

34 1.316-21 MAY COLYEAN / MAY COLYEIN

Head-note: 'Mrs Smith - or Mrs Williams, in Ayr, or rather the former'; 11.3 'on': 'and', which is deleted; 15.4 'my' should possibly be 'your', *cf.* Child D.d 17.4; 26.1 'tall': 'tauld'. On 1.316 Crawfurd has the reference '(See p. 158)' and attached to this page, which is now 1.168, is a chapbook without date or printer's name containing *The Historical Ballad of May Culzean* in twenty-seven verses equivalent to those known to Mary Macqueen.

35 1.206-8 MALL BOWIE

Head-note: 'old woman in Ayr Mrs Williamson'; 6.1 'no' is added above towards the end of 'for'; I give it before an inserted 'able' followed by 'for'.

36 1.54-8 LADY JEAN / LADIE JEIN

Head-note: 'From Nancy Walker the sister of William Sutherland's wyfe'. Nancy and Elizabeth Walker were daughters of Robert Walker, carrier in Kilbirnie (*Cairn* 2.291-4) and Elizabeth married William Sutherland on 27 June 1817 (Kilbirnie PR 596/1). The three verses concerning the sister, 13, 18 and 19, are not in Crawfurd but are given from Motherwell's *Ballad Book*, pp. 657-9. It seems quite likely that they were derived, possibly on a different occasion, from Mary Macqueen, for the text as Crawfurd first wrote it was incomplete, omitting verses 15 and 17 as well as the three verses noted above. He had to add at the end the verse beginning 'O late last night' with directions that it was to be inserted twice into his text. I have added the two verses at the points where they occur in M but Crawfurd says that they should appear earlier, 'Between the 12 and 13 and between the 14 and 15' of his numbered verses, and puts insertion marks there. This may have been a mistake on his part, but as the ballad may have been sung in this way I give the ending here as he indicates it:

12 Slowlie, slowlie, rose she up
An slowlie she gade hame
Until she cam to her faither's parlour
And there she did sigh and mane my love
An there she did sich and mane

O late last night as I came hame
Down by yon castle wa
O heavy heavy was the stane
That on my breast did faw my love
That on my breast did faw

13 And her faither he came trippan down the stairs
His steps they were fu slow
I think, I think, ladie Jean he said
Ye'r lyan far owr low my love
Ye'r lyan far owr low

14 Her mother she came doun the stair
Her steps they were fu slow
I think I think lady Jean she said
Ye'r lyan far owr low my love
Ye'r lyan far owr low

O late last night as I came hame
Down by yon castle wa
O heavy heavy was the stane
That on my breast did faw my love
That on my breast did faw

15 Her brither he came trippan doun the stair
His steps they were fu slow
He sank into his sister's arms
And they died as white as snow my love
And they died as white as snow

Although verses 13, 18 and 19 are introduced from M, 19 (which in M is identical with 15 and 17) is given from the 'O late last night' verse in the Crawfurd manuscript. In 13 and 18 the spelling 'love' is given as in the rest of the Crawfurd text to replace the spelling 'luve' used throughout in M, and a full stop after below (13.5) which comes at the end of a page in M is omitted. Two instances of overt changes to Scots made by Crawfurd in his manuscript occur silently in M: 'frem' for 'distant' (7.3) and 'yestreen' for 'last night' (15.1, 17.1, 19.1). Another alteration of this kind in the Crawfurd manuscript, from 'returned' to 'cam back' (8.4, 5), destroyed a half-rhyme with 'born' (8.2) and left:

The first time I came hame Jeinie
Thow was na here nor born
I wish my prettie ship had sunk
An I had neir cam back my love
And I had neir cam back

It seems rather likely that the M ending of this verse (8.4, 5):

And I had been forelorn my luve
And I had been for-lorn

was an adaptation by Motherwell for the sake of rhyme. M includes at two points words I have assumed were accidentally omitted in the Crawfurd manuscript and have included in the present text: 'the leaves' at 1.5 and 'to' at 6.2. I have also followed M in reading 'and spak' instead of 'bespak' at 3.3, 'into' instead of 'to' at 20.3 and 'O heavy heavy' in the third line of verses 15, 17 and 19 where the equivalent in the Crawfurd manuscript has 'O heavy O heavy'. There are also the following variations in M (shown in brackets) which have not been adopted in the text: 2.1 'stack' ('stuck'); 2.4, 5 'For to pu', 'nuts / nits and slaes' ('To pu', 'nit and slae'); 3.4, 5 'daurst thou' ('daur ye'); 3.4, 5 and 4.2 'this' ('the'); 4.1 'these nuts' ('the nit'); 4.4 'of' ('o' '); 6.1 'have' ('hae'); 7.1 'If' ('Gif'); 9.2 'nurse's' ('nourice'); 9.4 'seen neir' ('never seen'); 10.3-5 'I wiss I had die't on some distant isle / An never had come hame my love / An never had come hame' ('I wish my pretty ship had sunk / And I had neer come hame my luve / And I had neer come hame'); 11.2 'Doun' ('And doun'); 12.1 'Slowlie, slowlie, rose' ('Hooly Hooly rase'); 12.2 'slowlie' ('hooly'); 14.1 'And her' ('Her'). Crawfurd gives the repeats in full in all verses.

37 1.66-70 Earl Richard / Erl Richard

Head-note: 'From Peggy Thomson a lass in this town - sum time from Mithill parish in Perthshire'; 3.1 this line is written at the end of the previous verse, the first two lines of which are written as one; 6.1 'bow': 'board'; 6.4-5 the blank may be supplied from Child D 4.4: 'Wherewith she wound him deep'; 7.4 'Loves': 'Lives'; *end-note:* 'The last line of the stanza is to be repeatedly sung'. The repeats, line 5 of each verse, are not written out.

38 1.80 and 85-7 The Laird o Kelty / The Laird o Keltie

Cf. Appendix No 6 *The Pretty Parks of Cailty O*; *head-note:* 'From Peggy Thomson'; 1.4, 2.4, 7.4 I have added the 'O' at the end of these lines; 2.3 'horses': 'houses'; 2.4 'The young laird o' Kelty' is written and deleted on a separate line after this one; 5.1 'an': 'when'; 5.3 'will turn back again':

'offended thee'; Crawfurd has anticipated words later in the line, and I have inserted words taken from 5.2; 7.3 the line is not written out, but I have repeated 7.2, *cf.* verses 1 and 3-5. This song is not clearly set out in verses but there are short lines indicating division after verses 2-6. 1.1-3.2 is written on page 80 and 3.3 to the end on pages 85-6. The last line, 8.4, occurs again at the top of page 87 as 'And she is lady (of) o the pretty (of) o Kelty O -', but is deleted there.

39 1.87-8, 81-4 THE MASON'S DOCHTER

Head-note: 'From another Peggy Thomson in Lochinnoch - from Kilbirnie - now wife or concubine of James Millin - weaver from Dalry - She is a millener'; the date 'St Andrew's night' is deleted; 1.3 'The fairest o faces but the fausest o hearts': 'O the fairest o the faces but the fausest hearts'; 3.3 'I'll': 'intil I'; 7.6 'I'll never wad you I avow to wad you' is written and deleted on a separate line above this one; 'the': 'my'; 8.3-9.1 include the words 'and he fix it weel (out our the draw well / And he fixed [it weel and] a net out our / Supposing she) An he fixed a net out owr the draw well / supposing she' with the words in square brackets deleted separately and replaced by the following four words. 9.3 'draw': 'drew'; 11.5 'Till by good fortune he': 'Till (by) he by good fortune he' with the first 'by' deleted by Crawfurd; I have omitted the first 'he'; 14.3 'amaze': 'a phraise'; 14.4 'as braw a bairn': 'as a bairn as braw'; 15.1 'if': not in the manuscript at this point in the line but there is a deleted 'if' after 'lane'; 16.3 'intended': 'intented'; 16.4 'yon babie is': 'your babie be'; 18.1 'grippit' = arrested, 'suffered' = was executed; 19.1 'you': 'your'; 19.2 'If ever': 'A fe' deleted and followed by 'I fear'.

40 1.192-5 THE THRIE RAVENS

Head-note: 'From Peggy Thomson from Dalry'; 2.4 'quher'll we': 'quher we'll'; 9.1, 2 'fir': 'fire'. In verses 1-9 the four lines are written out in full, but in verses 10 and 11 only two lines are written, the first (understood to be twice repeated) and the last. The refrain 'hey doun' is written at the end of the second line in verses 1-9; in verse 1 only there are commas before and after it. The refrain line 'Hey doun hey derrie day' is written in full in verses 1 and 2, and is indicated in other verses apart from the last two by 'Hey &c.' or alternatively by 'hey doun' (verse 7 only) or '&c' (verse 8 only). The other refrain line is given by Crawfurd in full in the first verse as 'And sing lay doo-an-la doo-an day', but in the other verses it is indicated merely by 'And sing &c.', or, in the case of 9, by '&c.' only.

41 1.113-16 THE DEIL'S COURTSHIP

Head-note: 'From Jamie Orr of the Fairhill'. This branch of the Orrs receives mention by Crawfurd at *Cairn* 15.50 where, with reference to the year 1772, he speaks of a 'Wm. son of James Orr in the Fairhill', and in the Kilbirnie Parish Register, 596/1, where there is a record of the marriage on 14 May 1806 of 'William Orr farmer in Fairhill of Lochwinnoch'. This song also occurs in Motherwell's *Ballad Book*, p. 309, where it has the title *The Deil's Wowing*. The following readings of M have been accepted as making good omissions in Crawfurd's text: 1.2, 2.2 'the way'; 1.3, 4, 2.3, 4, 3.3, 4, 4.3, 4 'alang'; 2.1 'pennyworth o' (but 'of' is read as in Crawfurd 1.1); 12.1 'now'; 12.3 'And' (but 'An' is read as in Crawfurd 12.4). The following alterations are made from M: 4.2 'other ten' instead of 'other tymes' (*cf.* 3.2), 6.2 'stripes' instead of 'strips' (and 'stripes' is also read at 5.2 where M and Crawfurd have 'strips'). The following M variations shown in brackets have not been adopted: 'If' ('Gin') at each occurrence; 'I'll' ('I'se') at 5.1, 6.3, 7.1, 9.1, 10.2, 3, 4; 1.1 'of' ('o' '), 3.1 'I'll' ('Oh I'll'), 4.1 'or' ('nor'), 4.2 'Ten' ('Tho ten'), 6.1 'gown' ('soun'), 6.2 'other' ('the ither'), 7.2 'when you' ('when ye'), 10.2 'gang' ('gae'), 11.1 'a' ('ae'), 11.2 'the heel' ('his heel'), 11.3 'wi you' ('you'), 12.1 'have' ('hae'), 'you fast' ('ye fast'), 12.3, 4 'I'll no' ('I winna'), 13.2 'At every mile that dulefu sang' ('At ilka mile end she dulefu sang').

42 1.214-16 POOR GREITAND WILSIE / POOR GREITAND WILLIE

Head-note: '(Johns) John Greenlee's wyfe - Old (John) William Houston's daughter at the Clochodrick'. This was Mary Houston, daughter of William Houston, farmer in Clochodrick, Kilbarchan parish, the proclamation of whose marriage to John Greenlees weaver in Lochwinnoch was recorded on 9 May 1818 (Lochwinnoch Parish Register 570/1, *Cairn* 1.284-5 and 5.25). 6.1, 2 'will we': 'we will'; 7.1, 2 'what way'll we': 'what'll we'; 7.3 'draw': Crawfurd has deleted 'get' and substituted 'draw'. The first verse is written in full except that the repetition of 'O I will gang to the wood wi thee' is represented by '&c.', and the second verse is written in the form: 'O what an I wad lay thee down / Quo Wilsie quo Wilsie / &c. / Quo poor &c / O can I no rise again / Quo &c / &c. / Quo bonnie &c.' From verse 3 onwards the verses are represented by an abbreviated form on the pattern of: 'O quhat an I wad fyle thy goun / &c. / &c. / &c. / Can I no wash it again / &c. / &c. / &c.'

43 1.156-7 SLIGHTED LOVE /

Head-note: 'Sally Monie'; 3.3 'nae mair': 'the neir' originally written, 'the' deleted and 'nae' inserted; 3.4 'it break': 'it' followed by word covered by binding strip, perhaps 'brak', with 'it break' written below; 6.1 'large': the 'r' apparently written over 'n'; perhaps 'lang' was originally written; 6.2 'merval' = marble.

44 1.275-80 THE ENSIGN AND THE LADY GAY / THE ENSIGN & THE GAY LADIE

Head-note: 'Old Mary Maclean'; 1.3 'The ensign': 'Then (since they) the ensign'; 12.4 'The ensign's': 'Then since'; 16.1 'my': 'the'; 16.4 'There': 'They'.

45 1.127-30 THE UNCO KNICHT'S WOUING

1.1 'tae': perhaps begun 'th', with 'a' written over 'h'; 4.2 second 'be': superimposed on 'is', apparently by Macqueen; 13.2, 18.2 'wuss' = wish, curse. Crawfurd has written in the title and made three other additions: 'g' at the end of 'bedmakin' ' in 6.1 and alternative rhyming words added at the end of 19.1–2, 'As sune as she the Fiend did name - caw / He flew awa in a fierie flame - low'. This ballad is in Motherwell's *Ballad Book*, pp. 647–8. The following variant readings in M seem to have been derived from alterations made by Crawfurd into older or more distinctively Scottish forms: 'nor' in place of 'than' in every line from 9.1 to 18.2; 'or' for 'ere' (4.2), 'thir' for 'these' (5.2), 'Clootie's' for 'the Fiend is' (18.2). In 1.1 M has 'Sing the Cather banks, the bonnie brume' for 'Sing the claret banks tae the bonny broom', and evidently Crawfurd was responsible for substituting the River Calder (which runs through Lochwinnoch parish) under its old name of 'Cather', which occurs *e.g.* on the cover of a letter dated 1740 that was in Crawfurd's possession and is now in Paisley Central Library, PC 2844 *Brigend Papers* No 106. The omission of 'tae' in this line in M may indicate that the copy used by Motherwell had as its source the text in the Crawfurd manuscripts written by Macqueen where the 'tae' is not clear and may have been read as a first 'the' to be replaced by the 'the' which follows. At 8.2, the replacement of 'Tomorrow' by the Scots 'To morn' meant the loss of a syllable and the word 'made' later in the M line seems to have been added to supply this: 'The morn ye sall be made my ain' for 'Tomorrow ye sall be my ain'. There are also a few other variations. 'An' ' is omitted at 3.2, and there are the following replacements: 'And' for 'Or' (10.2), 'woman was' for 'woman's wuss' (13.2, 18.2), 'Hunger is' for 'Hunger's' (17.1) and 'blazing' for 'fierie' (19.2). None of the M variant readings has been adopted in the present text.

46 1.159–63 ROSIANNE

5.3 The words 'but her sister deir' are written over the rubbed out words 'ails thee Rosiann'; 6.2 'Rosie s' is partially rubbed out at the edge of the page, *cf.* 7.1. This ballad, the last three verses of which are in Thomas Macqueen's hand, occurs also in Motherwell's *Ballad Book*, p. 398. I have preferred the M readings where the Crawfurd manuscript has obvious instances of Crawfurd's Scotticizing: 'Weeping' for 'Greitand' at 1.2, 3.2, (5.2), 7.2; 'Wha' for 'Quha' at 3.3, 5.3, 7.3; 'what' for 'quhat' at 3.4, 5.4, 7.4 (10.1), 13.1, 14.1; 'A deal a deal' for 'A hantle' at 2.1, 4.1, 6.1, 8.1; 'reason' for 'cause' at 2.2, 4.2, (6.2), 8.2; 'little babe' for 'wee bairn' at (4.3, 6.3), 8.3; 'Between' for ' 'Tweisht' at 2.4, (4.4, 6.4), 8.4; and 'point' for 'neb' at 10.1. At 12.3 I read 'hae killit' as in 10.3 and 11.3 instead of the Crawfurd manuscript 'hae slain' or M's 'did kill'. There are also the following M variations, in brackets, which have not been adopted in the present text: In M 'saying' is at the end of 1.3, not the beginning of 1.4; 3.3 'Quha' ('& Wha'), 'by' ('doun'); 5.3 'Quha' ('And wha'); 7.3 'Quha' ('And wha'), 'by' ('doun'); 8.2 'hae I to mane' ('I hae to cry'); 8.4 ' 'Tweisht me an thee, deir brither John' ('Between yoursell and I'); 9.4 'An gae her deep wounds three' ('And he cut her fair bodie in three'); 10.3 'hae killit' ('did kill'); 12.1 'free' ('fresh'); 14.1 'bonnie' ('bonny bonny'); 14.3 'in anither' ('on some other'); 15.1 'little' ('wee'); 15.4 'ye in mind' ('in remembrance'); 16.1 'lan' ' ('lands'); 16.3 'dear' ('my dear'); 16.4 'Tae maintain my wee' ('To keep my own'); 17.3 'Moon' ('the mune'); 17.4 'that will never' ('that ll ne'er'). The spelling 'mune' at 17.4 and the reading 'wee' for 'little' at 15.1 in M strongly indicate that the text came to Motherwell through a copy made by Crawfurd. Where verses are highly repetitive, Motherwell has not written them in full and the line references given in brackets above are to forms that are understood, not actually set down. In the Crawfurd manuscript the following lines (*cf.* 9.1, 10.1-4) are written and deleted before verse 9:

> Weil ye hae tauld father the neb of your knife
> Dear son cum tell to me
> It is my horse that I hae killed
> Dear mither

47 1.204-5 THE PRINCE O ORANGE / THE PRINCE OF ORANGE

2.3 'willow': 'wallow'.

48 1.322-8 THE NUT BROUN BRIDE / THE NUT BROWN BRYDE

10.3 'Anie yet' = Annie's gate; 16.3 first: forest; 18.2 'side' = aside; 19.1 'eard' = yard; 20.3 the letter after 'e' in 'rached' is not clear; it could possibly be 'x'; 24.4 the 'O' at the end of this line is an editorial addition; it is present in Crawfurd's rather free copy of verses 22-6 at 1.328 (see introduction, note 38); 25.2 'Queer' = Choir; *end-note in Crawfurd's hand:* 'Gathered from Meg Walker widow of Horn (Caldwell) Johnie - at present at Brigend'.

49 1.329-34 THE LAIRD O OCHILTREE

1.4 'nows nows' is written and deleted on a separate line above this one; 3.4, 4.1 a blot obliterates 'a' of the second 'wrang' and 'e' of 'she'; 7.4 the 'b' of the second 'liberty' is an inserted letter which Orr has mistakenly put after 'e'; 13.4 'To pay' is written and deleted on a separate line above this one; 14.2 'string' = ribbon; 20.1 'nappey' = small wooden vessel made of staves; 22.1, 23.1 'Tod' = fox; 25.2 'key' was deleted by Orr and replaced by 'kine', but 'key' is read for the rhyme with 'by'; 27.4, 5 'goodman' = husband; 29.3 'guidfather' = father-in-law; *end-note in Crawfurd's hand:* 'Meg Walker at the Brigend'. The fifth-line repeat and syllabic bridge are given in full in verses 1, 2 and 6. Otherwise the fourth-line word is repeated and '&c &c' added in the following line, except that in verse 30 there is only one '&c' and none in verse 4, and that verse 5 does not indicate the repeat of either the word or the line.

50 F 15-16 JEMIEE DOUGLAS / JAMIE DOUGLAS

4.3 'He': 'I'; 7.2 'no' = not; 'ilded' = aged, caused me to age; 7.3 the missing line is indicated by a line of nine crosses; 9.3 the reading 'new' is doubtful, perhaps 'now'.

51 F 16–17 The fahill Shearing / Fawhill Shearing

1.1 'I live at fa hill' is written and deleted on a separate line below this one; 1.4 *etc.* 'To make amens' = As recompense; 'tiol' = toil; 3.1 'kempting' = contesting as to who can work the fastest; 4.3 'cries drough' = exclaim that they are parched with thirst; 5.2 'a': 'of'; 6.2 'burrey' = berry, thresh; 7.1 'study' = smithy; 7.2 'the irns to lay' = to weld new edges on the plough irons; 8.1 'Fil' is conjectural; the manuscript has only 'Fl' or possibly 'Tl' or 'H'; 9.2 'shap and shew claise' = make clothes.

52 F 17–18 LUCKEDAT GARLING OR WHEN MY OLD HAT WAS NEW / MY HAT WAS NEW

This song is also given the title *Luckidat Garland, or my auld Hat was new* in the index in F; 2.5 'Toy' = head-dress with flaps coming down to the shoulders; 4.1 a line of eight crosses before this line indicates an omission; 4.3 'ranting kirn' = iproarious harvest-home celebration.

53 F 18–21 / SIR DONALD AND LEIZY LINDSAY

This ballad is also given the title *Assembly at Edinburgh or Eliza Lindsay* in the index in F; 2.3 small blots over 'He' partly obliterate it; 'co' = quo; 8.2, 15.4 'derre', 'Derre Dei' = dairy-woman; 25.1 'Lindsay': 'Lind' at the edge of the paper, which may have been cut; 'Ye are welcome hame to me' is written and deleted on a separate line below this one.

54 I.345–9 / THE ROSE SMELLS SAE SWEITLIE

11.2 'Hooly' = slowly. The first line of the refrain appears throughout as printed. The second line appears as printed 'And the rose it smells sa sweetly' in the first four verses, but from verse 6 to the end it runs 'And the roses smells sa sweetly' and a transitional form 'And the roses it smells sa sweetly' occurs in verse 5. There are two false starts with the wrong refrain line: 'With a hey an' is deleted following 7.2, and 'With' following 17.2 where the line is completed by 'the roses smells sa sweetly' without the usual 'And'.

55 I.352–3 / THE SUN SHYNES OWR THE VALLEY

11.2 'slim' = crafty, but the word is not clearly written and although it looks rather more like 'slim' than anything else it might possibly be 'slew' = sly; 17.2 before 'maidenhead' the letters 'md' with 'a' inserted between them have been deleted. The refrain lines are given in full as printed throughout, except that the first line has 'they valley' in verse 2 and 'shine's owr' in verse 3 and is abbreviated to 'As the sun—' in verse 17, and that the second line often has '&' for 'and', omits 'blew' in verse 7 and is abbreviated to 'Doun amang the' in verse 18.

56 I.334–6 /A YARMOUTH STORY

7.2 'ove' = of.

57 2.198 LADY BELTREES / LADIE BELTREES

1.4 'Laddie': only 'Laddi' is visible but final 'e' may have been bound in; *end-note:* 'Meg Walker got it from Anne Adair daughter of Susie Stachers the wife of the gager'.

58 2.273-6 LORD THOMAS AND LADY MARGARET / LADIE MARGARET AND LORD THOMAS

2.4 'her face I dow na see' = I can't endure seeing her face; 7.4 'made': 'garrit'; possibly the manuscript line 'And he garrit her his ladie gae' should have been emended to 'And he garrit her be his ladie gae', but I have supposed that Crawfurd has silently substituted 'garrit' for 'made', *cf.* the overt substitutions of this word for 'caused' at 20 8.1 and 21 3.3; 13.2 'And to': 'Unto', but *cf.* 12.2 'And to'.

59 3.7-10 JOCK T' LEG AND THE MERRY MERCHANT /

2.2 'quarterers' = lodgers; 3.4, 5 'hauffers thou sal be' = you will have an equal share of the expenses; 12.1 a line of four crosses precedes this line as if lines were missing at this point, but the repeat at 11.4-5 shows that these lines come at the close of a verse and it seems that it is the opening two lines, 11.1-2, that should be regarded as absent. On analogy with the repetitiveness of other variants, they could be supplied from 10.3-4 as 'Tak eleven o thy well armed men / Thy sell the twelfth to be'; 13.1, 14.1 'links' = Lincoln green; 13.3 'come': 'came'. The repeating words at the end of the fourth line are given in all verses. The fifth-line repeat is also written in full in all verses except 5-7 and 12-13 where only the opening words of the fifth line appear as 'Till day &c.', 'He'll take &c.', 'For what &c.', 'Was a thing, &c.' and 'Gude billy, &c.'

60 3.71 [THE LAIRD OF JOHNSTONE AND MISS JEAN MACDOWALL]

Head-note: 'The last laird of Johnstoun and Miss (Jean Mary) Jean (McDowall the) different one than Miss Mary MacDowall'.

61 3.81 [THE BRAES OF KILLIECRANKIE]

1.8 'Killiemankie' = calamanco (a woollen material); 3.4 'pockmankie' = portmanteau, pack; *side-note:* 'A Song printed in Burns' Works (Motherwell and Hoggs Edition,) called "the Captain's Lady" like the Braes of Killiecrankie, or Glimmering. Burns' III. 16'. In *The Captain's Lady*, reprinted in *The Poems and Songs of Robert Burns* ed. James Kinsley (Oxford 1968) 2.520, a woman is invited to 'mount and go, / And be the captain's lady' as in this variant of *The Braes of Killiecrankie* a woman is asked by a soldier to go with him, but there is no close resemblance between the songs. This song is written as five four-line verses, which are numbered.

62 3.86-7 LORD EGLINTON'S SONG /

2.3 'endearing': 'enduring'; 4.3 I give 'aroving' for manuscript 'amusing', which does not seem to make sense. This reading suggests that Crawfurd was copying from a text written by Orr where the letters 'rov' and 'mus' would be easy to confuse. It is with this in mind that I have made the less necessary emendation from manuscript 'enduring' to 'endearing' at 2.3 for 'u' and 'ea' are very similar in Orr's hand; 6.1 'and make an end': '(and) an end'; 6.2 'all maidens that are fair and pretty': 'all fair maidens fair and pretty'; 6.3 'Never to leave off'; the sense does not follow clearly here, and there may at one time have been a connection like that in the broadside, BM 1875.d.16 No 8: 'Advising all maids that are both fair and pretty, / Never to forsake . . .'; *end-note:* 'it was [said] to have been written by the Earl of Eglinton shot by Mungo Campbell at Saltcoats: as it is preserved in all the neighbourhood in the people's memories as Lord Eglinton's Song. Old Saunders Barclaymore who bought the Bourtrees was the cause of his murder. He suggested to the Earl to come out and take Campbell's gun'.

63 3.106-7 THE WEE CRAP /

1.2 'crack my crack' = talk things over as I usually do; 2.1 'sin ever I was born': 'sin I was ever born'; 2.2 'o neither': 'or either'; 2.3, 3.4, 6.3 'The year' = This year; 3.3 'was': 'wad', with 'd' caught from following 'made'; 3.3 'sair' = serve; 4.3 'rug' = portion; 4.4 'bows o meal' = bolls of oatmeal; 'baken': 'bacon'; 5.2 'easy': Crawfurd appears to have written the 'eas' of 'easy' and then superimposed the word 'eithly'; 6.1 'that': 'it'; *end-note:* 'See Vol. II p. 275'. This page is now numbered 277 and the reference is to the quotation from the *Glasgow Chronicle* about the dry summer of 1826 which is given in the introduction.

64 F 23-4 / BONNIE BELLEIN

4.3 'her friends were gane': 'his friends were gane(?)', with the last word not clearly legible; 4.5 'seamaw' = sea-gull; *end-note in Crawfurd's hand:* 'Peggy Walker committed this from a book which was belonging to Miss Jamieson'.

65 2.157 / AIRLIE HOUSE

Head-note: 'Earlee house was burnt in the year 1715 the time of the first Rebellion by Lochail'; 2.2 'she': 'ye'; 4.3 'tour': 'tourl'; the 'l' seems likely to be the beginning of a mistaken 'ly' ending as in 'Early' and 'fairly'. Small pencil marks added by Crawfurd divide the verses as printed.

66 2.158-61 YOUNG LOCHINVAR COURSHIP / YOUNG LOCHINVAR

2.3 'young': 'yound'; this emendation was made by Crawfurd; 3.5 'ranked them and reaied them' = drew them up in ranks; 4.4 'fuie' = few; 5.8 'Fra': 'From' with 'm' deleted; 8.7 'learn' = teach.

67 2.166 [THERE WAS AN OLD MAN WAS SMOKING HIS PIPE]

1.3, 2.1, 3, 4 are scored through, leaving very little visible of the words 'arse' and 'ee' in 2.1 and 'Shite farder' in 2.4. Of the word read as 'damnd' in 2.3 only what appear to be 'd's at the beginning and end can be seen. 2.1 'sparks' = fragments; 2.2 'the divel a stiem he could see' = he couldn't see a thing.

68 2.167 [As I Was A-Walking by yon Green Garden]

The ends of lines 2, 3 and 4 are scored through, leaving only parts of the words visible from 'wife', 'old' and 'young' onwards, so that they may not be correctly given. In particular the 'ie' of 'bitchie' and the reading 'Rogue' depend on conjecture. 2, 4 'claw(ing)' = scratch(ing).

69 2.163 / Black Jock

1.1, 2, 2.2, 5.2 and the refrain lines are scored through. At 1.1 and 2.2 where 'wee' is read, all that is evident from the manuscript is that a short word without strokes above or below was present. The words 'black thing' and 'hairy' in the first verse, 'covered' in the second, 'you or your wee pickle' in the fifth and 'belley' in the refrain are heavily obliterated and may not be correctly given. The whole of the refrain is written out in the first verse but thereafter only its first four words.

70 2.177-8 / Johnie Millar of Glenlee

3.5 'penches' = paunch; 4.3 'genies' = genius, natural aptitude; *end-note* 'William Gemmel to the tune o' the banks o the Dee'.

71 2.209-10 / Lintock Race

1.3 'couth' = quoth, 'win' = ween; 1.5 'gast' = state of confusion; 2.6 'ean' = even; 2.7 'sike a raerd' = such a noise; 2.8 'hea mine' = remember; 3.5 'shirping' = chirping; 3.6 'shill' = shrill; 4.5 is written in the space normally left between lines and seems to have been added later; 5.3 'Neathing but run an'd won in heast = Nothing for it but to gallop all out to win; 5.4 'set out' = put up; 6.7 'sadly to the score the sought' = they strove towards the finishing line in a bunch; 7.4 'sten' = spring; 7.8, 8.4 'took the gree away', 'took awa the gree' = won pre-eminence; 8.1 'Fair fa' = Good luck to; 'walley hakie' = wall-eyed horse with white face-markings; four sets of broken lines before this line indicate that the first half of the verse is missing.

72 2.214-15 The We We Man / The Wee Wee Man

6.3 'King': 'Queen'. Small pencil marks added by Crawfurd divide the verses as printed.

73 2.153-5 / The old Bachelor

7.4 'They', possibly 'a' not 'e'; 8.1 'musing': 'viewing'; 8.2 'Mark what came': 'mark it gane'; 12.2 the 'a' of 'wad' is blurred; 13.4 'It's no be what may be' = what could happen, *i.e.* their marriage, will not happen; 14.4 'get the slip' = be cheated.

74 2.336 The Blackbird

1.1, 2, 2.1, 2 'wild' should perhaps be 'wide'; 3.2 'of her': 'offer'; 3.3 'and': 'I'; 3.4, 5 original sense of 'alake!' was evidently 'I'll hawk' as in LC 2890:14 n.p. n.d. pp. 3-4 *The Pretty Grey Hawk* which has the line 'I will Hawk with her now and then', but this sense may have been lost. The bridging 'brave boys' at the end of the fourth line occurs in verses 2 and 3 but not in verse 1. The repeating lines 1.5, 2.5 and 3.5 are not in the manuscript, but have been supplied on analogy with other texts. *End-note:* 'John Smith tailor &c. as before His grandfather retained it from his infancy. He forgot the rest of it.'

75 2.337-40 Moss Grove / Mess Grove

3.1 'give': 'gave'; 6.1 'he': 'she'; 14.3, 15.3 'a (a') at the turning' = ay (always) at the change; *end-note in Crawfurd's hand:* 'John Smith got it from (a bo) an Irish boy who was his (fellow) comrade being apprentice to his father - at Stranraer'. The only final repeat shown in the manuscript occurs in verse 15 where one word is altered: 'Misgrove I wish you begone / Misgrove I bide you begone'. I have supplied the fifth-line repeat in the other verses. The bridging repeats of a single syllable are not represented in nine of the verses and are shown variously in the others. A single repeat appears in verses 3, 17, 18 and 20 as 'wife wife'; 'sleep / Sleep'; 'sleep / sleep '; and 'mare / mare'; double repeats appear in verses 16, 19 and 21 as 'bedfeet / feet feet (feet feet)', 'man / man man', and 'on / on on'; and triple repeats in 1, 2, 7 and 14 as 'all / all all all', 'Sun / Sun Sun Sun', 'ran / ran ran ran' and 'ill / ill ill ill'. I have taken it that the single repeat is an incomplete rendering of the singer's words, and that the triple repeats, which show three words in a line on their own, are an imperfect way of rendering a double repeat, *i.e.* the word sung three times, and so I give a double repeat throughout; *cf.* Bronson 41. The verses are divided as printed by spaces or small pencil marks added by Crawfurd, except that Crawfurd has marked off as a separate verse two lines (3.1-2) which are given here as the beginning of an exceptional seven-line stanza.

76 2.341-3 / The Widow's Dochter

2.1 'It': 'That'; 2.3 'jinker' = dodger; 3.2 'lunders' = blows; 4.3 'Sayand': 'Syne'. Although this song is in Crawfurd's hand, there are insertions and deletions by William Orr. Orr's deletions can be clearly distinguished since, unlike Crawfurd, he uses double lines. Orr's insertions are as follows, with words he has deleted shown in brackets: 2.1 'on a bonnie simmer's day'; 4.2 'hie' ('be'), 5.4 'is', 6.4 'us' ('not'), 7.3 'was', 8.2 'she' before 'micht' ('she' after 'micht'), 8.4 'ye' ('as'), 9.2 'ng' following 'gane', 11.1 'the', 13.1 'lyin'. I have incorporated all Orr's alterations in the text, and have also, on analogy with the correction at 4.2, emended 'be' to 'hie' at 8.2. Possibly 'not' at 5.4 should be emended to 'us', on analogy with the correction at 6.4. At 8.4 Crawfurd had deleted 'you' apparently by mistake for 'as', 'As the first nicht as (you) bore me'; Orr's correction removed the 'as' and restored the pronoun in the form 'ye'. Short lines divide up the song into four-line verses, except that verses 9 and 10 are shown as a single six-line stanza.

77 2.347–9 The Mailen / The Mailin

Title, r. 3 'mailin', 'mailen' = farm; 1.2 'auld' = eldest; 1.7 'mounting' = outfit; 3.5 'have': 'had', 'd' perhaps caught from the preceding word 'soud'; 3.7–8 'Sen he is my fortune / I can na let him be' is conjectured from the obscure 'Sen my fortune / I can let him be'; 4.5 'faces and': 'face is ance'; 4.6 'mair grace' = better success; 4.7 'But': 'And', perhaps caught from the start of 4.8; 5.3 'their': possibly 'a' not 'e'. For the sense of 'wont be linings' (5.3) *cf.* a rather similar fragment, Greig *Words* 4.13, which runs:

He's a dark man, he's a black man
  He's nae match for me
He'd scarcely be linin'
  To the lad that likes me.

Other men are worthless in comparison with the lad. *End-note:* 'John Smith got it from his grandfather. and Mrs Orr Auchinhane got it from her mother'. Crawfurd mentions a James Orr born in 1738 whom he calls 'old Auchinhane' and 'Mrs Orr Auchinhane' may possibly refer to his wife, Margaret Barclay. Her mother was Isabel Thomson from Dundee (*Cairn* 1.50–1; 1.338–40). At the end of the first verse come the words 'Still abiding still providing' and then there is the heading 'Chorus' followed by the four refrain lines as given. The refrain is indicated after verses 2–4 by 'Still abiding &c', and after the four lines of the fifth verse by the variation 'And still abiding, &c.' Possibly the refrain was sung twice over at the end, once to fill out the verse and then again as the refrain proper.

78 2.349 The Weaver's Dochter

The eight lines are divided as two four-line verses. *End-note:* 'and so on in this same doggrel style and he introduces Doctor Hutchison a man of skill – likewise his brother John and lastly his apprentice viz bold Stafford – This young Doctor Stafford was her trew love. She was sick of love for this gallant – unknown to Stafford – She died although Stafford declares he would marry her. John Smith got it at Stranraer'.

79 2.350–1 / Jockie and the Fair Maid

1.3 'there': 'therie'; 2.1 'she said as like a Goat she ran': 'or like Goat she ran'; 2.4 'Going into yon: I am unable to make sense of the word, apparently of eight letters like 'Sounting', before 'yon' in this line.

80 2.351–2 / The Wooer Came to the Widow's Door

1.2 *etc.* 'fain' = glad; *side-note:* 'John Smith got it at Galloway at Stranrear in his infancy'.

81 2.353-5 / THE MAID'S COMPLAINT TO HER MOTHER

r.1 'I swear': 'is sweir'; 2.2 'And make no': 'And to make', with 'Unto' written above 'And to' and crossed out; 4.4 'in cloth of sack': '(with) cloth in sack'. The four lines of the refrain occur in exactly the same form after verses 1 and 2 only. The stops in the text have been added on the model of the chapbook form, Appendix No 8 *The Longing Maid*, where they seemed essential to indicate the breaks in these long lines, except that the comma after 'mother' in 3.3 in the manuscript.

APPENDIX

THE CHAPBOOK and broadside texts given in this appendix are from the following sources. I have added the numbering of the verses, and also made the few slight alterations which are indicated below.

1 Harvard College Library chapbooks 57(iii):10 *The Unfortunate Grazier's Daughter.* Shewing how a rich Squire married a poor Grazier's Daughter; afterwards he married a rich Lady by the Persuasions of his Friends, and slighted the Grazier's Daughter. Shewing how the Grazier's Daughter miscarried, and soon after died with Grief. Shewing after her Death, how she and her Infant came to his Bedside, and upbraided him for his Perjury; and how she killed him in the Arms of his new Bride, and wrote his crime in blue Roman Letters about his Body, to be an Example to all false-hearted Lovers. Belfast; Printed in the Year, 1767.

2 Madden 24, No 322 *Fair Rosamond.* J. and H. Baird, 20, Paul-Street, Cork. 8.1 'down' ('dowm'); 10.4 'divine' ('n' reversed).

3 BM 1870.c.2 'A collection of the publications of J. Kendrew, etc., 1803-51,' No 286 *The Wedding.* Sold at J. Johnson's, Goodramgate [York].

4 GUL Mu52 - e.22:42 *Three Songs.* Scottish Glory, Displayed at Waterloo. Braw Jean, Or will nae Bonny Laddie take me awa'. Neighbour Hark. Edinburgh, Printed by J. Morren, pp. 7-8. *Title:* 'Neighbour' ('Neighbour'); 3.4 'And' ('n' reversed), 'many' ('may'); 6.4 'lose' ('love'); 7.2 'feet' ('f' only).

5 BM 11621.i.12 'A collection of ballads. Collected by Thomas Bell, 1780?-1820?' f. 57 *Bonny Bush of Broom.* (No place, but probably North of England like other items in this collection.) 2.1 'Guisborough' ('Guisborouuh'); 8.2 'four' ('four').

6 BM 11602.gg.30 'A collection of ballads printed chiefly by C. Croshaw, York, and by J. Pitts, London, 1820?-40?' f. 28 *The Pretty Parks of Cailty O.* C. Croshaw, Printer, Coppergate, York. 2.4 'you' ('u' reversed).

7 BM 11621.c.2:36 *The Longing Maid's Garland,* Composed of five delightful New Songs. I. The Longing Maid. II. A new Irish Song. III. The young Man's Request to his Mistress IV Robert Wilson and John West. V. The Norfolk Maiden: A New Song Licensed and Entered according to Order, pp. 2-3.

1 THE UNFORTUNATE GRAZIER'S DAUGHTER

cf. 8 *The Grazier's Dochter*

1 Attend you lovers, and give ear
Hereto, with true attention,
For these few lines I do declare
Are true, and no invention:

But in perfect truth I'll write,
As it hath been reported,
How a young squire ruined quite
A damsel whom he courted.

2 She was his father's servant maid,
And daughter to a grazier;
Behold how he her heart inveigled,
At every time and leisure,
With all the arguments of love
That passion could discover,
Protesting by the powers above
How dearly he did love her.

3 With modest blushes she reply'd,
Pray stop your fond proceedings,
For I am no way qualified
For you in birth or breeding:
You may have choice of ladies gay,
Of noble loins descended;
Therefore let me alone I pray,
Your friends will be offended,

4 When e'er they come to understand
Your foolish fond pretences.
Therefore young squire out of hand,
For to avoid offences,
Discourse to me of love no more,
But strive to please your parents:
I'd rather wed a man that's poor,
Than live with you at variance.

5 Says he, you jewel of my heart,
Don't fear my friends displeasure,
Whoever shall frown I'll take thy part,
And love thee out of measure:
No lady born of noble blood
Shall fall within my favour,
I honour thee by all that's good,
And so I will for ever.

6 If not, let fearful vengeance fall
Upon me when I leave thee:
'Twill be but just if that I shall
In any case deceive thee:
For by this hand and heart of mine,
If parents they should slight thee,
'Till I my vital breath resign,
Dear jewel I will right thee.

7 With these arguments and many more
He strove for to enflame her:
She gave consent to wed therefore,
No one alive could blame her;
This damsel soon was made his wife,
In strictest ties of marriage,
But she at length did lose her life
Thro' his ungrateful carriage.

8 Unknown to friends or parents dear,
She with the squire wedded,
And for the space of half a year,
After they both had bedded,
It seems she prov'd big with child,
Her looks began to show it,
But 'till his friends were reconcil'd,
He wou'd not have them know it.

9 Then up to famous *London* town
Immediately he brought her,
And jewels, rings, and silken gowns,
He very freely bought her,
That she might like a lady gay
Appear in all her beauty,
And for some time while there she stay'd,
He own'd a husband's duty.

10 Some how his parents came to hear
By private information,
That he lodged near the Strand,
With a miss of recreation.
Then having miss'd their servant maid,
They presently concluded
That she some cunning prank had play'd,
And certainly deluded

11 Sweet *William* their only son,
Who was by birth a squire,
For the deed that she had done,
A jail should be her hire.
They sent a letter full of wrath,
And threatned her with ruin,
Which griev'd him so, that in troth
As he these lines stood viewing,

12 Tears from his eyes flew amain,
She asked him the reason;
Says he, my friends do thee disdain:
They both wept for a season.

She read the lines as well as he,
And found them harsh and cruel;
Be kind to me, my dear, said she,
Be kind to me my jewel.

13 Let me not suffer for thy sake,
Consider my condition,
For if you don't my heart will break;
'Twas not my ambition
To be a lady you well know,
'Twas long e'er I consented,
Why do they seem to threaten so?
I strove for to prevent it.

14 But since I am your lawful wife,
As you were pleas'd to make me,
Your smiles perhaps may save my life;
I'll die if you forsake me.
He took her by the hand, and said,
My dear, my joy and sweeting,
Pray in your lodging now abide
'Till our next happy meeting;

15 I'll make the matter clear and plain,
And in all cases clear you.
He went, and ne'er return'd again,
He never more came near her.
In melancholy thoughts she pass'd
The time, one month and better;
Then did she travel down at last,
Having receiv'd no letter.

16 But when she came unto the town,
She was told how he was married
To a young lady of renown;
With grief she then miscarried.
When his parents came to hear
She lived with a neighbour,
To whom she did her conscience clear,
When in her extreme labour.

17 They threatned her with punishment,
For talking of the squire;
But fatal death did them prevent,
For she did soon expire.
The minute just before she dy'd,
In her friends and neighbours hearing,
She wrung her hands, and wept, and cry'd,
What is there no appearing?

18 Will you not come and see me now,
You husband most false hearted!
In just vengeance I will you have,
When my wronged soul departeth.
It came to pass as it was said,
The wronged grazier's daughter
Her ghost did come where he was laid
In bed, some minutes after.

19 And in the midst of all their joy,
To their amazing wonder,
The room was fill'd with dreadful noise,
Like claps of roaring thunder;
About the stately marriage bed
They saw the flashing fire,
A voice they heard that often said,
You most deceitful squire,

20 The lady which lies by your side,
She shall not long enjoy you,
It's I that am your lawful bride,
Just vengeance shall destroy you.
The apparition of his wife,
And little infant crying,
Whom he had bereav'd of life,
Came both like furies flying

21 Against him as he lay in bed;
At which they were affrighted.
The lady much discomforted,
Her snowy breasts she smited,
With arms as cold as any clay,
The spirit did enfold him,
And took him thence by force away,
His lady could not hold him.

22 She screech'd and cry'd, but all in vain,
The apparition gave him
That very night, his fatal bane,
For there was none could save him.
The family arose with speed
At this sad consternation,
And on his body they beheld
These words of lamentation,

23 In perfect *Roman* letters blue;
This wretch was my undoing,
For being done, it proved true
My death and dismal ruin;

When I was left he scorn'd my cries,
My grief I cou'd not smother,
He for a cursed golden prize,
Must needs go wed another,
Leaving his wife and child to fall
A sacrifice together;
These are my accusations all,
And so farewell for ever.

2 FAIR ROSAMOND

cf. 18 *Fair Rosanne*

1 There was three Lords in Salsbury, one day was riding by,
Some of them talk'd of fox and hounds, and more of Ladies gay,
I have a Sister Lord Clifford he said, most glorious to behold,
I would not for her weight of Gold, King Henry would her know.

2 My Sister's locks of golden hair, do shine like diamonds bright,
Her skin's far whiter than the snow, that falls from yonder height,
Her eyes do glitter in her head, like diamonds in a row
The bloom appears all on her cheeks, like drops of blood in snow.

3 King Henry sat in his Bower Window, Lord Clifford was riding by,
Hearing these words express'd, call'd him immediately
I'm the King of old England, my orders now obey,
Here's a letter seal'd with Gold, my messenger you must be.

4 Lord Clifford he mounted his milk white steed, his grievous heart was sad,
Although he was one of the finest Lords, that e'er King Henry had,
And when he came unto the court, he knock'd loud at the ring,
There was none so ready for to rise, as Rose to let him in.

5 Here is a letter my lovely Rose, here is a letter said he
Here is a letter my lovely Rose, King Henry sent to thee,
Here is a letter my lovely Rose, most glorious to behold
With her pretty fingers long and small she broke the seals of gold

6 The very first line that she read o'er, she seem'd to be satisfied,
The second line that she read o'er, she wrung her hands and cried,
Oh! cursed brother are you now, and cursed may you be,
Could you not talk of fox and hounds, and not to brag of me.

7 Go bring me down my plannet-book, that lies in my private room,
Go bring me down my plannet-book, 'till I see what is my doom,
Her plannet-book it was brought down, and plac'd all on her knee,
It said the time was come to pass, that poison'd she should be.

8 Go call me down my waiting maid, 'till she combs back my hair,
Go call me in my stable-groom, 'till he saddles me my mare,
With four and twenty Lords of honour convey'd her to the King,
And when she enter'd the palace gates the royal bells did ring.

9 And when she enter'd the Palace Gates, she fell down on her knee,
Saying my Liege if I dare but speak what is your will of me,
My will my lovely Rose, is to embrace my Royal Bed,
No sooner than these words he spoke, she blush'd like scarlet red.

10 What makes you blush my lovely Rose, what makes you blush said he,
What makes you blush my lovely Rose, will you unhappy be,
There's not a lady in the land, can purchase your desire,
Your charming smiles are so divine, you have won my Royal heart.

11 A Garland of the finest flowers, made for this ladies head,
A Garland of the finest flowers, this lady was put to bed,
A Garland of the finest flowers, all for this lady fine,
All for to hide her modest looks she being a Concubine

3 THE WEDDING

cf. 21 *The Penitent Bride*

1 Being invited to a wedding,
A fair maid that prov'd unkind,
She remembering her former losses,
Her own true love run in her mind.

2 The wedding supper being over,
Every one was to sing a song,
Then began the former lover,
And unto me you do belong.

3 How can you lay on another man's pillow
When you have been my true love so long,
Leaving me here for to wear the green willow,
O false maiden what have you done!

4 The bride being set at the head of the table
Marking every word that was said,
When she could no longer bear it,
Down at the bridegroom's feet she laid

5 A favour I have for to ask you,
If you will grant it to me,
The very first night for to lie with my mammy,
The second night I will lie with thee.

6 Such a favour ought not to be granted,
You should have considered before you had wed,
Leaving me here to lament in sorrow
When your heart to another was inclin'd.

7 This favour being already granted,
Weeping and wailing she went to bed,
Early the next morning
He found his new bride lying dead.

8 My green willow don't carry the blossom,
Buds in the spring time of the year;
Young men and maidens spend many an hour
In courting, but they are never the near.

4 NEIGHBOUR HARK

cf. 24 *The Reeking House*

1 Neighbour hark, come here and speak,
Yonder's a house, I see has reek.
Yonder's a house, hut and a lum.
I'm sure this house belongs to some.

2 Then honest man for to be free,
I want a wife a wife to bide with me,
Now lasses they're not easy tane,
I do not like to bide my lane.

3 You are a fool for saying so,
Where you have one you might have two,
The lasses they are not so scant,
And many a one a man doth want.

4 Perhaps that you do climb too high,
Or doat on one that does deny;
To answer you at your request,
Who's void of love within her breast.

5 But fare you well, I must away,
Seek not a lass that gangs o'er gay,
Nor yet a lass with a deal of siller,
'Cause that's the motto that leads you till her.

6 For riches is a blinding blinding bride,
Does many faults and failings hide,
And afterwards it doth appear,
When you begin to lose your gear.

7 And beauty also is a cheat
Leads many a young thing off their feet
And after this I'll let you know,
Beauty's nought but a vain show.

8 Fare you well, take my advice,
Seek not a lass that is too nice,
But if the lass be young and douse,
You may take her into your toom house.

5 BONNY BUSH OF BROOM

cf. 27 *The Bush of Broom*

1 As I was in walking one May morning,
For to gaze what I could see,
Who should I spy but a very bonny lass,
Enquiring the road to her own country.

2 Where are ye going, my bonny lassie,
O where are ye going then, said he.
Its I have been at London that pretty place,
And at Guisborough town I fain would be.

3 If you have been at London, my bonny lassie,
And at Guisborough town you fain would be,
Then come and sit by the bonny bush of Broom,
To bear a young man's company.

4 Fain would I sit by the bonny bush of Broom,
For wet and weary may I be,
But I connot sit down by the bonny bush of Broom,
To bear a young man company.

5 He took her by the lilly white hand,
And kindly gave her kisses three,
Wo be to thee and the bonny bush of Broom,
I wish I was in my own country.

6 What would you do, my bonny lass,
As what would you do in your own country?
I would take my cup and fill it to the top,
And drink to the bonny bush of Broomberry.

7 He put his hand into his pocket,
And kindly gave her guineas three,
Here take this, thou bonny bonny lass,
It will carry thee to thy own country.

8 She had not been in her own country
Weeks four, months six and three,
Till she sent him a son, and a very fine son,
And she bade him nurse him on his knee.

9 So now he has got his bonny lassie,
And he sits smiling on his knee.
Its this reminds me of the bonny bush of Broom,
And the welcome girl in her own country.

10 I wish I had that bonny lassie here,
And have her in my own country,
I would make her a lady of all that I have,
And set her young son on her knee.

11 So now he has got his bonny lass here,
He is got safe in his own country,
He has made her a lady of all that he has,
And he has set her young son on her knee.

6 THE PRETTY PARKS OF CAILTY O

cf. 38 *The Laird o' Kelty*

1 Where are you going my bonny lass, where are you going so late,
Are you not afraid of meeting some ill fate,
Are you not afraid of some ill fate,
If you meet with the young Laird of Cailty O.

2 She passed by the harrows she passed by the ploughs,
It was on a summer's evening when they was going to loose,
O stay my bonny lassy till our horses we let go,
And we'll convey you through the pretty parks of Cailty O.

3 She turned herself right courteously she thank'd him with a smile,
I've travelled this road late and early many times,
I've travelled this road late and early many times,
And I never saw the young Laird of Cailty O.

4 She had not travelled through the parks scarce half a mile,
She heard a voice behind her saying stop my pretty child,
She heard a voice behind her saying stop my pretty child,
Don't you know you're in the pretty parks of Cailty O.

5 She turn'd herself round about the tear stood in her eye,
Saying I will turn me back again if I have offended thee,
I will turn me back again if I have offended thee,
I perceive you are the young Laird of Cailty O.

6 He took her by the middle and he gently laid her down,
The grass grew up on every side the tree grew feeble down,
The grass grew up on every side the tree grew feeble down,
It was all in the pretty parks of Cailty O.

7 When he had had his will of her he lifted her up again,
Saying if any should ask you who has done you this wrong,
If any one should ask you who has done you this wrong,
Don't deny it was the young Laird of Cailty O.

8 This fair maid being tender most delicate and young,
This young man repented the folly he had done,
He has made her his wedded wife before the child was born,
Now she is Lady of the pretty parks of Cailty O.

7 THE LONGING MAID

cf. 81 *The Maid's Complaint to her Mother*

1 O Mother let me marry, I long to be a Bride,
And have a lusty young Man to daddle by my Side:
For I think it tis well known I am a Woman grown,
Therefore tis a Pity, one so pretty, e'er should lie alone.
O Mother do not deny me therefore I pray,
Consider I am young and may chance to go astray.
For my Maiden-head I swear, does fill my heart with Care,
The Burden, Burden, O the Burden! is more than I can bear

2 Why are you so eager to be a married Wife?
The greatest Joy and Pleasure is in a single Life:
Daughter, now you live at Ease, and can ramble where you please;
But if you marry you may tarry, Sorrows will you seize,
House keeping is chargeable my dear Child;
But *Nancy*, she reply'd, Mother I am almost wild.
For my Maiden-head I swear, &c.

3 Am I not a Beauty, and in my youthful Prime;
So now to have a Husband I think it is high Time:
Let me have my hearts Delight, though I labour Day and Night;
It will be a Pleasure out of Measure, Mother, if I might
Have all the Pleasure that I ever saw,
Without a loving, a loving Man, I do value not a Straw.
For my Maiden-head I swear, &c.

4 O Daughter don't provoke me, but hold your idle Tongue
And talk no more of Men, for you are seven Years too young
Mother, pray what do you mean, am I not above Fifteen,
Let Gallants try me, dont deny me; Thousands I have seen
That hath been married before my Age,
And if I longer stay you will put me in a Rage.
For my Maiden-head I swear, &c.

5 O Daughter, I was Nineteen before that I was wed,
Yet was not over-burden'd with my dear Maidenhead
Loving Mother that may be, but 'tis otherwise with me
I'm brisk and airy, therefore weary of my Virginity.
Cupid hath given me a fatal Wound,
Therefore a Man I'll have if he be above the Ground.
For my Maidenhead I swear, &c.

6 If you are so pamper'd, I'll pull your Courage down
By hard and painful Labour, strip off your silken Gown,
With your Garments rich and gay; to the Fields this very Day
I'll send you packing, Clothes and Sacking, then perhaps you may
Leave off your Longing for a young Man:
No, no, I never shall, reply'd her Daughter *Nan.*
For my Maidenhead I swear, &c.

7 O Mother, if you set me to labour in the Field,
Young Batchelors may tempt me, and I may come to yield,
To the Thing I will not name; therefore never lay the Blame,
Upon your Daughter, if therefore I should play the Game:
For I am certain it will be so,
A man I needs must have whether mother will or no.
For my Maidenhead I swear, &c.

8 If you are resolved to play at Hooper's-hyde,
There's honest *Frank* the Farmer for you I will provide;
He's lusty, tall and trim, and hath Courage to the Brim:
I thank you Mother, there's no other that I love like him.
And as for the Torments which now I do endure,
I make no longer doubt but to have a speedy Cure.
For my Maiden-head I swear, does fill my heart with Care
But not much longer, not much longer, I'll the burden bear.

GUIDE TO AIRS OF SONGS IN VOLUME 1

THE FOLLOWING list of airs is not intended to be exhaustive. For ballads included in Bronson, reference has generally been confined to that collection. For other songs I note all instances in the Greig-Duncan manuscript collection and also attempt to indicate for each song a tune available in print, giving preference to tunes recorded in Scotland.

1 LORD BANGWELL'S ADVENTURE. In this collection; also Bronson 1.103, No 5 tune 2.
2 BOB NORRICE. In this collection; also Bronson 2.318, No 83 tune 4.
3 MY LORD DERWATER. Bronson 3.264-7, No 208.
4 THE HAWTHORN GREEN. Simpson p. 165, No 104 *Dargason*; Fred Hamer *Garners Gay* (London 1967) p. 15.
5 WILLIAM AND THE YOUNG COLONEL. In this collection; also Bronson 2.412, No 88 tune 2.
6 FAIR ROSALIND. In the table of tunes in *The Charmer*, this song is included in the group which may be sung to any of the following: *Ye frolicksome sparks* (Bodleian MS Mus.e.19, p. 68), *Can love be controll'd* (John Gay *The Beggar's Opera*, London 1729, repr. New York 1961, music p. 13 No 8 *Grim King of ghosts, &c.*), *Tweedside* (*SMM* 1.37, No 36), *My banks they are furnish'd* (music by Thomas Arne for song in William Shenstone's *Pastoral Ballad* Part I 'Hope').
7 THE CRUEL STEPMOTHER. Simpson pp. 96-7 Nos 63 and 64 *Chevy Chase* and p. 368, No 234 *In Peascod Time*; see Simpson's comments p. 370.
8 THE GRAZIER'S DOCHTER. The tune title given with the chapbook text printed in the appendix, No 1 *The Unfortunate Grazier's Daughter*, is *The Battle of Almanza*. The words of this song are printed in W. H. Logan *A Pedlar's Pack of Ballads and Songs* (Edinburgh 1869) pp. 82-4, but Simpson, though mentioning the title (p. 154 n. 1), was unable to trace the tune.
9 LORD MEANWELL. Bronson 2.428-45 and 4.479-80, No 93.
10 SIR HUGH. In this collection; also Bronson 3.100, No 155 tune 56.
11 THE KING'S DOCHTER JEAN. Bronson 2.495-506 and 4.481, No 100.
12 THE CRUEL MOTHER. Bronson 1.276-96 and 4.456, No 20.
13 LORD GREGORY. Bronson 2.218-28 and 4.472, No 76.
14 THE WANDERING LOVER. Greig *Tunes* 2.12 beginning 'Arise arise it's your own true lover'; Bronson 4.20, No 248 tune 10.
15 THE SQUIRE'S SON OF AIZLING TOWN. Bronson 2.515-29 and 4.482-3, No 105.
16 THE MERRY LYKEWAKE. In this collection; also Bronson 1.306, No 25 tune 3.

17 YOUNG BETSY. *Journal of the English Folk Dance and Song Society* 3 (1936–9) p. 244 *Cruel Mother.*

18 FAIR ROSANNE. Eloise Hubbard Linscott *Folk Songs of Old New England* (New York 1939) p. 194. Simpson p. 137, No 88 *The Court Lady* is the tune associated with the broadside form, which is in double stanzas.

19 WILLIE TAYLOR. Greig *Tunes* 2.62 and 4.74; William Christie *Traditional Ballad Airs* (Edinburgh 1876–81) 2.208.

20 LORD LEVEL. Bronson 2.189–217 and 4.471–2, No 75.

21 THE PENITENT BRIDE. Greig *Tunes* 1.32, 2.46, 47 and 86, 3.69 and 147, 4.107, 113, 158, 163 and 180 *The False Bride*; Duncan pp. 10, 208 and 287, Nos 15A–C *The Inconstant Lover*; John Ord *Bothy Songs and Ballads* (Paisley 1930) p. 132 *The Unconstant Lover.*

22 THE THREE JOLLY BUTCHERS. Greig *Tunes* 1.137.i and ii and 4.29; Duncan *Tunes* pp. 209 (No 264), 438 and 450; Frank Purslow *Marrow Bones* (London 1965) p. 89.

23 WISE WILLIE. *Tocher* 1 (1971–2) p. 233 *Hunting the Wren.*

24 THE REEKING HOUSE. Greig *Tunes* 1.64, 122 and 123 *The Teem Wa's.*

25 THE AULD WIFE AND THE PEAT CREEL. In this collection; also Bronson 4.258, No 281 tune 1.

26 THE YORKSHIRE RAMBLER. Greig *Tunes* 2.84 *When first to Lunnon Town* and 3.42 *When first in London*; Frank Purslow *The Wanton Seed* (London 1969) p. 55 *I'ze Yorkshire, Though in Lunnon.*

27 THE BUSH OF BROOM. Duncan *Tunes* p. 201, No 253 *To Newcastle I wad be* and p. 205, No 258 *The Bonny Bush o' Broom.*

28 MOTHER BUNCH. Possibly Greig *Tunes* 1.49 where the accompanying stanza runs:

> My mither is turnin' auld
> And she wad ha'e me to behave
> But oh, gin she were young again,
> She wad jist be like the lave.

This has some similarity to verse 16 of the text printed here, but the mother is not addressed directly in this fragment and it may not be the same song.

29 THE HILLS O' GOWRIE. Lady Nairne's version of this song is to the tune *Loch Eroch Side* (*SMM* 1.78–9 No 78).

30 THE SHEPHERD'S SON. Bronson 2.547–63 and 4.489, No 112.

31 THE FAUSE KNICHT. Bronson 1.34–8 and 4.442, No 3, and *Scottish Studies* 9 (1965), pp. 9–14.

32 THE LAIRD OF OCHILTREE WALLS. In this collection; also Bronson 3.340, No 217 tune 9.

33 THE BONNIE BLUE-EYED LASSIE. No tune located.

34 MAY COLYEAN. Bronson 1.39–100 and 4.442–3, No 4.

35 MALL BOWIE. Frank Purslow *The Constant Lovers* (London 1972) p. 93. On the manuscript from which Purslow prints the tune (Cecil Sharp House H.235) it is suggested that the tune may have been recorded in Scotland.

36 LADY JEAN. In this collection; also Bronson 1.407, No 52 tune 1.

37 Earl Richard. In this collection; also Bronson 2.64, No 68 tune 6.

38 The Laird o' Kelty. Greig *Tunes* 1.120; 2.79; and 3.3 and 26 *The Parks o' Keltie*; Duncan *Tunes* pp. 77-8, No 110A.

39 The Mason's Dochter. Greig *Tunes* 2.137 *In fair London city* and 4.87 *Fair Isabel.*

40 The Three Ravens. In this collection; also Bronson 1.310, No 26 tune 2.

41 The Deil's Courtship. Greig *Tunes* 2.96, 3.207 and 4.9 *A Pennyworth o' Preens*; Duncan *Tunes* p. 518 *O, I'll gie to Ye a Pennyworth o' Preens*; Norman Buchan *101 Scottish Songs* (Glasgow and London 1962) p. 143 *If You Will Marry Me.*

42 Poor Greeting Wilsie. Greig *Tunes* 3.93 *I'm gaun to the wud*; see also Simpson's comments at pp. 423-4, No 269 *Lady, Lie Near Me*, and James C. Dick *The Songs of Robert Burns* (London 1903) pp. 95 and 383-4, No 101 *Laddie lie near me*, and pp. 129 and 399-400, No 142 *Lang hae we parted been.*

43 Slighted Love. Duncan *Tunes* p. 402 *In Halifax Town; Journal of the Folk-Song Society* 5 (1914-17), 184-5.

44 The Ensign and the Lady Gay. Bronson 2.83-4, No 69.

45 The Unco Knicht's Wooing. Bronson 1.3-8 and 4.439, No 1.

46 Rosianne. Bronson 1.403-6, No 51.

47 The Prince of Orange. Greig *Tunes* 3.163 *The Rambling Beauty*; William Christie *Traditional Ballad Airs* (Edinburgh 1876-81) 2.6 *The Rambling Beauty.*

48 The Nut-Brown Bride. Bronson 2.88-154 and 4.468-70, No 73.

49 The Laird o' Ochiltree. Bronson 3.338-44 and 4.500-1, No 217.

50 Jamie Douglas. Bronson 3.258-61, No 204.

51 The Faughhill Shearing. No tune located.

52 When My Old Hat Was New. Greig *Tunes* 1.138 and 2.132; W. G. Whittaker *North Countrie Ballads, Songs & Pipe-Tunes* (London and Philadelphia 1921) pp. 78-9, No 23.

53 Sir Donald and Eliza Lindsay. Bronson 3.365-8 and 4.502, No 226.

54 The Rose Smells Sae Sweetly. Bronson 1.185-90, No 11 and *Scottish Studies* 9 (1965) pp. 17-18.

55 The Sun Shines Over the Valley. Bronson 1.305-7, No 25.

56 A Yarmouth Story. No tune located.

57 Lady Beltrees. Greig *Tunes* 1.108.ii and iii, 4.51 and 139 *Hey bonnie laddie, mount & go*; Duncan *Tunes* pp. 9-10 (No 13A), 30 (No 44), 250 (No 300), 383 and 462 *Mount and Go* or *My Parents hae Married me owre Young*; Norman Buchan and Peter Hall *The Scottish Folksinger* (London and Glasgow 1973) p. 75, from Grieg *Tunes* 1.108.iii.

58 Lord Thomas and Lady Margaret. Bronson 4.70, No 260.

59 Jock t' Leg and the Merry Merchant. Bronson 4.278-81, No 282.

60 The Laird of Johnstone and Miss Jean Macdowall. *The Collier Laddie* in Grieg *Tunes* 2.104 and 4.59; Duncan *Tunes* pp. 3-4, No 4A; John Ord *Bothy Songs and Ballads* (Paisley 1930) p. 40.

61 The Braes of Killiecrankie. James C. Dick *The Songs of Robert Burns* (London 1903) p. 104, No 113 *The Birks of Abergeldie.*

62 Lord Eglinton's Song. *Journal of the Folk-Song Society* 5 (1914-17) p. 92 *A Sweet Country Life.*

63 The Wee Crap. No tune located.

64 Bonnie Belleen. No tune located.

65 Airlie House. Bronson 3.191–7, No 199.

66 Young Lochinvar's Courtship. Bronson 3.352–8, No 221.

67 There Was an Old Man Was Smoking His Pipe. No tune located.

68 As I Was A-Walking by yon Green Garden. No tune located.

69 Black Joke. *The Poems and Songs of Robert Burns* ed. James Kinsley 3 vols. (Oxford 1968) 1.60, No 46.

70 Johnie Miller of Glenlee. This song is stated in the manuscript to be to the tune 'The banks of the Dee', *SMM* 6.532, No 516.

71 Linton Race. No tune located.

72 The Wee Wee Man. Bronson 1.326, No 38.

73 The Old Bachelor. *Robert Burns: Selected Poetry and Prose* ed. Robert D. Thornton (Boston 1966) pp. 97 and 258 *I am a man unmarried*; Frank Purslow *The Wanton Seed* (London 1969) p. 100 *The Roving Bachelor*.

74 The Blackbird. Frank Purslow *Marrow Bones* (London 1965) p. 39 *The Grey Hawk*. I do not know of a Scottish record of a tune for this song, but there are several records of a closely related one with the same stanza structure: Duncan *Tunes* p. 164, Nos 207 and 208 *I once loved a Boy*, and *Journal of the English Folk Dance and Song Society* 3 (1936–9) p. 246 *My Bonny Boy*.

75 Mossgrove. Bronson 2.267–315 and 4.474–6, No 81.

76 The Widow's Dochter. There is a traditional singing of this song on the disc *Folk Ballads from Donegal and Derry* collected by Hugh Shields, LEA 4055 (1972).

77 The Mailin. This song has not been located elsewhere, but there may possibly be a musical connection with *Tocher* 1 (1971–2) p. 180 *He's providin for me*, which has a similar refrain.

78 The Weaver's Dochter. Greig *Tunes* 3.171; Duncan *Tunes* p. 34 (No 49) and pp. 17–18 (No 25A) *Doctor Stafford; or, the Rocks o' Penn; or the Weaver's Daughter*.

79 Jockie and the Fair Maid. P. W. Joyce *Old Irish Folk Music and Songs* (Dublin 1909) pp. 180–1, No 375 *Searching for Young Lambs*.

80 The Wooer Came to the Widow's Door. *Journal of the Folk Song Society* 7 (1922–6) p. 136, the Manx *Haink Sooreedeyr nish gys Dorrys ven Treoghe* (*A Wooer came to the Widow's Door*).

81 The Maid's Complaint to her Mother. Simpson p. 636, No 412 *The Scotch Haymakers*; in combination with *Whistle, Daughter, Whistle* Duncan *Tunes* p. 119, No 165, and Cecil J. Sharp *English Folk Songs* (London 1920) 1.100–1, No 43.